AFTER
YOU'RE
OUT

Also edited by Karla Jay and Allen Young
Out of the Closets: Voices of Gay Liberation

by Allen Young
Allen Ginsberg: Gay Sunshine Interview

AFTER YOU'RE OUT

PERSONAL EXPERIENCES OF GAY MEN AND LESBIAN WOMEN

edited by Karla Jay
and Allen Young

links
New York
London

International Standard Book Number: 0-8256-3056-8
Library of Congress Catalog Card Number: 75-17447
Printed in the United States of America.

Distributed by Quick Fox, Inc.,
33 West 60 Street, New York 10023; and
Gage Publishing Limited,
164 Commander Blvd., Agincourt, Ontario,
Canada M1S3C7.

Book design by Richard Spector
Cover design by Iris Weinstein
Cover photograph by Duane Michals

The publisher wishes to thank the following for permission to reprint
material in this book. Any inadvertent omission will be corrected in
future printings upon notification to the publisher.

"Lesbian Sexuality: An Unfinished Saga" is from manuscript and is
printed by permission of the author. Copyright © 1975 by Nina
Sabaroff.

"What's a Dyke to Do? and What the Dyke Is Doing" is an expanded
version of two articles. One was entitled "What's a Woman To Do?"
and was published in the Lesbian Tide, Vol. 3, No. 7, April 1974. The
other was part of a roundtable entitled "A Kiss does not a Revolution
Make," which was published in the Lesbian Tide, Vol. 3, No. 11, June
1974. Copyright © 1974 by the Tide Collective. Printed by permission
of the author.

continued on page 293

Editors' Dedication

In Memoriam
Lydia French
Lee Mason
Ralph S. Schaffer
Eddie Rastellini
Rev. Robert Spike
"New Orleans 32"
Frank Bartley
Larry Turner
Camilla Hall
Patricia "Mizmoon" Soltysik
Lige Clark

Contents

FOREWORD

Allen Young

Once upon a time, there was the closet. Inside the closet, I hid. My homosexuality was something I feared and loathed. It is with some relief that I now realize that such fear and hatred almost killed me, as it has, in fact, taken the lives of many. The gay liberation movement has meant a great deal to me, as it has to countless gay people all over the world. Coming out of the closet was, for me and many others, a vital act of liberation, a rebirth.

Coming out was a joyful experience, not only of simple self-acceptance and freedom but also of appreciating for the first time the special value of being gay—the fact that it is a way of loving and that it is an important part of transcending the stifling masculine and feminine roles developed and enforced by our patriarchal system.

It's hard to remember all the details of those days in late 1969 and early 1970 when my consciousness was overwhelmed—my mind blown—by the ideas of gay liberation. What gay writers wrote then was very important to me. I specifically remember an interview with members of the New York Gay Liberation Front published in *Rat*, articles by Konstantin Berlandt which were published in the Berkeley *Tribe* and which were reprinted by Liberation News Service, and Carl Wittman's classic "Gay Manifesto," initially published as an article in the San Francisco *Free Press*, which was shown to me by Jimmy Fouratt in his apartment on the Lower East Side of New York City in December 1969. Suffice it to say that these articles and the ideas they represented were all very exciting and dramatic. Although it was all threatening on some level—and still is!—I probably had the mistaken notion that with gay liberation I would achieve nirvana, and coming out would put me right on easy street.

Not so. Creating a gay identity for myself was only the beginning. It has brought me many joys, not the least of which is a greater appreciation for the sensual, the aesthetic, and the emotional sides of life. Coming out has enabled me to lead a more integrated life, as it has enabled many gay people to end the hiding and the "double life" demanded by the closet.

There are many who still stay in the closet because our example is not meaningful enough, or because those of us who are out seem somehow strange. It is probably true that a majority of up-front homosexuals are people employed in traditional gay areas of work, or who have lifestyles associated with the more tolerant environment of Bohemia or the counterculture. While many gay people choose to remain in the closet because they fear they have too much to lose (jobs, friends, family, religion), there always remains the lingering question about to what extent the closet is a self-imposed prison. Employment is probably the crucial stumbling block. We all have to eat. No doubt, this is why gay organizations place such an emphasis on civil rights legislation. Without such legislation, someone who comes out in the wrong place at the wrong time will lose his or her job. But some might suggest considering the maxim that we cannot live "by bread alone."

This question of coming out, ultimately, is a decision for each individual. There are a thousand nuances and degrees of coming out, but there can be no doubt about it: in any form, coming out of the closet is a great celebration of human freedom. However, the integration that emerges from it and the emotional impact of an uncloseted life, compel the individual to confront a new, more whole but still very difficult reality.

If "out of the closets!" was the rallying cry of gay liberation (as it was the title of an earlier anthology edited by Karla Jay and myself), it also proved to be inadequate as a total political statement for the gay movement, or as a total way of life for gay people. As with most of the social movements of the late 1960's, shrill dogmatic voices rang the loudest, and "ideology" or "organization" took precedence over personal experience and feelings. At least some gay people became turned off to the gay movement because some of the "movement heavies" in it seemed so devastatingly unappealing as people. At our best, we were often dull and humorless; at our worst, we were judgmental and hypocritical. While more and more gay people rallied to the ideas and feelings behind gay liberation, fewer and fewer thought of themselves as "movement people." Today, the gay movement reflects diverse attitudes, actions, ideologies, and organizations. By buying this book, or even reading it in the aisle of a bookstore, you have become a participant in the gay liberation movement.

After You're Out is not designed to set forth the ideology of gay liberation, nor does it pretend to suggest that specific programs or actions are "the only way." An underlying assumption of this work is that aside from any organizational efforts by gay people—and we support such efforts—there must be a realistic and clearly understood notion of survival by gay people—by individuals, by couples, and by groups. At the same time, we mustn't lose our sense of ourselves as human beings in a larger, very complex society undergoing vast social change. The issues raised here, therefore, are only a portion of those we have to deal with in our lives.

With this notion of survival in mind, we have divided this book into three sections: one on identity (realizing who we are); another on survival in a world that often does not welcome our transgression of its "morality"; and a third dealing with our efforts as gay people to form a community, to work together to improve our lives and the lives of those people who share with us the gay consciousness and the gay experience. Of course, in this process we will also help ourselves.

Although *After You're Out* is seen by us as reflecting a later stage in the gay liberation movement, it is motivated by the same concern that produced our first book, *Out of the Closets: Voices of Gay Liberation*. That concern has to do with the need to break through the walls of falsehood and silence that have kept gay people from understanding each other and even our own inner selves. As writers and editors, we have felt that the mass media in this country (and indeed all over the world) have failed miserably to portray the gay experience in a way that is helpful to gay people. To the extent that the movement has been reported on, such reports have tended to be trivial or incomplete or hostile. For example, virtually nowhere in the mass media has there been a discussion of the vital connection between gay liberation and feminism, while this link has been the subject of many articles in the gay and lesbian-feminist press. While we welcome efforts to influence the mass media, we feel it is essential that we do not sit back and wait for the big-shots of the communications industry to throw us crumbs.

Our collaboration came about initially in 1971, when Karla Jay and I were independently collecting what we considered the best writings on gay liberation in the hope of compiling them in book form. Most of these writings consisted of mimeographed leaflets or clippings from underground gay newspapers with an average circulation of four or five thousand. At that time there was not a single book available that reflected the ideas of the gay liberation movement, then two years old. I had met Karla early in 1970 when she was chairperson of the New York Gay Liberation Front and I was attending my first meetings.

When we both learned about each other's plans to put together an anthology, we decided to collaborate.

For all the affection that has been generated by our collaboration, it has not led to marriage and a life together in the suburbs. It has led us, rather, beyond our first book to this volume. *After You're Out* represents for us a logical follow-up reflecting the development of the gay liberation movement to a more pragmatic view, toward a commitment to the long haul.

While our first book contained a good deal of radical rhetoric, *After You're Out* should not be mistaken as an indicator that we choose reform over revolution. Rather, it is a reflection of our belief that people engaged in a revolutionary process such as gay liberation still have lives to lead, still must survive in their own minds, with their friends and lovers, and with all the creatures of this planet. Rhetoric does not a revolution make; people do.

There are many topics relevant to gay people and our struggle which are not covered in this book. I do not believe the articles selected adequately reflect the vital gay sensibility in the arts, nor are there enough examples of our sense of humor. It is also unfortunate that we have no full article on gay people and the back-to-the-land rural lifestyle. Not only are we missing some articles, but we as editors do not agree with everything that is said in the articles we have chosen. But there are many different ideas and viewpoints that will be helpful and comforting and perhaps stimulating for gay people. Hopefully, these essays will communicate something to our readers, gay and straight, about the contemporary gay experience—and about the consciousness of gay liberation in the mid-seventies.

Grateful acknowledgment is made to the editors of the various gay publications where some of these writings originally appeared. These small periodicals have been published against difficult odds, and the people who put them out deserve more thanks than they usually get. Karla and I had the good fortune of dealing with the informal and good-natured world of two smaller publishing houses, and there we have worked with Danny Moses, Ross Firestone, and Carol Fein, all of whose labor and assistance we appreciate.

Thanks also to all the working people in the publishing and printing industries, and to the lovely green trees who have all helped make this book possible.

Part One
Identity and Lifestyles

INTRODUCTION:
Identity and Lifestyles

Karla Jay

It is no accident that "Identity and Lifestyles" is the first section of this book, for the first step toward true liberation that a gay person should take is the awareness or search for who he or she is. He or she must also decide which lifestyle suits him or her best.

Part of the oppression of being in the closet was the isolation from other gays and sometimes even isolation from knowledge about other gays. What we were forced to accept were heterosexist stereotypes of us as either "nelly hairdressers" or "hardnosed truckdrivers." Yet while the oppressor saw and still sees us as all cut from the same mold, one of the truly positive and beautiful aspects of gay life is that there is great diversity among us. Sometimes it seems that there are more types of homosexuals than heterosexuals, despite society's assumption that we are an insignificant minority.

Therefore, part of the purpose of this section is to celebrate that diversity among us. Who are we? We are people moving toward defining ourselves as gay and people moving away from defining ourselves as gay. We are people committed to the gay liberation movement, people torn between the gay movement and the other movements, such as feminism, and people with no movement commitments at all. We are people who form lifelong commitments to one person, people who never form a commitment to any one person, people who believe in promiscuity, and people who believe in celibacy, asexuality, or masturbation. We live alone, in couples, in threesomes, and in groups or communes.

So when you ask, "Who am I?", you must decide for yourself, for we are as diverse as can be imaginable. The articles in this section are just a sampling of some of the identities and lifestyles some of our sisters and brothers have chosen; we have not been able to include all lifestyles and identities. Communal living is one example of a style we had to omit. Most of the people we contacted found the problems and pleasures of communal living to be so complex that they felt they could not deal with the issue in one article. Readers are urged to read an

3

entire book devoted to the subject: *Great Gay in the Morning* (Times Change Press).

Another problem we had was in dealing with some groups which have caused great debate within the homosexual community. Transvestites and sado-masochists are two of these groups. For example, many lesbians feel oppressed by male transvestites since they feel that transvestites further the role oppression of women by presenting a "super-feminine" image of women. Other lesbians object to transvestites portraying women for entertainment or for profit. In short, most lesbians will not tolerate men defining women. But there are also female transvestites, male transvestites, and gender-fuck men (men who dress in female clothes without the intent of passing for female) who believe that they are breaking down rather than building up roles. (See the forum on "Can Men and Women Work Together?" in Part Three for a further discussion of this issue.)

As for sado-masochists, many gay people feel that the entire concept is antithetical to gay philosophy, which aims at breaking down roles and at breaking down oppressor/oppressed relationships, while S&M is based on master/slave constructs. S&M people argue, on the other hand, that S&M is consensual and that fantasies should be lived out. A final problem is that since many transvestites and sado-masochists are straight, it would be important to relate the unique aspects of these lifestyles as they relate to being gay.

Another group omitted here is transsexuals, those who change their sex through surgery and hormones. The reason for this omission is that it is debatable whether a man who becomes a woman to pursue men is really a homosexual (although some men say that they are lesbians after their operation). Again, this is a complex problem.

The editors believe that each of the above-mentioned categories needs a full and honest discussion in an entire book—not just a few brief articles. And while it may seem like avoiding these issues, it would be wrong to deal with them in a superficial way, or to have one article against these groups without an adequate defense also presented.

Finally, the editors would like to point out that this section is not an invitation or even a proposal for the reader to label him/herself. To label ourselves (except as we find it convenient and helpful) would be just as harmful as the negative labeling heterosexist society has put on us. Rather, this section suggests some alternatives for gay people. The contributors to this section have written about one important aspect of their lives, and their articles do not imply that the authors have excluded other choices.

LESBIAN SEXUALITY:
An Unfinished Saga

Nina Sabaroff

The story of our sexuality is the story of a species of crippled ones who have begun to run. The story of a dark room with the windows flying open. The story of a desert where irrigation has finally come. My story, the story of a girl who was programmed to serve men but will no longer. Who doesn't have visions of the way it will someday be?

I like to think that this article is the unfinished saga of a girl who was always a lesbian but had to become a lesbian; of a sexuality that was always free but had to become free. I cannot speak honestly for the bodies and spirits of all women who will read this, but I know my strength comes from not being unique. It feels like an enormous task to stop history from orbiting long enough to crawl into my own body, connected up as it is with everything else . . . I hope as you read you will be encouraged to do the same.

I was 17 when, living in a rented room on a work-study from college, I looked between my legs and discovered a pearly bump, pink and translucent. I stared at it in disbelief. "Cancer!" I thought. (Until I touched it.)

One year later I was lying on my narrow bed on another work-study in New York, eyelids slightly lowered, the late afternoon sun splintering through the round leaves of the thousand-leaved tree into my room. Patterns of green and gold danced on the wall.

I was slowly touching my body . . .

I was thinking of Angie, my best friend in college, who was on *her* work-study, now in Chicago. I was thinking of her smiling at me, and I was smiling too. Her smile was entering me like a cool light turning into a warm light as I was raised off the bed a dreamwalker into the air, where I lingered until I broke into a million pieces . . . each one was brightly colored then soft, as I floated down to the bed, my fingers strangely wet.

I had had a mystical experience, or so I told whoever I told, never once admitting I had

MASTURBATED.

But go back further, much further.

Lying in bed after finally giving up thumbsucking, and rubbing my left nipple as I would fall asleep, night after night after night. Until at age ten I went to camp, and in the showers noticed my left nipple was like the nipple of my counselor, on a flat child's breast, my right nipple like everybody else's tiny button. Why did I feel secret pleasure from this premature glimpse into the mystery of breasts, and only a little shame at being different?

Or further back. When I was a little baby all I needed to start sucking was a little tap on my lips. I would eagerly take my mother's nipple into my mouth. For years after nursing ceased, my parents could steal into my bedroom at night as I lay sleeping, tap my mouth, and I would perform a little lip dance: kiss suck kiss suck . . .

Is kissing sucking inborn? Is love inborn? Do you love to kiss and suck, your fingers and toes

DON'T PUT THAT INTO YOUR MOUTH!

I played in the blue lupin in a wild gully near my home when I was growing up in San Francisco with my friend Kay. This day we were wearing felt beanie caps on our heads with little springs sewed on that vibrated as we jumped in the flowers, like little Martian girls. First we held hands and ran in unison and jumped over a puddle . . . then we picked little bouquets of lupin and gold poppy and gave them to each other. Then we whirled and twirled and fell down and heard in our bodies the pulses that come from excitement and exertion, and our beating hearts . . .

My memory dies there. Did we roll over to meet in the middle, hug each other, kiss, our beanies fallen off, our hair free? Did we touch like that, never shy because never knowing? Or were we content, girlfriends, to lie, simply, inches apart, and breathe together at four o'clock on a child's endless afternoon?

To feel, as I feel now, lying next to but not touching my lover, the warmth and smell of her body, its mystery filling up the small space between us?

Then it was one spring night, and I was eleven, playing kickball with the kids on the block. It was getting to be dinnertime, I was at home

6

plate, and the pitcher was rolling the ball toward me. I was ready for it, focused and full of adrenalin. I still remember what I was wearing: my favorite sweater, turquoise blue wool and snug. I looked down and suddenly saw two small round warm shapes pushing out my sweater. Breasts! Giddy, I kicked the ball hard, my foot tingling from the connection. The ball rose high high into the air, almost disappearing into the dusk, and I ran to first base, drunk on the power of my life, my strength, my beautiful new breasts!

That's the moment I can point to—just before puberty—when I was still a whole person, free and sexual and growing, the me I now recognize as my lesbian self. The being whose sexuality was an unfragmented response to her life in the world as she made sense of it, the tomboy girl scout whose mastery of her body was far more complete and more in harmony with her emotions and her brain than mine are now, almost twenty years later.

What became of her? What became of her when the pieces were carved out of her being so she could fit into the jigsaw puzzle of nuclear heterosexual patriarchal life?

She stopped dancing to school, stopped turning cartwheels, stopped arguing in class, stopped kissing her girlfriends, stopped playing basketball, learned to flirt, learned to pluck her eyebrows, learned to fear the smell of her vagina, learned to listen, to admire, to hold back, to say no, to say stop, to stop, to *not* stop, to think orgasm was "hills and valleys" and not the delight of abandon, suspension, explosion. Except in the privacy of my own room where somehow I remembered where my clitoris was, and would so gratefully, and without any fuss, rub it gently, lying in my dormitory room, my roommate sleeping fifteen feet away.

I became a female. I was socialized, acculturated, mystified, and alienated; I had crushes; I felt inadequate; I hated parts of my body. I dieted, was jealous, was competitive, put other women down. I had pimples, my breasts were too big.

(When I was first coming out, two lesbian friends lived upstairs. I confessed to them in all my confusion that I wasn't sure lesbians would be attracted to me because I had big breasts. Men like big breasts. Lesbians, I was sure, liked little ones.)

How long I clung to my freedom to be a person, I don't know, till fourteen or fifteen maybe, and maybe it always lived inside of me like a clock that ticks, its sound insisting I AM, beneath the masks, the pleated skirts, the strapless formal, the rolled-up jeans, the short dress,

7

the workshirt, because my self burst out like an angry moth when women's liberation finally struck me.

TWO LONG-TERM RELATIONSHIPS WITH SENSITIVE MEN AND MANY STRUGGLES LATER ...

Coming out at the same time many of my friends were, I felt a new security. Now there was nothing to hide. Now I could love myself and all parts of myself and my sisters and all parts of my sisters. Now everything would be clear and honest. Now my sexuality would come out too. At first it seemed to be true. It was so easy! Soft lips wonderful breasts cuddling and stroking and finding out about my body by finding out about hers. How naive I was to think it was going to be that easy, that I could throw away all those years of crippling to become innocent again. Nothing flows uphill, and uphill was the way back to myself.

My first lesbian lover used to masturbate after I had kissed her cunt or touched her clitoris with my hands when she hadn't had an orgasm. So she's *frustrated*, I thought. I felt excluded, mortified. Couldn't I do anything right? Couldn't I know exactly how to touch her at any given moment. After all, she was just like me, wasn't she? (As if all women are alike! As if all lesbians are alike!) Maybe I wasn't a lesbian at all, I thought, if she has to masturbate to orgasm after making love with me.

Also, she was a bi-sexual and I was her first woman lover. Sometimes I even felt guilty I had no penis. I felt guilty I could not "ravish" her. That my muscles could not crush her, since it seemed that was what was missing, for her, in our lovemaking. I felt guilty, because her lips on my breasts made me feel so passionate, so needy. I would lie next to her and crave her. We rarely kissed, and I wondered why. Wasn't I a "good lover"? Didn't I have it in me? Shouldn't I have stayed with men. At least *they* like sex with me. Oh god, I thought, won't lesbianism give me a rest from this kind of thing?

I was angry when women spoke of lesbianism as a panacea to all sexual problems. I was a lesbian but my relationship wasn't satisfying.

Finally it fell apart, and I found myself in another relationship, this time with a woman who was, incredibly, a *real* lesbian: a woman who loved women! not men! A woman who loved what *I* had, what *I* was, who loved *me*. I wrote a song: "Then I fell in love with a woman like me, didn't know I could feel so free, my heart and my body laughing

8

with discovery, something new every day and twice as much on Sunday."

It was in this—my present—relationship, that I finally began to trust and explore my lesbianism and my sexuality.

Journal Entry of First Night with S.

...ended up going home with S. and feeling so all right and like an adventure of heady possibility—so relaxed and high. The kiss and followed by another another lips tongues lips lips soft wet hard biting moving gentle, feeling all my tissues so open so responsive heating up, the beautiful little noises the bodies tumbling all dressed in clothes. S. likes to kiss! I like to kiss! Forgetting what that's like to kiss and kiss so deeply so telling each other who we are why we are that way. These two intense people being so soft, so astonished to find ourselves so open so generous so stimulated so free! Feeling my lesbianism like my body. Aching and tumbling and laughing, all my parts compact organic moving as a body will when its free. S. and I making love to each other *with*, not one to the other then one to the other. Finally taking off our clothes and overlapping and me feeling so trusting and so passionate. And S. telling me how beautiful I am, and me telling S. how beautiful she is. Making love hour upon hour—so that's how women make love all night (The Insatiable Woman!) with pauses and changes of rhythm, how exciting to feel us moving together in those rhythms that are so instinctual. Touching her clitoris feeling it throbbing—how different/same/different we are! My lips feeling like polished stones, my body responding anew every time we turned over. Feeling so with her wishing we didn't have appointments the next day. And on no sleep!

I'm in transition, and so is my sexuality. It has only been two and a half years since I have been a conscious lesbian, and for many years before that I struggled, as all of us have, with my sexuality. I agonized, in childish journals and journals not so childish, hoping to discover my real needs, and to separate those from artificial needs that cripple and drain me. I used to ask: Can you have sex without love? Can you have love without sex? I used to ask, how do I know if someone loves me? How do I know who to trust? I had no scale to weigh things on. I had

9

no analysis of this culture as patriarchal, with male supremacy affecting even my physiological capabilities.

Writing this article, I have had to face up to the paradox that the topic represents. On the one hand, I want to stress—in opposition to straight society—the joys of my lesbianism: the ease, the delight, the natural flow that I have felt of one woman loving another, awakening feelings in each other and fulfilling each other. I want to speak of the innocence, the familiarity, and the power of our sexuality. On the other hand, I recognize that when you live against the grain of society, when you refuse the awful compromise of roles, refuse the games and the goals of their sexuality, you are also in the uncomfortable (if necessary) position of having to separate the rot from the real. It makes everything suspect.

The very body I am learning to really accept and love still plays tricks on me. Along with the intensity and sweetness of lesbian love (for love, too, has to submit to our piercing gaze) is the fear of falling into patterns that stunt, or having expectations that deny someone else their freedom. Sometimes it feels awkward to "make love," for what exactly are we saying to each other?

To sometimes be feeling open and loving and when it turns into "making love" to feel everything change, to draw back or to feel her draw back. *Is* the natural progression from affection to sensuality to sexuality natural? What *is* natural?

I have read visionary lesbian literature of women loving women and I have written some. But the truth remains we are still in a primitive place, a self-conscious place, compared to where we want to be (which is in lesbian heaven!) and we want to be there RIGHT NOW.

I can list some *negatives* that are now gone for me: no more sperm dripping down my legs, no more "foreplay," no more "afterplay," no more "ACT," no "best position," no birth control, no "did you come?" or faking orgasm, no wondering if I'm wet enough, no sex every night like clockwork, no accommodation to a penis, no thousand-year-old roles haunting my every move.

On the other hand, there are no models for love and sex between women, between equals. My lover has the same rights I do: the right to be asexual, the right to be passionate, the right to orgasm, the right to masturbate, the right to have her own room and her own bed, her own work and her own friends, the right to need something different from what I need. This is easy to agree upon intellectually but working it out is something else again.

10

As lesbians, we understand the myth inherent in patriarchal romantic love that says two become united into ONE. All of us who have tried that or fallen victim to it know what it is to live crippled, to live for another person, to feel like half, to feel like a shadow, to be dependent, to be lonely, to be crazy, and finally, if we're lucky, to rebel . . . to break free, to go looking, to grope, to question, to throw out everything we've learned and to feel frightened, to struggle not to again be submerged, to struggle not to give ourselves up, to find and hold onto and stick with a new vision. I feel it sometimes in the arms of my lover, I taste the taste of how it will someday be to love, to be free.

I keep thinking of the words to a song by Bonnie of the Red Star Singers. She sings, "We don't want crumbs . . . we want the *Whole Meal*."* That's how I feel about my sexuality. I want it to be free, not just better. (It's better now that I'm a lesbian, but it's still not *free*.)

I want our feet to love as well as our genitals. The tender place behind my knee. Her delicious cheek. I want to roll over and over, like in the fields of childhood, I want to giggle, laugh, sing, grunt, mutter, groan, pant, smile, be suspended in time, go over the waterfall . . . I want to feel our breathing all over my body. I like touching myself when we make love. I like touching her touching myself touching herself touching ourselves touching each other touching our fingers our nipples our clitorises our vaginas our gentle rhythms and hear our noises welling up inside, whose noises, our noises. I don't want crumbs I want the whole meal.

I think of the patriarchal image of good sex: he enters your room where you lie reading . . . he looks at you . . . he tears open your blouse . . . he must have you! Your head falls back, he is ravishing your throat your breasts. How exciting, how raw, how animal, how truly sexual! While he is raping you you are crying out for more . . .

I think of my lover coming into my room as I am writing this. I try to imagine her tearing open my blouse, eyes half-crazed, saying "I must have you!" Yet this is the model of sex we have to go by: your animal desires burn in you with a fire that cannot, however you struggle, be put out. Whatever degradation, disease, or betrayal follows, yield all, abandon yourself to primal obliteration . . .

That raw, hurtful, passion is the other side of romantic love. It is the story of two species at war, with sex the white flag that brings you

*From "Still Ain't Satisfied" by Bonnie Lockhart. Copyright © 1973 Paredon Records.

11

together in momentary harmony.

It's not that lesbians aren't passionate: we melt, cry out, and are abandoned. But this we want to do without surrendering ourselves to the death of our own being. My lesbian life—and that includes my sexuality—means, basically, never surrendering myself out of existence, but instead enduring and multiplying. Imagine a society where you could afford to be open, without defenses, most of the time. How would that change your sexuality? If there were intimacy and sharing in plenty, not in low reserve. If there were no stares on the streets when we embrace or hold hands, no pretense, no closets, no parental disapproval, no alienation or anger that comes from being trapped when you want to fly.

Besides welling up out of animal need, sex in the patriarchy is also great entertainment. Has sex gone out of your life? Well, go get some. Try for the big orgasm. Try one partner, try them all. If the lights flash twenty-five times, you're a winner. Count your own contractions. If it is THAT BIG, it HAD to be good.

It isn't just "good sex" we want, but good friendships, work, knowledge, and the real power to make our visions of a better life a reality.

How separate can sexual energy be from life energy? I no longer believe that sex is an overpowering drive. This kind of sexuality—the kind that takes over your life—must be exposed as part of the patriarchy that feeds it. I want to be able to have a healthy sexuality, but more than that, I need not to be isolated and to have more control over my life. When I think about sex like this, I feel angry about the sufferings sex has caused me in the past, when I confused my search for it for the larger search for well-being.

How do we explore and build an honest sexuality in a culture that makes millions on pornography, degradation, sexual objectification, violence, a culture that is genitally-oriented, product-oriented, that says it is "normal" to "do it" this many times a week and suggests promising new positions to "do it" in. A society built on sexual and emotional repression.

Men, in the form of culture, still control our sexuality even when we no longer sleep with them, even if we never did. I haven't figured out all the components of patriarchal sex, how many ways my sexuality is still "perverted," but I'm sure there are many devious ones that I am still working out.

I laugh when I think, at age thirty, that I am supposed to be "reaching my peak" sexually. I may be reaching a peak in my evolution, from one who serves men to one who loves—how shocking and obscene!—herself and other women. This is seriously at breach with all that is male and woman-hating in this culture, the culture that tells me that loving women is a case of arrested development! I tell myself I won't be sacrificed to the terrible power of those who want to destroy me, my new culture, my vision, my sexuality, my LIFE. Sex, as sex is presently constituted here in the predominant culture, has *never* been less important to me than it is now. Since the consuming trauma of puberty began me on that tread-mill rat-race that said I was a woman equals sex equals love equals marriage equals babies equals tide me over until death. Paying all my life for sex which was supposed to be free. And people are supposed to be free to love each other. And to have free choice of whom to love. And to be free to like yourself and to think you are worthy of love, great love. If you're a good person, if you're a strong person, if you don't hurt others, then, we are told, you are supposed to get help from all the resources on earth so you will grow up healthy and free.

Well, we want what we deserve.

We want, and are beginning to have, the friendly, soothing, affectionate free touching between friends, as it once was in childhood. Lesbians holding hands, as we talk, at the movies, at meetings, at the beach, walking down the street together. Telling all the world how women feel about women. Stroking each other's hair. Dancing, running, doing karate, massage, sleeping in the same bed. Beginning to be generous with each other like we used to be.

This sensuality that is so free from tension . . . but then, what makes us feel *sexual*? What is our *real* sex drive?

For me, the two basic components of lesbian sexuality seem to be: (1) self-expression (physical and psychological); and (2) the expression of love (physical and emotional) for another woman. Ideally, these two become an interwoven theme, to be elaborated upon, like the beautiful fugue of flute and recorder intermingling, each instrument carrying its melody line, taking its cues from a familiar, overlapping scale.

I try to counteract the myth that I've internalized that sex is all-important—sex the romantic shuck, the magic potion that is supposed to cure all your ills, that so often takes energy away from fighting for what ELSE you need to be happy.

Sometimes I see celibacy (that includes masturbation) as a transitional way to deal with the contradictions and the unresolved paradoxes of sexuality and of relationships. Sometimes being in a

13

sexual relationship (how hard it is to say this!) is a real drain. Sex can spark the fights, the tensions, that lead sometimes to a lack of friendship among lovers. I know that celibacy is not sublimation, or giving up, or copping out (that argument is also used against lesbianism!) just as dancing or practicing karate is not sublimation of sexual energies. Celibacy is a chance for us to put our creative energies elsewhere, and to weigh how much energy we really want to give to another sexual relationship . . .

Masturbation, really experimenting with masturbation, was the big transition for me between heterosexual and lesbian sexuality. Not masturbation the antisocial, narcissistic, infantile fixation that Freud dreamed up, but an acknowledgment that sexuality is *inside* each one of us, not a gift or a lesson another bestows if we only surrender ourselves to it. I define masturbation in the broadest sense as a woman understanding and loving her own body, learning to give sensual and sexual pleasure to herself and exploring her changing rhythms, paces, and needs. All that I learn I am free to celebrate and share whenever I choose with my lover. Free to begin to break down the rigid categories of what is sex with another and what is sex with yourself.

The summer I was coming out I traveled in Europe by myself. I carried Violette Leduc's autobiography (*La Bâtarde*) around with me and would read a chapter in it every night before going to bed. I would read about Isabelle & Thérèse and their first orgasm (yes, a clitoral one). Isabelle and Thérèse are young adolescents in boarding school. They sneak into each other's cots in the cubicles of the dormitory sleeping room and make love with each other. Make love! Swoon, feel the fire, and melt, sigh, call out love words and encouragements ("a little to the right, a little softer, AH . . . yes Thérèse . . . ") and the smells and the heat would come into me. There I was alone, nobody even knew where, with Violette . . . on a journey taking place on so many levels.

Over the summer my body became brown and strong. I felt like the healthy unself-conscious creature I almost wanted to be (since I was a tomboy). I was coming out. I was going to be a woman-loving-woman. I already *was* a woman-loving-woman, but now I was going to live it!

One day I hiked up on a mountain of big red boulders that rose away from the road, away from the ocean, toward the sky. I climbed until I was out of view of the road, lay down and stretched out my arms and legs. Then I threw off my clothes and let my pale breasts look up at the sky, let the sun touch them, let my thighs and belly feel the heat and the light ... thinking *am I really doing this*?! I lay there, half-awake half-dreaming, rejoicing to be alive and indestructible. I could feel the force of my blood running in magic circuits deep in my flesh, my nerves, my soft skin ...

When I got back to the hotel, I masturbated. I always regretted that I didn't masturbate out on top of that mountain, the free daughter of earth and sky. Since that time, masturbation has been for me an important part of the process of self-discovery, self-love, and of liberation.

The struggles my lover and I are now going through are metaphors of new feeling and new life. Our bodies reveal the pain and the freedom inside coming out. The shy, the unfinished motion, the transitional, the clumsy, the graceful, the visionary. Our bodies the living signs of our dissatisfaction and hunger, the bearers of powerful change and desire. I know our bodies have gone through many revolutions and are giving birth to more. Like the thousand spokes flying into and out of a giant wheel, I feel women set into motion: self-perpetuating, gathering momentum, and inexhaustible. ...

We have a lot to struggle against, but we also have a lot to win. I think of the prophetic line from the *Lavender Jane Loves Women* album:

"We ain't got it easy, but we got it."*

---

*From "Talking Lesbian" © 1974 Alix Dobkin, Women's Music Network, Inc., 215 West 92nd Street, New York, N.Y. 10025.

WHAT'S A DYKE TO DO?
AND WHAT THE DYKE
IS DOING

Jeanne Córdova

PART I: WHAT'S A DYKE TO DO?

I have been a lesbian for seven years and I used to think I knew what being a lesbian meant. But I must admit over the last years the feminist reinterpretation of lesbianism has thrown my political activity in the gay, lesbian, and feminist movements into a quandary.

Recently a friend whom I call a *nouveau* lesbian (because she recently came into lesbianism from heterosexuality via the women's movement) told me, "A lesbian is not a homosexual." Last week I read a button put out by a radical lesbian-feminist collective which read, "We are angry, not gay."

In 1968 B.F. (Before Feminism), I read in Webster's, "a lesbian is a female homosexual . . . a homosexual is one who sleeps with his [her?] own sex." In 1970 I read in that now-famous radical lesbian document, "The Woman-Identified Woman," that "a lesbian is the rage of all women condensed to the point of explosion . . . but lesbianism is also different from male homosexuality, and serves a different function in the society."

Clearly these are somewhat conflicting definitions. Clearly they come from different perspectives. The former is what men like Webster understand about us; the latter, apparently, what my feminist sisters saw in our lifestyle. In recent years I have come to understand that lesbianism is *not* like (male) homosexuality because in a sexist society such as ours, no behavior of women is the same as that of men. Having come out "gay" four years before feminism, I first identified as *homosexual*, then *gay*, then *gay and lesbian*, then *lesbian but also gay*, and now finally as *lesbian*. It took me a long time to understand that in a society where women and men have become fundamentally different, lesbian women and gay men are also just that different.

The word "gay" comes from the French word "*gai*," which became popular in France in the Middle French burlesque theater as it was used to describe mock-feminine (swish?) roles. Because women were not allowed onstage, all the mocking and burlesque was done by *gai* men. Later the term came to be applied to any and all men who appeared feminine, on or off stage. The word was never meant or used to describe lesbian women. European tradition, closer to Greek, still uses the words "sapphic" and "lesbian" to refer to the daughters of Sappho of Lesbos. Sexist society lumped gay men and lesbian women together as "homosexuals" because they never took their "research" beyond our bedrooms. Now even the most blatant heterosexist researchers write that the culture and practices of lesbians differ strikingly from those of homosexual men. The difference is lesbians are women and gay men are men.

When women *love* (men or each other), they don't "love" like men do. What physical and emotional feelings women derive from sex are not the same as those that men experience. When women work *together*, it is not the same experience as when men *compete*. When women talk to each other, they don't talk about the things (money, status, power) that men talk about. Ad infinitum. Knowing this helps men understand that when women love each other and attempt to build a life around that love, they do not live or build as men who love straight women and they do not live or build as men who love other men. After I got this through my consciousness I was still left with another sticky conflict which I am now hoping to work out.

I was a lover of other women four years before I found the women's movement. During that time I, like so many of my sisters who had the misfortune of falling into pre-feminist lesbianism, spent much of my energy in *the bars* and *the roles*. Having left the latter, I still vividly remember the former. I still remember walking down the street and having men, and *yes, women*, point *"queer."* I still remember the cops coming in and lining me up against the wall and throwing other sisters into the wagon outside. I still remember when *The Ladder* used to say, "We homosexuals deserve our democratic rights to live and love the same as heterosexuals." I still remember my father throwing my short-haired lover out of the house and saying, "Don't you ever bring a woman *like that* in this house again!" I still remember others in my Abnormal Psychology classes saying, "We oughta take all those dykes and faggots and shoot 'em." I guess that means I remember what it means to be *homosexual* in this society.

In the last three years I have seen that to be *woman* in this society is just one step up from the bottom of the dung heap. I've always known being *queer* is being part of the dung heap. Maybe being woman isn't

17

even one step up, but I don't want to argue about which part of me (as if I wasn't whole) is more oppressed. It's all lousy. What I mean to say is this: I came into the women's movement via the gay movement. I now realize when society busts a faggot they are showing contempt for "a man who would be a woman," and when the courts take away a lesbian's children it is because she is *not really a woman*. For many years I have known that the "faggot-swish male" and the "dyke-butch lesbian" come in for far greater harassment than the butch male or latter-day femme lesbian. I know this is because the former are overtly breaking role behavior while the latter are okay because they still *look* like *real* men and *real women*.

Laying aside this crap, I as an activist question whether my place is with the movement which seeks to lift discrimination off my sexual orientation or the movement which seeks to redefine the one-down position of my gender. Does a lesbian belong working in the gay movement? The feminist movement? Both of the above? Neither?

Sometimes I sit in large gay community meetings and watch gay men subtly put down their femme-male lovers. Sometimes I sit in large feminist meetings and listen to my "sisters" say, "No, Jane can't be the one who gives the TV speech, her hair is too short, she wears men's boots—what will people think?" I know damn well what a lesbian thinks in either situation! I also know that a lesbian in the women's movement isn't doing much to help her sisters keep their kids in court cases, and I know a lesbian in the gay movement is not doing much to help her sisters prevent rape. Emotionally I so totally identify with women that it's hard to feel a part of Christopher Street West parades, it's hard to recognize "brotherhood" with John who got busted on "lewd and lascivious," when last week he asked me, "What do you see in women?"

For starters, what I see in women is, yes, indeed, being a lesbian is totally different from being a gay man. We have little in common but the society that mislabeled us—and right now we are rejecting that society and all its labels.

I am tired of telling my gay brothers, "No, you can't do that to women." I am tired of telling my straight and lesbian-feminist sisters, "I'm angry *and* gay." Sometimes I think my sisters who have found loving another woman through the rosy enamel of high-gloss feminism forgot-or-never-learned that loving another woman is also *queer*. No, being a lesbian is *not* the same as being a homosexual, but how do you fight against a society which says it is?

18

This year I don't see any real place in the male-identified gay movement for the feminist-identified lesbian. Yet this year I still question, "What is a lesbian-gay-queer woman's responsibility to the thousands of her sisters who still suffer under anti-gay as well as anti-woman prejudices?" Next year maybe someone will write about how to fight a society which would lock me up on two counts. Both, I hear, carry life sentences.

PART II: WHAT THE DYKE IS DOING

I now define myself as a lesbian separatist. I define myself as lesbian, rather than lesbian-feminist, in the sense and with the belief that lesbianism is the state of total woman identification, in the sense that lesbianism is the complete realization of sisterhood among women, in the sense that lesbianism is the bonding principle between women. I also define myself as socialist, not in the male-abused sense of that word, but because I know that a system which legislates power, wealth, and privilege as the prerogatives of an elite can never give rise to a culture based on the emotional and economic welfare of women or any other minority. I am a socialist in the humanist and feminist sense of knowing that socialist principles of collectivity and economic equality best serve the interests of women.

In my last four years after feminism, I have chosen to remain an activist in the lesbian, as opposed to gay, women's, left, and/or Trotskyist movements, because my emotional identification prescribes that the lesbian movement is the most honest place for me to work. And my politics, while recognizing our dialectical relationship with the world oppressed, dictate that there can be no better world for me than one in which I and my sisters can live in total openness. While I believe and hope for a socialist revolution in my lifetime, and I see that struggle as imminent, I believe whoever is in "the vanguard" of that revolution must be reminded that they are creating a better world for lesbians as well as other classes or races. The only way they will know this is if a strong and independent lesbian movement is around to kick their ass—if it's not already moving in the right direction. In that sense, I am a lesbian separatist.

Now then, a word of caution about the politics of our new Lesbian Liberation Movement. Knowing that male values, since the beginning of written history, have artificially separated art and culture from economics and politics, dubbing the former "a female invention" and the latter "the prime male contribution" to so-called civilization, I recognize no dichotomy between culture and politics. Validating the so-called cultural/political split is male-conditioned thinking. Western society's "thinking" is rooted in Aristotelian logic, linear, either-or, male *or* female dichotomies.

Being involved in several movements which seek the rebalance of human relationships along gynadrous lines, I believe every "politico" has to see in cultural expression the reflection of new laws that she is promoting, and every so-called "culturalist" must see in our proposed laws and redistribution of powers, the foundation which will support or negate her creative expression.

I think it is on a practical, rather than theoretical, level that this pseudo-dichotomy arises. We see some activists working on democratic rights and large-scale organizing, while others express their politics in small group discussions or art. And again, I think that both the civil-rightist who has no time or capacity for developing her emotional/creative self, as well as the artist who refuses to recognize that the world of (someone else's) law dictates her freedom to create, are half-persons, falling into male-constructed identities.

In my opinion the Second Wave of feminism has theoretically crested out . . . and in its demise, or perhaps temporary dormancy, we are now in a period of practical consolidation. As I see it, conditions which brought this about were:

> a. The January 1972 end of the Vietnam war and consequent dismantling of the single biggest radicalizing force of the last two decades, the antiwar movement. However much of it ran in principle antithetic to feminist values, many of us are left over and into feminism.

> b. The February 1972 Supreme Court pro-abortion decision which victoriously, but thoroughly, knocked the wind out of one of the two largest overground issues in the women's movement.

> c. The campaign for the E.R.A.—which abruptly put to sleep the other visible section of our movement.

> d. Last and most important—the sudden reactionary shift in this country's atmosphere as brought about by inflation, tight money, and the return to survival, as opposed to quality and equality, life issues.

20

We are living in a survival-oriented time; we can't fantasize our way into the revolution. As always in social movements, the most liberal, or easiest-to-stomach issues, such as equal pay for equal work, fair employment, abortion, civil rights in marriage and property, etcetera, have met with the most success. And the more radical issues of class conflict, lesbianism, and psychic genocide remain. In my opinion, class and freedom of sexual expression will emerge as forefront issues in the Third Wave. In this country's future, race will continue primarily as a class issue. Liberal waves in the ethnic minorities movements have done much to "liberate" some upwardly mobile blacks and Chicanos into mind-fuck middle-class homogeneous closets. The real issue we see here now is class.

I see the women's movement as the mother of the lesbian movement. But the lavender daughter has come of age! In the spring of 1974, *Lesbian Tide* magazine began to identify itself as a feminist-lesbian, rather than lesbian-feminist, publication. We in our dyke-rite have begun to take on the challenges our mother fears. We mean to tell the world we were not a miscarriage.

WITH ALL DUE RESPECT:
In Defense of All
Lesbian Lifestyles

Jane Rule

Several years ago I volunteered to set up a seminar called "Lesbian Lifestyles" as one of a number of offerings for a large, non-credit women's studies course at the University of British Columbia. I did not limit enrollment because it did not occur to me that very many women would feel free to attend. On the first night forty women registered, and through the twelve weeks the seminar met there was a floating population of well over fifty. Those with some experience in the women's movement wanted an open discussion without a chairperson, and, though the group was obviously too large for many of the women to feel free to speak, no one was willing to break up into smaller groups. At first, perhaps, it was the pleasure of being in a room with so many women willing to call themselves lesbians; but quite soon it was the fear of being isolated in smaller and more vulnerable numbers. For that room (it was my own living room) had become a very dangerous place to be, heavy with mistrustful silences, defensiveness, and hostility. Having been asked not to direct the group in any way, not to sit in my "Archie Bunker chair" (yes, I'm afraid I do have one, and it even looks very like my father's chair where we used to fish in the cracks for loose change to go to the movies), I waited out the first few weeks with hopeful patience, telling myself that we probably just had to get through a period of testing to a time when people would be willing to move into smaller groups and speak with the open candor I had come to associate with other women's meetings. But the atmosphere didn't improve; it deteriorated. I could not understand why people came back week after week. If the meetings had not been at my house, I would have given up in a month.

There were plenty of explanations for what happened. The age range was from eighteen to fifty-five; occupations were as diverse as laundry worker and professor of psychology. There were Maoists and devout Catholics. Some were members of a commune. There were monogamous couples, married women living with their husbands and female lovers, single parents who hid their lovers or explained their lovers to their children, women who had never dared approach the women they loved for fear of rejection. Such diversity doesn't need to get in the way of sharing experience, but in this circumstance it did. One by one every woman who was willing to speak was disqualified by others in the room as inauthentic, not a "real" lesbian. Women without sexual experience were rejected; women who associated with men were rejected; monogamous couples did not have the political consciousness to be lesbians; political lesbians were only using the label as a gimmick. Night after night people did nothing but defend their own right to be lesbian and discredit others whose notions were different from their own. A great many people never spoke at all.

To be a public lesbian, to dare to wear the label even in a group like that—or perhaps particularly in a group like that—is to insist that the psychic and moral content of the word be changed, its connotations made positive rather than negative. But what is positive to one lesbian is negative to another, and differing values become at once conflicting values. For, if one woman asserts her right to wear boots and a jeans jacket as an image of her freedom to be who she is, another who wants people to understand that "lesbians are just like anybody else" feels profoundly threatened. If one woman is trying to work out a loving and open relationship with both her husband and the woman she loves, another with a partner who is tempted by the safety of a heterosexual marriage feels betrayed and morally outraged. The lesbian who is willing to sacrifice everything for the privilege of being public in every circumstance, who sees any other choice as cowardly, confronts the lesbian mother with the loss of her children, the schoolteacher or nurse with the loss of her job.

I don't know how much the atmosphere of those meetings was also my inadvertent doing, my assumption of a basic goodwill among people which simply didn't exist, nor do I know how much of the hostility people directed at each other might really have been meant for me, but I did feel a heavy responsibility for the damage done to so many people who could ill afford attacks by those from whom they might expect support. My frank disapproval of what was going on only added another flavor of bitterness to the experience.

Finally, with only two meetings left, I couldn't stand it any longer. I sat down in my Archie Bunker chair and made my reactionary speech. It was *my* house, and I was left every week to clean up the psychic blood that had been spilled. If people wanted to go on with the destruction, I'd get them a room at the university for the last two meetings. If people came back to the house again and if they still refused to meet in smaller groups, I would assert my right to chair the meeting, to dictate topics, to cut off hostile speeches. Some people decided to meet elsewhere. Some came back. The day after the last meeting a couple of young women appeared at my door with a single rose, saying, "We met and fell in love in your seminar, so it couldn't have been all bad."

The conflicts that I saw in my living room are also being played out in the larger public world. Robin Morgan discredits Jill Johnston for being politically incorrect. Others discredit Robin Morgan because she is married and has a child. And Kate Millett can't figure out, moving from community to community, whether she's supposed to call herself bi-sexual or lesbian, because what is momentarily all right on the East Coast turns out to be wrong on the West Coast. There is not, apparently, an authentic lesbian in the land, except perhaps those who have yet to admit it. To discover this at a time when thousands of women are choosing to take the risk of being public lesbians is at first disconcerting and then for many really terrifying. It ought, I think sadly, to be funny.

For those of us who were public lesbians long before there was a movement which seemed to promise support, the rule-making, the testing, and the infighting are not as threatening as for those women who have counted on some sympathy and protection in order to take the risk in the first place. I don't mean to suggest that we pre-movement lesbians are either wiser or more courageous. The choice for many was forced upon us and had to be dealt with more like a broken leg than an heroic stance. For others the choice had more practical advantages than disadvantages, in providing a defense against marriage or relief from burdensome family relationships, or a way out of work we didn't like in the first place. Even those few who were actually crusaders usually enlisted in the battle under pen names when writing for magazines like *The Ladder*.

In those days when we met other lesbians, we did not automatically assume sympathy. On the contrary, we accepted the danger of increased visibility and usually avoided each other except at carefully arranged private meetings. "Don't worry about dress," I was told by a lesbian in her sixties who was inviting me to Sunday lunch, "we'll be just queers." We all knew people who had lost jobs or children just by having been seen with one of us. We learned to be negatively protective. There was no illusion that, when we walked in the bright light of day, we would have the support or even the approval of our sisters. What we did learn was to live without it, to come to terms with our own lives without the aid of the threat of the group. It's not an easy lesson, and it leaves some people in places of fear and bitterness who know, when they see what is happening among lesbians now, that people are really no damned good, and the only solution is to go on marching through life fully armed. (We grew up on Steig cartoons.) But for others of us the movement has provided some real support, new choices and new friends. Since we aren't as badly shaken by disapproval and rejection, having learned to live with it, perhaps we have a special job in the movement to work against what divides us and for a kind of solidarity that is real.

"Support" is a much-used word in the women's movement. For too many people it means giving and receiving unqualified approval. Some women are awfully good at feigning that for long periods of time and just as good at withdrawing it at crucial moments. Too many are convinced that they can't function without it. It's a false concept which has produced barriers to understanding and done real emotional damage. Suspension of critical judgment is not necessary for offering real support, which has to do instead with self-respect and respect for other people even at moments of serious disagreement. I have been critical of Jill Johnston's pressuring of other people to be as public as she is, not because it threatens me for I stand very much with her in public, but because I don't believe total visibility would necessarily achieve the better world she believes in. I have been critical of the amount of fear and hostility Robin Morgan has found it necessary to express because I think those emotions are contagious. I don't like Kate Millett's occasional flirtation with the role of public victim chiefly because I care about Kate Millett. I do, however, respect the right of each of those women to choose what she chooses, and, given the privilege of arguing with any one of them, I would contend as I do with a lover, to know and be known, without will to discredit, without will to win or lose, in a contest designed to strengthen both people. That attitude is possible only when I first of all accept that none of these women ever speaks for me, any more than Gertrude Stein or Radclyffe Hall or Vita Sackville-West speaks for me. I speak for myself. We must all finally speak for ourselves. I don't mean each of us should be able to command large audiences. Frankly, the dangers of serving a large audience often outweigh the values, for too many women are tempted to think of people like Robin and Kate and Jill as "leaders," therefore required to represent all women, though none of them has ever stood for election. They are self-appointed only as we are all self-appointed to speak our own minds. Each of us is, in that sense, alone, and if there is terror in that knowledge, there is also relief. No one else can discredit my life if it is in my own hands, and therefore I do not have to make anyone else carry the false burden of my frightened hostility. The paradox is that when I really stand alone, I realize what remarkably good and large company I am in. There are authentic lesbians everywhere: yes, asleep in their husbands' arms, yes, nursing their children, yes, three in a bed, yes, faithful into old age, yes, alone. Each has to stand alone before we can walk together, even in twos or threes, never mind as an army of lovers.

ON HUMAN IDENTITY
AND GAY IDENTITY:
A Liberationist Dilemma

Allen Young

There's a very old joke about the white liberal who attended a party where there was only one black guest. Anxious to get into a conversation with this black man, but unsure of how to do it, he finally walked over to him and said, "That Joe Louis sure is a fine boxer!"

I realize there may be some readers of this book who don't even know who Joe Louis is, so I will tell you that he is a black man who held the World Heavyweight title in championship boxing for much of the 1930's and 1940's. It is probably fair to say that he was the most famous black person in America at that time, and perhaps of all time—more famous than Frederick Douglass or Marcus Garvey or W.E.B. DuBois or Bessie Smith or even Billie Holiday or Louis Armstrong. His victories over white boxers were an early symbol of black power, of racial equality.

Now while black Americans loved Joe Louis and identified with Joe Louis (whose nickname in the white press was "the Brown Bomber"), one can only assume that the black man at that party did not appreciate the white liberal's lame attempt at conversation.

The point is, of course, that the white liberal was unable to relate to the black man as another human being, and so felt compelled to relate to him on the basis of skin color. Well-intentioned, the white liberal thought he would be more likable in the eyes of the black man if he showed appropriate recognition of a black hero.

At the heart of this joke is the question of identity, a crucial issue facing the gay liberation movement. I believe that the affirmation of gay identity has been simultaneously the greatest strength and the greatest weakness of the gay liberation movement. This contradiction is our greatest dilemma—my greatest dilemma.

The advantages of a strong gay identity have already been written about extensively in the gay press, but I will sum them up here.

First of all, identifying ourselves as gay is *truthful*, and brings with it the righteousness of spirit that comes with the truth. That sounds religious, and perhaps suitably so, as we proclaim our gayness to the world with a fervor that has religious overtones to it.

Second, saying "I am gay!" has the important element of *self-definition* to it. It is not the negative definition of others (homo, lezzie, queer, pansy, fruit) but a positive term we can call our own. (Even if the term is not an ideal one—there have been objections to the trivializing aspects of the word "gay" from within our community—still it is the one most generally favored.) The word "homosexual" is far less satisfactory, though we use it a lot, too. It has a medical, clinical feeling to it which we dislike, and besides, most of us have not always been (or are not now) exclusively homosexual. Most important, the term homosexual does not comply with the need for self-definition, because the term was given to us by doctors and other "scientists" who have not generally been our friends. "Faggot" and "dyke" are used in a special way, turning terms of put-down into proud affirmation.

Third, the affirmation of gay identity allows us to get together and achieve *unity* with others of like identity. This has obvious advantages for our sexual and social needs, but it also means we can share life experiences which cannot be shared with people who are not gay. This sharing is important to our self-image—to overcome the prejudice and lies of straight society—and to our sense of solidarity and awareness of our vast numbers, as opposed to our isolation. This leads quite naturally to the discovery of gay culture and gay history, the development of gay media, international communication and understanding among gay people, and, perhaps most important, action against our oppressors.

The price of suppressing one's gay identity, the price of closetry, is a very high one to pay. We have all known the closet in one form or another, and we abhor it. The experience we know as gay pride and gay militancy/revolution is a direct response to the dismal closet experience.

But once a person is out, once it is no longer traumatic or innovative for one to say to one's friends and to the world, "I am gay," once some time has passed, then the joy, the victory, the sheer relief at being one's self is no longer such an overwhelming part of one's day-to-day reality. In other words, coming out is great, but it isn't everything.

The gay liberation movement's stress on gay identity, gay pride, and gay militancy, as we all have said from the beginning, directly contradicts our larger message about human liberation. On the one hand, we want to affirm our oneness with the human species, while on the other we insist on our separateness (for the good reasons I have already summarized).

28

There was a time a few years ago, when I was active in the New York Gay Liberation Front (GLF), that I felt guilty for the few evenings a month I spent with straight friends, some of them married. I felt guilty not only because I wasn't spending my time with my "gay sisters and brothers" (some of whom were not my friends), but also because I failed to denounce my straight friends for their straightness and their marriages. I have since discovered that this was a rather specialized hang-up resulting from movement dogmatism, actually the product of a mere handful of individuals who laid heavy trips on those of us who were vulnerable to such trips. And I was vulnerable because I had previously put so much energy into the straight New Left movement, and because I had "passed" for straight.

Of course, as with all dogma, there's a kernel of truth to be dealt with. My married friends tend to follow the norms of that institution, and it is difficult if not impossible for us to have the kind of full and open relationship I would prefer. And it was good that "heavies" in gay liberation helped me move away from the New Left into involvement with the gay movement, just as they helped me discover and affirm my "femininity" and reject aspects of my "masculinity." So, hopefully, I have been able to contribute something to the gay movement.

But not everyone who is gay, or even gay-and-proud, is going to be my friend, or is going to share my values as a whole. It is unreasonable for us to expect ourselves, or any gay people, furthermore, to drop everything, to obliterate past lives and past interests, in order to further the gay cause. There is something about the very idea of gay liberation as a "cause" that bothers me. There were definitely "missionaries" in the New Left, and there's a lot of the same mentality in the gay movement. It doesn't strike me as healthy; I find it very restricting, and I think that is one reason there is always a shortage of activists.

Let me illustrate with an example. I am thinking of two friends, both of them writers, whom I knew in the New Left. Both of them were secret homosexuals, just as I was, but both of them came out somewhat later than I did. While both have become involved in aspects of gay liberation, neither has become involved or known as a "gay liberationist." Neither has become widely known as a public gay, yet both of them function in gay social circles and have carried the ideas and language of gay militancy to their straight environments. They are both quite well-known for their non-gay achievements; both are beautiful, deeply concerned people who believe that peace and justice are possible in this world. I have responded to these two friends with a

29

mixture of resentment and envy, most of it unspoken. I am resentful because I feel that if I burned all those bridges, they should too, that gay liberation should be a priority (some self-righteousness here!). But I am envious because I often wish I hadn't burned so many bridges, I often wish I could get my head together to write about something other than gay liberation (I find it almost impossible), and I somehow sense that they are more talented and more whole people, that I in contrast am a mediocre, hack "professional homosexual." But it is my friendship with them that seems most important, and I am concerned that the dogma of gay liberation not interfere with friendships that are valuable to me. Similarly, I am concerned that I can be me, the whole me, and not only a "gay liberation spokesman."

I do not want to be routinely asked about the gay perspective on this or that, any more than the black person in the joke wanted to hear praise for Joe Louis. But here again is my ambivalence: I do find I can express a gay perspective on this or that, and I do enjoy communicating it when I have a chance—and I feel that this is rewarding and socially meaningful. Still, I don't like the idea of being a full-time homosexual.

I feel a similar ambivalence when I am socially involved with my gay friends, especially my gay friends in Boston or New York. A typical relaxed conversation involving myself and other faggots is likely to involve such topics as sexual achievements (hopes and failures), a gay-oriented critique of movies, gossip about mutual friends and acquaintances, and news and views about a gay-oriented event, publication, or political action (plus a little chatter about the depression). The time goes quickly and we have a really good time. Sometimes, these conversations are beautifully intimate, warm, and personally rewarding. I depend on them for my emotional survival. But sometimes in the aftermath of such a conversation, I say to myself, "Gay, gay, gay, that's all I ever think, say, or do!" I feel at those moments that I have become narrow, bored/boring, hung-up, and stuck in a rut. (I hasten to add that I have spent some boring times with straight friends, too, in recent years, acutely aware of their straightness and the barriers it creates between us.) But the fact remains that a one hundred percent homosexual lifestyle and a one hundred percent gay liberation mentality can place one in a very small box, given the totality of the human experience.

I think that this notion of the "box" is helpful to understanding the failure of political movements generally to attract a mass following. Too often, the emphasis on a political category precludes full human interaction. Where the political category is not recognized ("we're all people"), there can be opression. But where the category is emphasized above all, there can be dehumanization. I am reminded of a Puerto Rican gay brother—see, even that phrase "Puerto Rican gay brother" reeks of dehumanizing rhetoric—who came into contact in 1970 with some members of New York GLF. Some of us saw in him the fulfillment of our fantasy of the right-on-gay-Young-Lord, but in the process of recruiting him to the causes of gay liberation and Puerto Rican nationalism (for he was not a nationalist; in fact he was happy to have escaped from *el barrio* to Greenwich Village), we stopped seeing him as a human being and we ultimately lost his trust and friendship. I, for one, miss him very much, and I am sorry he is no longer my friend.

The dilemma of the "box" is the dilemma of gay identity, too, and it is one reason that the gay movement does not have the numbers of visible, committed activists it needs. I am no longer the activist I was, and though I occasionally speak in public and write for gay publications, I rarely (or never) attend meetings, plan marches, lobby, run dances, mimeograph leaflets, or even do any of the troublesome nitty-gritty tasks of putting out a publication. I admire and respect those who do these tasks, and I did them all in the past, but I feel I can no longer do them. Of course, more heads and hands are needed to do the work of gay liberation, but perhaps more would become involved if they could feel that their total human identity could remain intact and not be overwhelmed by the label "gay."

Arthur Bell, writing in the April 4, 1974, *Village Voice*, told about his experiences at a recent gay dance at Columbia University in New York City:

> I bumped into a few men I used to know when GAA [Gay Activists Alliance] was in its heyday [presumably around 1970-71]. Their anger is toned down. They're not trying to change the world any more but are grateful to the movement for instilling that sense of self-identity. GAA was where they went to school, and once they got their education, they left. They're indifferent about the present in-fighting and they don't give a damn if Intro 2 [the New York City gay civil rights bill] gets passed.

I suspect that many veterans of GLF and GAA in many cities would fit such a description of apathy and indifference. Is this depressing?

31

Should those people who *do* still want to change the world (and I count myself among them) be angry with those who are apathetic? I am neither depressed nor angry, for if I and others have withdrawn from the active gay movement in varying degrees, there are new people involved in new projects, and old people involved in new ways. In other words, the movement we knew in 1970-71 has created ripples that are still expanding outward. Gay people with a sense of self-identity are "liberationist," whether or not they are activists.

I said before that I felt ambivalent about being heavily identified as a gay person. One important way I have dealt with this ambivalence is by deciding (back in 1971) to move to the country.

The most common gay experience is that the strengthening of gay identity leads a gay person to move to a big city, or perhaps a different city, in order to seek out a social situation away from straight pressures, where the environment is markedly gay.

Here in rural America, the environment is markedly straight—but why should we allow sexual oppression to deprive us of birds, water-falls, lakes, rivers, rainstorms, wildflowers, sunshine, springtime buds, gardening, building a house? Are these things straight? In a sense they are, for up to now, rural America has stressed the nuclear family and thereby enforced straightness on its inhabitants, but we must fight for our right to live in a rural environment.

Of course, rural people have experienced homosexuality—lots of it. Lesbian homesteaders, for example, are an untold part of American rural social history. And for gay men, there's even the word "corn-holing," right out of rural America (though perhaps the phrase is British in origin). My own early homosexual experiences took place in open fields under sunny skies and in an old barn in the Catskill Mountains, where I grew up.

The recent struggle of gay students in Maine and New Hampshire testify to the straight, up-tight mentality in rural and small-town New England—and to the courage of the students there. But I am too old to be a student, and I am talking about the gay experience beyond school.

Gay liberation as an ideology and practice has yet to come to grips with the ideas and demands of the back-to-the-land or country commune movement. How terrible it is that in order to be gay we usually have to choose life in an urban ghetto. Yet there are many gay people, myself among them, who are fed up with the reality of city life. It is a widely held belief, especially in Marxist circles, that moving to the country is a "middle-class privilege." It is my experience that what it takes is not a lot of money, but only the will to make the move. It certainly does not take any more money than the amount an ordinary worker spends on a new car or a summer vacation. Life in the city has many advantages, and I was a loyal New Yorker for some time, but once I really got in touch with the disadvantages, the city lost its charm for me, perhaps for good. That goes for the noise and pollution, the crowded housing, the paranoia, the rip-offs and the violence, the artificiality and crass commercialism, as well as for much of the aura surrounding urban sexuality (baths and bushes, smoky unfriendly bars, unhealthful drugs such as downs and amyl nitrite, etc.).

I risk sounding self-righteous, so I hasten to add that I have been back to the baths and the bushes and the smoky bars more than once since moving to the country. But I am glad not to have them around me as part of my environment.

Living in the country as an open gay person is an entirely new experience for me, and I cannot write about it in depth because it has not really happened yet. I have only been here for several months, and everything happens slowly.

But as I concern myself with building a house, growing vegetables, familiarizing myself with my natural environment, finding a place in a rural New England community, I am dealing with my broader human identity. That is a rewarding relief for me, to find myself relating to people once again on some level other than by using the vocabulary of gay liberation. Of course, I am still a faggot, and I am not proposing a return to the closet.

Do our neighbors "know?" We think some of them might. But some of them don't, and I have found that I simply do not overtly communicate my gayness here as quickly as I would in the city. I don't consider this to be closetry, but it is different from the kind (degree?) of gay identity one can have in a big city. Even in the city, of course, there are very up-front gay people who are "discreet" in their workplace—for the sake of survival.

Being gay here, my friends and I will have to confront two kinds of straightness: first, the rural New England Yankee nuclear family (or at worst, redneck); and second, the country commune folk who often adopt their own brand of sex roles (he-man farmer and earth mother, etc.). There are faggots in these woods, too, and we will find them! I know I am still part of the gay liberation process. I do much of what the he-man farmer does and much of what the earth mother does, yet I am neither. Here the process of gay liberation is bound to have unique characteristics, both in the area of being "out" and in the area of sex roles. We are only beginning to feel our way. Though at the present time we are all gay men, we don't consider our place to be a "gay commune." We hope for an integrated community that will eventually include women and children.

Like most people, I am seeking a meaningful, happy life. Recognizing the oppressive nature of this society, and my own place in it as an oppressed person (gay on the one hand, moneyless on the other), I do not choose to allow my sense of oppression to define my life into misery, martyrdom, and gloom. For me, the rural life, with its emphasis on creation (growing and building things) and simplicity, is particularly meaningful at this juncture in my personal history and in the history of America. I do not believe that rural life should be equated with isolation or withdrawal from social reality; I certainly don't see it that way, though I recognize that some people do. I don't feel the onus is on me to justify my choice. In fact, I am concerned about the city people who generally prefer to ignore the ecological crisis and the collapse of technological-urban America that is already upon us.

Above all, I suppose I feel that a rural lifestyle will provide me with an identity that is ultimately more satisfying than the other identities I have had to deal with in my past, such as student, Latin Americanist, professional journalist, New Leftist, or gay liberationist. These former identities do not, of course, fade away, but rather merge into a newly defined place in my current personhood. For one thing, my life here demands more physical labor from me, which is good for both mind and body.

I am motivated largely by my hope to transcend the experiences I have had as a homosexual and to explore my broader human potential. Humility as a human being amid the earth's many creatures is a crucial characteristic I can link to my gayness, or at least to the part of me that has rejected typical male notions of dominance. Just as we blame the *macho* mentality for war and other forms of coercion and control, we should also blame it for humankind's foolish insistence that nature be dominated rather than lived with harmoniously.

If I succeed in building a meaningful life here, however, it will be largely because of the incredible support that I have felt from the gay liberation movement and from the gay people who have been, and continue to be, my acquaintances, friends, and lovers.

SURVIVING GAY COUPLEDOM

Karla Jay

I. EXTERNAL STRESS

There is a persistent myth among both heterosexuals and homosexuals that long-term relationships are a trait of heterosexuality, whereas social interrelations among homosexuals comprise brief and frequent encounters in dark bars, tea rooms and bushes in the local park. This so-called "promiscuous" homosexual is the one put forth to the public in novels and movies with rare exceptional "stable" couples shown in movies such as *That Certain Summer*. Undoubtedly, the promiscuous homosexual *does* exist in visible numbers, just as the stereotypical fag hairdresser or designer is also a reality.

However, there are no reliable statistics to show what percentage of gay people do *not* fit this stereotype. Although my contacts are large and international in scope because I do a great amount of traveling and speaking on behalf of gay liberation, even I am relying here on my own sampling, which is naturally biased because one would assume that I associate with those who have something in common with me—that is, other couples.

Despite the unscientific base of my sample, my conclusion is this: the proportion of gay couples is probably almost as large as the percentage of heterosexual couples, and the spectrum of types of relationships is at least as large—that is, gay couples range from those who are completely monogamous to "swingers" and "spouse-swappers," and gay singles range from asexual (but gay-identified) or "one-at-a-time" individuals to numbers-counters who notch their bedposts.

Legally, of course, all gay people are considered "single"—that is, one can't file a joint income tax form with one's lover and one can't pass on any benefits or rate reductions such as social security or health insurance to a gay spouse, so I'd like to make it clear that I use the words "single" and "couple" only in a social context. I'm sure, however, that no one will argue this point, nor will many people of any sexual orientation deny the wide range of gay sexuality. However probably many gay liberationists as well as heterosexuals will want to deny for different reasons that a relatively large proportion of gay couples exists.

Naturally heterosexuals have a vested interest in seeing us as "the Other," as Simone de Beauvoir might put it—that is, the more unlike them we are, the more they will be able to point us out and hopefully keep us at a safe distance, for if they can't do that, how will they distinguish us from them? And if we are just like them, a further step might make us them—or worse yet, them us. For homosexuality—unlike blackness or womanhood—is "contagious." A white man won't wake up one morning to find himself black or a woman, but he might become "queer" just as millions in this country are gay without any adequate medical, psychological, or sociological explanation. We are inexplicable, and, ergo, no one has a clue to immunity! We are greatly to be feared. It is thus no mistake that the phrase "Pinko Commie queer" emerged. If we deny the majority's vested sexual interests, we must be "Commies"—against the family, God and Country, haters of Mom and apple pie, and fancy-free, footloose hedonists.

It's all a neat package. Again, some of us fit this description; others don't. Many gay people, including myself, do oppose the nuclear family and with good reason, for it is this neat foursome (Ozzie, Harriet, and two kids) which was always held before us and which was a prime instrument of an oppressive atmosphere which conspired but failed to make us "straight."

Some of the "radicals" go even a step further: They automatically eschew any traditional heterosexual value, just as heterosexuals have condemned in wholesale fashion the lives and loves of gay people. To this way of thinking, since heterosexuals have traditionally lived in couples, such a lifestyle must be pronounced "perverse," and one is told to live in threesomes, foursomes, collectives, and alone—in short, everything but . . .

Of course, monogamy—the preached but rarely practiced virtue of the heterosexual—has got to go, too. In addition to being a trait of those other people, monogamy is flagrant capitalism. The argument, if I can put it succinctly, is that having a "mate" is part of the whole hang-up of having property. Marriage and its ills are even traced back to when the nomads became cultivators and thus the first capitalists.

This argument is also supported along anthropological and biological lines, just as homosexuals have argued (and rightly so) that

36

homosexuality is frequent and "natural" in many animals (such as monkeys) and should therefore not be considered unnatural in humans. This reasoning also rightly points to human cultures in which homosexuality was (ancient Greece) or is almost institutionalized. When applied to monogamy, the homosexual theorists point to all those animals out there hoofing it with more than one—dogs, elephants, and so on. The trouble with this type of argument is that it tends to neglect those animals that are monogamous, such as the wolf, and many species of birds. In fact, much like the Bible, the animal kingdom can be looked at to support any type of lifestyle: should we applaud harems just because they are supported by the wild stallion with his herd of mares?

Worse yet, such dogmatic attitudes against monogamy and coupledom, along with downright condemnations of other heterosexual values such as a straight-male-God-the-father, drive people from our midst. Like the preachers who promised Heaven if only we would give up sex, liquor, and all worldly gain, we often promise people the abstract pleasures of liberation and self-love providing they first give up monogamy and coupledom in general, and that male chauvinist God and role-playing in particular. In short, we attempt point-blank to pull their entire value system from under their feet, and the result is that those who don't cherish anomie or who lack the proper spirit of adventure/liberation dash right back into the closet and bolt the door.

Of course, one can point to our gay churches and synagogues replete with marriage ceremonies and say that only "those radicals" are seeking another way of life, but that would deny the reality of the threat of gay liberation to the nuclear family, its traditional role-playing, and even to the nature of God him/herself. This emphasis also neglects the very real waves the radical is making, if only because those homosexuals who look and act just like the heterosexual have been so coopted into the system that they are practically invisible. Ask any newsperson! Only the ugly or different stories make the paper—if 210,000,000 do it daily, that ain't news.

It is ironic, I suppose, that I do not deny the validity of most of the "radical" concepts I have just described, whereas I do object to the usual belligerence and absolute dogmatism of the arguments. Having been told all my pre-liberated life by straights how to catch a man, I resent being told by gays how to order my current sex life. Furthermore, we who have been regimented all our lives into one neat hetero box should allow for variety in others. Can't there be both monogamous and polygamous creatures among us as well as in nature?

Of course, we should encourage people to experiment with other ways of life, but let's have an end to this fascistic way of shoving our points of view down the throats of fellow homosexuals. And if we "radicals" have come to the conclusion that monogamy and/or role-playing is "wrong," we have reached that point only after months or perhaps years of raising our own consciousness on a personal/political level. Why do we expect others to grasp in a day what it took us so much blood, sweat, and years to understand? And how can we be so absolutely sure that our way is the "correct" way? We must finally realize that consciousness can be passed onto others only in a general sense (such as the fact that homosexuals are oppressed) but deep individual change comes slowly—especially change in one's whole way of relating sexually—and we must allow others the same time, mistakes, and plateaus of consciousness we ourselves had. If we insist on being dogmatic, we should aim our fierceness at dogmatism.

In addition to the heavy rhetoric driving people away, there is an underlying ambiguity. A few of the people who have the heaviest anti-couple rap have come up to me privately and informed me that they envy my long-standing relationship with my lover but fear that such a destiny is not to be their lot for a wide variety of reasons— usually based on failures of past attempts.

Even more confusing is when some of the people who swear by anti-couple lifestyles come to me for advice on how to keep together in or form new relationships, which they supposedly reject politically and personally. Why do they want me to help them when they continually scorn the nature of my relationship or put me down indirectly—when they speak abstractly of "those couples," I'm part of one too!

I suppose, however, that the ambiguity is preferable to some of the wounding put-downs. One concrete example of this is when I protested the proposed picketing of a movie on the grounds that my lover and I felt it had more merit than fault. In the heat of the discussion, all of another woman's latent hostility toward my relationship emerged. She announced that our opinion only counted as "one opinion" since we "always think alike." I'm sure that if she really knew us, she would have heard of the heated "discussions" we have continually over movies, books, and politics (to name a few areas in which we sometimes disagree), and that idea would have been quelled in a hurry! Perhaps she was implying that we are together because we like to see all our thoughts mirrored or that we naturally have the same thoughts. Sure, people must have something in common to relate, but a continuous echo would be dull and nauseating—for us at least.

More insulting was the trip she way laying on us—a trip laid on heterosexual couples too, I'm sure, especially before the advent of women's liberation; that is, whatever hubby likes, wife will like too. When the wife of this model heterosexual couple finally spoke up, and loudly too, men finally realized that she had her own mind, no matter how close her relationship to her mate. If we haven't learned this lesson from women's liberation, what have we learned?

Finally, this opinion expresses a great fear of the couple: that is, in a society of supposed singles, the couples have two voices and could form in theory a political bloc in decision-making. Again, this type of thinking about couples does not give us the credit of having individual ideas.

Furthermore, anti-couple people insist that as a couple we are unrepresentative of lesbians, without realizing that lesbianism today is predominantly represented by couples, such as Phyllis Lyon and Del Martin, Sidney Abbott and Barbara Love. They lay on us such a set of "couple" stereotypes that I sometimes feel that we should do an "Amos 'n' Andy Show." They insist that we are monogamous, which we are not. They act as if we are physically tied as if by an umbilical cord and show great surprise if I mention I have some friends who are not also friends with my lover. Or if either one of us shows up alone, they suppose the other has malaria. They must think all our mail comes addressed to Ms. and Ms.

Since we are backward enough to be in a couple, they also assume we are into role-playing, and they proceed with great authority to tell us who is who, in case we've forgotten. They forget, I suppose, that a lot of role-playing was and is enacted in the singles set as well as among couples. In any case, since I am a writer, they assume me to be the "butch" and think my lover sits home knitting. They cannot or will not see that we merely have different talents—I am verbal and my lover visually artistic—and some are shocked when they discover that two of my hobbies are cooking and gardening, and hers is ham radio, a supposedly "masculine" hobby. We *do* play roles—but only *survival* roles, and who does what best does it.

If other couples are treated this rudely, it's no wonder couples are not seen nor heard as often as they should be. However, I don't want to leave the impression that the only flack couples get is from the uncoupled. Unfortunately, other couples also oppress us. As soon as a relationship is on thin ice, the couple runs over to us for help. We have been together longer than they, so we must have the magic formula. They naïvely ask us what we do about various matters, as if our solution will automatically apply to them. Since they see us as stable, they lean on us—and lean and lean. To a rocky couple, and to some singles too, our stability makes us parent figures, so they feel safe to come to us to have their nervous breakdowns. You may think its flattering for people to have so much faith in you, but after the tenth nervous breakdown each month, we disconnect the doorbell. I know of another "stable" couple who got so many advice-seekers they had to set up a special "crisis room" with a ten-day limit to make room for the next impending crisis. Of course, we care about our sisters and brothers, but we have only so much energy and would rather spend what we have on those we feel close to.

Individuals are also oppressive sometimes, making thoughtless remarks they think are compliments. For example, lots of couples and singles think they are flattering us when they tell us how pleased they are that we have managed to stay together so long—as if our function is to be their North Star in an ever-changing world. It's hard enough to have a relationship without all these people following us around with egg timers wondering if and when we will make the *Guinness Book of Records*. For us, our relationship is a matter of quality not quantity, and we stay together because we love one another. Pleasing others is extremely incidental.

Needless to say, but necessary to repeat, all types of gay people have something to contribute to the movement. If love and constructive thinking (i.e., show people alternatives, but leave the choice to them) operate, with any bitterness going to our true oppressors, then couples will feel free to come out more openly among movement poeple, for certainly the cause is the same one. Of course I don't speak for *all* couples, but I have a feeling that all we really want is to be treated like normal *individuals* (just as singles are treated) with a basic recognition of our lifestyle as couples and a recognition of the unique types of suffering couples undergo in a singles world.

II. INTERNAL PROBLEMS

The preceding analysis of the pressures and difficulties gay couples experience from the gay singles community in no way implies that external problems are the only ones that gay couples have to cope with.

40

In fact, despite all external difficulties, it goes without saying that gay couples most often break up due to *internal* turmoil, although outside social pressures may be a contributing factor.

It is also true that the specific difficulties that gay couples experience within their relationships are more difficult to analyze, because we suffer from many of the same problems that beset heterosexual couples. Like heterosexuals we may fall into sexual or behavioral roles which eventually prove destructive to one or to both members of the couple. We often also suffer economic inequalities in the relationship, with one partner making more money than the other, a disparity which may cause strain in the relationship by making one partner feel "inferior" to the other or in some way inadequate. Finally, each person comes into a relationship bringing her or his own personal and cultural values which may conflict with those held by the other partner.

But while many books have been written for heterosexuals on the problems experienced within relationships, we have very little written directly for us. Often we are forced to read about how some heterosexuals have dealt with their problems and then have to transfer their solutions onto our own relationship. This process may or may not work, but at best it is inadequate. It also seems that it would be inadequate and unfair for me to offer "general" or "total" solutions in an article of this size. Therefore, I have decided that it would be better for me to relate how I have dealt with these problems in my own lesbian relationship; perhaps my own experiences will be useful to others facing the same difficulties.

First there is the problem of roles. Since neither my lover nor I was into butch/femme roles, we only had to combat other kinds of divisions of labor, which had their origins in what we came into the relationship equipped to do. For example, since I had lived by myself for six years, I was an able cook, whereas my lover had lived with her parents and knew only how to thaw food or open cans. For sheer survival I did most of the cooking until I gradually taught her how to cook, and now she does half the cooking. On the other hand, I had never learned to drive a car, and frankly I didn't particularly relish the idea of doing so. However, she taught me how to drive, and now I do half the driving. We divide even the most pleasant and unpleasant tasks equally, and the only role division is based around survival necessities. For example, I get deathly ill if I have to empty the carpet sweeper, as I am very allergic to dust, and so my lover does that task. I do other work to make up for this lopsided division of work.

41

As for economic differences, luckily we have none. We are both impoverished! However, what money we do have we keep separately, since we each want to feel financially independent. Having our own separate checking accounts allows us to feel free to spend money on whims, such as books or records of no interest to the other person, without feeling guilty about "wasting" communal funds. However, we pay equal amounts for most things (such as rent, food, electricity, etc.), including the car, and each item we purchase together becomes common property. In the event that one of us would make inordinately more than the other, we would divide what we put into rent, food, and so forth on a proportional basis with the larger "breadwinner" paying more.

Differing social values are the hardest to deal with, and we each came into the relationship with opposite views in many important areas. My lover believed in monogamy (although she no longer does), and I don't. She wants to spend more time with me than I care to spend with her, since I have a very strong need for time alone. At times, these differences seemed insurmountable. However, we both have an enormous amount of love for one another and try to understand and relate to the other's views and needs. I am still uncomfortable with her monogamy (since in practice she is still monogamous) as she is with my lack of it, but we have each grown more tolerant of where the other is at. And she respects my time alone, as I have come to an understanding of her need for my time and attention. The struggle has not been an easy one, nor has it ended, but it has not torn us apart either. To expect a relationship with no tension is unrealistic, but it is also impracticable to be completely obdurate about one's own position.

Finally, I would like to write about the one problem which seems to confront most homosexual couples far more than heterosexual couples: jealousy. "The jealous lesbian" seems like a stereotype laid on us by heterosexuals, but there is a lot of truth to this image for a very simple reason, which is that we socialize in groups which are usually all men or all women. In other words, each time I go out to a party or a dance, every woman in that room is a potential sex partner for my lover or me. In a similar heterosexual situation, a man would only have to worry about his female partner being attracted to another man, or vice-versa. We have fifty percent more people to worry about and thus more cause to be jealous!

And because we live in a single-sex environment, a jealousy problem among non-monogamous couples can become much more complex than in a similar heterosexual situation. For example, once my lover was jealous not only because I had another lover, but also because she too wanted to sleep with the woman I was relating to.

In addition to the jealousy problem, we face one other problem in social situations that heterosexuals don't—that is, one partner of a gay couple may be used or played with merely to get to the other partner sexually. For example, my lover was befriended and much sought after by a woman whom she thought was interested in her affection. She was then astonished to discover that the woman was really interested in becoming my lover and was using her for this end. The reverse has also been true. I have even witnessed situations in other couples in which a woman has slept with first one member of a couple and then with the other member of the couple just to separate the couple so that she could retain the first woman!

I don't really know what can be done about this situation, but I suspect that half of the solution lies in a recognition that a lot of paranoia is justified. Every woman in a lesbian community is a potential sex partner, and in many communities of limited number, breaking up another couple is the only way to obtain someone for oneself. Realizing that all involved are oppressed by such a situation, we can perhaps have more tolerance for all involved.

But no matter how many potential sex partners are out there, couples should realize that whether the relationship ultimately stands or falls depends on themselves. We stay together because of our own love or willingness and desire to stay together, and others are actually only a catalyst that may ignite an already troubled situation. For despite all external and internal problems and pressures, only the members of the couple control the course and outcome of the relationship. And that knowledge that we alone have this ultimate authority on the direction of our lives may help us survive and flourish in gay coupledom.

SOME THOUGHTS ON MONOGAMY

Julie Lee

Because I lived monogamously for over twenty-two years, then started a multiple relationship while trying to preserve the relationship with my original long-term partner, the discussion of monogamy vs. non-monogamy has been much on my mind for the past sixteen months.

I had known for many years that the concept of monogamy was oppressive, originally developed as a way of keeping women enslaved, and that it was no longer a viable idea in the 1970's—and I had said so in public many times. The funny thing was that I never expected to be personally involved in anything other than a monogamous lifestyle myself, having lived this way for all those years, and not having been really dissatisfied with it. I had what seemed to be an exceptionally good relationship with my life partner. Sure there were areas of disagreement; there were bitter disappointments, especially in the early years; there had been the usual struggles to adjust to each other. But on balance we certainly seemed to be as happy a twosome as any I knew. I had lots of self-expression and status within the movement, and my partner was totally supportive of me in that role, which seemed to fulfill my needs sufficiently so as to blind me to what was really going on inside of me—the *real* inside where I lived. I did not realize that this happiness was partially a result of my having given up the struggle for self-expression and status within the relationship.

One thing that I had always taken for granted was that my companion was not only my lover and life partner, but that she was also my best friend. This seems to be a common fallacy—I know many women who thought this about their husbands, only to find that the husband turned against them when they confided to him situations that did not fit into his preconceived idea of what a wife should be and do. I found the same in my lesbian partnership.

I suddenly and totally unexpectedly at age fifty fell deeply—almost desperately—in love with another woman. I had certainly *not* looked for this experience. I was neither ready for it, nor did I basically want it. As a matter of fact, if I had been consulted in advance, I would undoubtedly have said that it was the very *last* thing that I wanted. But sometimes fate plays peculiar tricks, and it seems that passionate love was to come to me at an age when most people are willing to settle down and be thankful for even a tolerably good relationship with almost anyone.

When the realization of what was happening hit fully, I was at first at a loss as how to handle it. I was much too affected by this experience to be willing to ignore it—if I could have, which I doubt—but on the other hand, I had no intention of "exchanging" this new love for the woman at whose side I had lived for the past twenty-two years. I never could understand "exchanging" one person for another; I still cannot understand it, and I had no intention of doing this—ever. I knew the popular opposition to "more-than-one lover," especially at the same time. I also knew that most people live that way—secretly—and I was determined to show the world that it could be done openly. Presuming my life companion to be my best friend and realizing that I had done much—if not most—of the emotional giving in our relationship in the past, I was sure that now that I had a deep and personal need, she would surely understand (as I had in the past understood her needs) and would help me and my new love to work out a satisfactory multiple situation. It did not turn out that way.

At first my life partner seemed to feel that my involvement was merely a passing fancy—a short affair—and that if she "humored" me, it would pass within a few weeks. This belief in itself shocked me. I had thought that after twenty-two years she would know me better than to imagine that I would take my emotions for another so lightly. Some of her friends informed her that this was probably due to my menopause, and that it would go away in a short time. Others clicked their tongues in disapproval. In general, none of *her* friends (some of whom had pretended to be my friends also) seemed to consider taking me and the involvement seriously—a real blow to my feelings. After all, I had been totally monogamous with her for so many years, proving that I do not relate casually to others in an intimate way. I had always been totally honest with her, but when it came to something she did not want to face, I was considered frivolous, suffering from the menopause, and a "bad, unfaithful wife."

Being a feminist and having lived for many years with my companion, I was really floored by all these events. Hadn't she listened to *any*thing I had said in the past years? As it happened, she really hadn't but had attributed my opinions to "little feminine wiles." Had the feminist movement had no impact on her? Again I found that "women's things" were not to be taken seriously by a person who was career-oriented and strongly male-identified.

Somehow, despite unasked-for interference from innumerable people, very little support except from some few individuals within the radical lesbian/feminist group to which I belong, and every type of imaginable hassle, we have managed to stay together so far. Working things out with my new lover have been complicated by the difficulties my life partner has given us and is still giving us. But my emotional commitment to my new lover is strong enough to hold us together as is her love for me; and my life commitment to my life partner is somehow strong enough for me to survive every conceivable hurt and rejection. We are not yet out of the woods, and my life partner still threatens to leave me at times, but after sixteen months I have some hope that things will work out eventually.

Whatever the future holds, the last sixteen months have given me a tremendous opportunity to evaluate what monogamy has meant to me, what it most probably means to others, why we are so locked into this oppressive system, what the nature of this oppression is, and what we can do to free ourselves from the system and develop something better for all of us, especially for women-oriented women.

First of all, what really puzzled me was that lesbians—who have already rejected the status quo to a large extent—could still be so rigidly into monogamy to the point where they were eager to support the "injured" partner and condemn the "guilty" one. Words like "betrayed," "unfaithful," "immoral," and "promiscuous" and opinions like "how could you do this to her?" and "she supported you all these years" were thrown at me. No one, it seemed, could accept the fact that I had experienced extremely strong personal feelings and had developed a vital personal need that had to be fulfilled. No one seemed to recognize that a twenty-two-year monogamous relationship did not preclude the possibility of falling in love—even after all these years. No one seemed to care about *my* feelings—my need for the other woman, my intense desire to stay with my life partner. This denial of individual needs is one of the worst aspects of monogamy: the "joining together into one" of two people who used to be individuals. Monogamy—as we understand it in our culture—takes two individuals and molds them into one unit, then kills the individual, including that individual's needs, wants, desires, and independent action. In a heterosexual marriage this

46

works out to be a unit represented by the male—the female being totally "swallowed up" in the process. In a lesbian couple the one swallowed up is the one who, for the sake of unity, gives in and lets the other's needs come first and foremost. But the process is so insidious that most of us never notice it until it is too late.

Monogamy apparently can only work when one or the other of the twosome is willing to give up her personal identity and her personal needs, at least within the partnership. In some cases, as in ours, outside activities are tolerated to a certain degree, but within the inner sanctum, it is one or the other who represents "the whole." However, even the "dominant" one is expected to give up certain needs and desires in exchange for whatever advantages the monogamous relationship is supposed to bring.

If looked at closely, this role-playing is a master-slave relationship, although at times the relationship can be—and is—one between a benevolent master and his "beloved" slave. As in all circumstances, the master is permitted certain "digressions," as long as it is done discreetly. The slave has almost no freedom to do her own thing, and often has to give account of her every actions, her time away from home, and every cent that she spends of her "husband's" money. In a gay relationship the outward appearances are not nearly so blatant as in a heterosexual couple, but often the inside of the relationship does not look all that much different.

One reason why many gay relationships break off after a number of years—often before the tenth anniversary, and usually much sooner—is that one of the partners or both realize that the relationship is leading to such a slave-master situation. Those who become aware of this quickly disengage from such a predicament. Those who continue in the relationship for more than ten years almost always have set up some type of master-dependent thing, or the twosome could not have lasted. It is understandable that in the heterosexual world this role-playing is almost taken for granted, due to our early upbringing and religious training. We are told that we will all get married and raise a family, that the man is the head of the house, as Christ is the head of the church, and that marriage is "forever." Of course in 1975 we all know this idea to be a myth, but rigidly enforced "values" die slowly, and the conventional marriage vows still tell the wife to "obey" and tell both that the bind is "till death do us part." Polygamy is a crime in every state of the union; therefore if one partner in a marriage wants to love and live with another person, (s)he must get a divorce (that is, "discard" the mate) and enter into another marriage "for life."

The puzzle is why gays fall into the same trap, given that there are no legal bonds. There must be attractions in the monogamous way of life, even for gays, that make one of a couple want to give up her individuality in exchange for . . . what?

One major reason seems to be the matter of security. Most people need someone to be with, to be close to, to live with, to love and to feel part of and with. Probably influenced by our socialization, we put the emphasis on *one* such person, rather than on several. Even gays feel that it is desirable to have some*one* they can rely on when they go out, when they feel the need for closeness and/or sex, or when they need someone to tell their troubles to—much like young people feeling safe when they "go steady" because they are assured a date for the next party or the big prom. Also, our society is "couple-oriented," and even for same-sex-oriented men and women it is easier to be socially accepted when one is in what appears to be a stable couple. A coupled person is "safer"—whatever that implies—in the eyes of others, especially other couples. Unfortunately most of us cannot see that there is really no security in monogamy, and that what we give up for this phantom is our own independent selfhood and the expressions of our innermost and most urgent needs. This loss is especially so for the "weaker" or the more dependent partner in a couple, but it is also to a degree so for the stronger and more assertive one who may, however, go outside of the couple relationship for satisfaction without telling the other partner.

Why is security only a mirage in monogamy? For the very basic reasons of the one-to-one relationship, namely the dependence of one partner totally and completely upon the other. What could be less secure than for someone to depend upon only one other person? Since humans are frail both in body and emotions, depending totally upon one other person is a most precarious situation. For the stronger of the partners it means that (s)he can put pressure on the weaker one by threatening desertion, abandonment, and other dire consequences if the weaker will not adjust and cooperate fully with the wishes of the stronger. But also for the stronger partner, the one-only situation constantly poses a threat of being left alone. The very fact that two people form a couple indicates that both need closeness to one another, although this need may have different reasons and root causes. But, the ever-present possibility of losing one's partner is always in the background.

I think my situation is not all that atypical, in that I was fearful of being deserted and consequently did everything I felt necessary to "hold" my partner. It also meant that I worried a lot about her extensive travels by automobile and constantly feared that one day she would have a fatal accident, especially after she had two or three "close calls." It meant that every attractive woman she met was a threat to my "security," because if that other woman were able to interest my companion, then it meant that she was going to leave me and go with her. In other words, it meant that I had to watch every step I took or I would be alone and in the most *in*secure situation possible. It also built up in me an awful lot of resentment, naturally. No one likes to be in that precarious a position.

All this is, of course, a very important basis for the concept of monogamy. How otherwise could men have obtained free slave labor and a certain sex partner, unless insecurity was locked into the system? How else could society get a woman to have children—a real burden—and force her to bring up these children? The only way was to put her into a position of total jeopardy unless she did as she was told by her "master." Unfortunately this system was carried over into the same-sex realm, with the same destructive results. And even though the untenability of this system has been recognized, society nonetheless made sure it would continue by making any deviation from it a matter of not only moral but also legal sanctions—again carried over into the gay life, where "breaking" a monogamy elicits the most vicious and vitriolic attacks on the "guilty" party.

Another argument in favor of exclusive monogamy is the matter of intimacy. To my mind this is really the only valid positive advantage to be obtained from such an arrangement. Some intimacy must be sacrificed if one has more than one lover. The insecurities of a twosome, the exclusive togetherness of the two members of the dyad, the acknowledgment of a couple as a unit—all these help to increase intimacy in a working twosome. If such a relationship is good, it also tends to have a very beautiful intimacy between the partners. In a heterosexual marriage this intimacy is largely destroyed with the arrival of children, as most couples will admit if they are honest. In a gay dyad or a childless marriage, such intimacy can grow and develop, although it rarely does unless the partners are really sensitive to each other.

In my own case, intimacy did develop and increase up to a point, at which time something happened which I still do not fully understand—possibly a "taking for granted" of each other—and while we still looked like a devoted couple to the outside, we actually had started to live more parallel than together. Now living in a commune and a multiple relationship, I sometimes miss that very special kind of intimacy that we used to have when there were just two of us, in love and alone. When it was there, it was beautiful beyond anything that one could imagine.

Everything in life involves choices, however, and the choice between this rare kind of intimacy and what I now have in increased self-expression and security is a difficult one. My own personal choice is for less intimacy and an expanded living scope. For some the special quality of intimacy might, however, be an overwhelming reason for choosing exclusive monogamy.

The usual alternative to exclusive monogamy is, of course, serial monogamy. How anyone can see any security at all in this system is beyond me, but since true monogamy is obviously impossible for a large percentage of people, this second system has been accepted as the only other possibility, until rather recently. In serial monogamy we really do have an "aggrieved" party, namely the person who is left behind, usually alone, often without funds and joint property, and frequently with little access to emotional support from others who used to be common friends of the couple. For all these reasons it remains difficult for me to understand why the ideas of communal living, group marriage, and multiple relationships have been so strenuously resisted by gays who, to a large extent, have already kicked over the traditional heterosexual lifestyle of "one man, one woman, and children." What could be more natural, more "secure," than surrounding oneself with a group of loving individuals, carefully chosen for their congeniality? Why can't one of a dyad bring in another person, add this person to the couple, and love this person as well as the other partner? Why can't the other partner do the same, if (s)he is so inclined? But if not, why can't (s)he accept the fact that the other partner felt a need, did not want to "replace" the first lover, but rather wanted to *add* onto the dyad? Isn't it better for a couple to live with two, three, or even more people, in love or communion, not totally dependent on just one other person in every way? Wouldn't it increase one's feeling of security with a beloved if one knew that even if (s)he met another and fell in love, (s)he would not leave, but would add this other person to the "family"? My personal answer to these questions is a resounding "yes." It seems to me that ideally in such a situation, the destructive emotions of jealousy would be eliminated, emotions which our society encourages and admires rather than proscribes and which to my mind are among the most destructive emotions we can have.

I feel that lesbians especially need to rethink their values. That we need to realize that much of what we consider "right" is simply the instruction we received when we were growing up. That much of what we were taught not only no longer applies to society in general, but never did apply to gays in particular. I feel that serial monogamy must necessarily hurt at least one of a couple, but that multiple relationships have the potential for being the best for the most. I propose that when such relationships are developed in good faith and with high ideals by reasonably mature individuals, they can instill tremendous energies, can satisfy a wide range of needs, can increase the feelings of security and stability for every member of such a relationship, and in general prove to be far more satisfactory and stable than a twosome could ever be. Multiple relationships should certainly eliminate many of the power struggles and power plays that are inevitable in a one-to-one situation. They will minimize the power of the stronger and more independent over the weaker and more dependent, eliminating the fear of total abandonment of the weaker by the stronger if the weaker refuses to accede to the demands of the stronger. They will minimize the uneven distribution of labor which exists in most dyads, even in the gay world. They will help to alleviate most slave-master situations, if not all.

To see multiple relationships as the answer to all of our social ills is, of course, naïve and unwarranted. Such relationships bring with them their very own and different problems, such as the upper limit in size of such a household; acceptability of a new member to present members; the continuing presence of jealousy, which unfortunately still exists in multiple situations; and many other practical and economic problems which have not yet been begun to be solved.

However, in view of the fact that exclusionary monogamy has obviously and miserably failed a large percentage of people—certainly within the last twenty years and increasingly so—we must look to other ways of living and relating. We as lesbians have an especially good opportunity to try and develop new ways of living together, because we have already rejected society's norms for us as women, and are therefore less bound by tradition. I feel that multiple relationships may be one such possible way.

LIVING ALONE

George Whitmore

I. BEING ALONE

At some point not too long ago, at the beginning of the Nixon years when I got out of school, I decided I wanted to live alone. I wanted quiet. Like everyone else I was shell-shocked by the sixties. It had been a long time since I had been alone to think of myself as a person rather than as a generation. In addition, I was coming out. I hadn't been doing so well in what is still referred to in magazines as the "war between the sexes." I decided to retreat. No more roommates, and, please, no more lovers. The rest of the world was nothing but a group grope as far as I was concerned, a confused melange of sexy politics and political sex. Of course, it hasn't changed much since then.

Part of my desire for privacy has to do with the requirements of being a writer. But there's more to it than that. All kinds of people, if asked, would say they often long for that privacy, to live alone, lots of times. But few people do.

For one thing, it's expensive. You pay for all that space. So you are likely to be middle-class. For another thing, our society isn't structured to accommodate single people beyond the "acceptable age" of thirty or so; in many things we have to fend for ourselves with little outside help. Everyone, of course, pays for any small measure of the freedom he or she gets. But after you liberate yourself from the strictures against living alone—and it's mainly the strictures I want to talk about—there are other obstacles to prevent you from living alone well.

Living alone successfully partially depends on whether or not you regard it as a permanent or temporary situation. I tend to regard it as something of both, though I confess I'm not too optimistic (or too anxious) about the prospect of living "permanently" with someone else. The trick would really seem to be to settle in to your own lifestyle instead of regarding solitude as some sort of temporary detention. That depends, in turn, on how afraid you are of living alone and how committed you are to yourself. Whether you become resigned to it or not, most people who live alone after that certain age are going to continue to live alone. That's just a fact, or at least the way it's been.

If you do live alone, are you then the bona fide recluse we've all been taught to fear? I don't think so. The case could be argued the other way. That your social contacts can be more significant to you and to others. That people who live alone and make their own decisions are more free to act together out of mutual self-interest than are others. Perhaps this is another way that the cultural solidarity in the gay community has been underestimated. We should understand that none of us is alone in our isolation; all of us suffer and gain from isolation and solitude.

A distinction should be made between *living* alone and *being* alone. This is especially important for gay people. *Living* alone is a fact, a physical state to which some of the above considerations apply—space, money, class. *Being* alone is an existential state that everyone inhabits potentially. It is more likely to accompany living alone. When people contemplate living alone, their reluctance about doing so usually involves mistaking it for *being* alone. The gay person who feels trapped in either a homosexual or heterosexual marriage probably, on the other hand, longs for the freedom to make the existential decision to *be* alone as much as he or she longs to live apart from the family in solitude. The lack of choice is a major factor in either situation, solitude or claustrophobia. *Being* alone is a state gay people have traditionally had to cope with. Our writers have often described it to straight people who weren't clear-sighted enough to see the landscape for themselves.

So *being* alone is an existential problem. Telling you how I manage to *live* alone is one thing. Telling you how I manage to *be* alone is quite another. As a friend of mine said when I told him I was writing this article: "How do you write a positive article about living alone when every one of us who has done it knows that the gut feeling is one of sheer loneliness?"

Well, we all have to deal with that—right? But if you live alone there are other things you have to deal with alone that other people share with their spouses, lovers, children, etcetera. And there's another, invisible piece of furniture in your apartment that you stumble over all the time—it's a mass of loneliness.

Everyone knows that friendship is what really makes living alone possible. However greedy you might be in a material sense, and whatever means you devise to supply those superficial needs, self-reliance has its limits. There are, of course, good friends and bad. Sometimes you can get along with the bad because they are less demanding and the friendships have a shorter life expectancy. The friends you meet in bars serve the purpose of being both acquaintances (you aren't all alone there) and strangers (you don't have to be *so* friendly).

A bad friend won't turn up at your door at three in the morning and would never dream of having you do likewise. It is only good friends who are unembarrassed about sharing their tacky love affairs with you, or who will accept you for the shameless, short-sighted failure you often are in yours.

A lot has been said in gay circles about how friends (and even movement acquaintances) are our families. But our friends, unlike our families, are preferential relations—unless they are chosen out of the fear I alluded to above—and are thus different, if not better or worse. Good friends are individuals with no *contractual* obligations.

Some people even have sex with their friends.

No one can do without sex on a fairly regular basis unless they are determined to be chaste or have simply found sex boring. Just as sex isn't the big deal we always make it out to be, it isn't always a problem for the person living alone. Living alone facilitates sexual encounters by giving you the time and privacy poor people don't have. If you are male and live in an urban setting and are aggressive enough, sex should be as easy to get as take-out Chinese food, if often just that satisfying. Masturbation is a more reliable and pleasurable outlet for thousands of people than is a quickie or a one-night-stand. Yet some people, conversely, thrive on anonymous encounters without losing their warmth or curiosity. Those who aren't under the impression that you explode from lack of genital contact with another person do without it for long periods of time. Others just aren't overly enchanted with the promise of sex in abundance that an affair with one person offers.

Still, many of us who have put sex in its place are troubled by its frequent coincidence with love. Love screws everything up. (I'm even tempted to put love in quotation marks, since the word is so often used as a weapon against the solitary person, as in "but you don't *love* anybody!")

Likewise, many of us who have gotten to the point where we have chosen our friends carefully and have delineated the formal and informal "rules" of friendship—and these can range from semi-cohabitation to nothing more than dinner out together once a month—those of us who consider living alone a true, viable alternative nonetheless find ourselves alone when we don't want to be. Being alone when you don't want to be alone has little to do with sex. Sex is easier to get along without than is company. If living alone is now a choice for many people, why is it that *not* being alone is seldom a matter of choice for the same people?

Surprisingly, few of us ever expected we would be alone at all. For those of us who are gay, being alone can be a very bitter surprise indeed. That's why people lie to their parents, so as not to face that aloneness. It's the tension between the reality of being alone—the obstacle sitting smack in the middle of your living room—and all the expectations programmed into you that can make living alone a trial. No one has taught you how to do it.

We learn to expect the things our parents have encountered and have learned themselves. But for gay people, those expectations are always accompanied, early on, by the threat of alienation from the world of the family. All our expectations reinforce the strictures against being gay, against living alone, of course. In our society the expectations are created and marketed for that and other similarly repressive purposes.

My own generation was hoodwinked, I think, because we were idealistic in the extreme. My parents and others of their generation, having grown up themselves in the thirties and having learned one lesson (don't trust anything but your own will and stamina), prepared their children for a world that didn't exist any more than the bygone rural world of their own childhoods. It was the static world of the fifties, and it manifested itself mainly on TV. Everything else was made to resemble it.

We were prepared perhaps to be independent and (admiring our parents' struggles) resourceful. Perhaps we all shared the same secret to a greater or lesser extent: that we were not like the others, were somehow different. (This was, for some of us, the beginning of being gay.) We learned about beatniks and other "out groups" in sociology classes. How many of us felt secretly that we belonged to those categories? It seems many of us did if we count the number of us who dropped out, crashed, or blew ourselves up.

But we were not prepared to be alone in any but a vague, romantic sense. (Remember, the premise of the fifties was togetherness.) We were, some of us, ready to be regarded as eccentrics. That, after all, was the price you paid for individuality. (No thought of isolation.) We saw ourselves as perhaps like Thoreau, the objects of village gossip. Good old Thoreau, who shunned society but cared so much more for its institutions than the others did.

But there was, you see, no village, no cozy social unit to which we could belong. There never had been for some people. (The "gay community" in 1955?) It's hard to believe that this sense of solitude was such a revelation, but it was.

Some were not deterred in their efforts to succeed in business without really trying, to carve out a niche and crawl into it. They found sufficient reason to continue.

Others of us flip-flopped. We were sometimes the most eager of the consumers of Cold War hype—brotherhood of man, world citizenship and so forth—and thus were most sickened when we discovered the true nature of the flesh at the banquet. We were branded the enemy, exiled, ultimately invisible and isolated. Some of us were dead. That's the final kind of alone.

II. THE NATIONAL LONELINESS

Among the many promises made to me over the course of growing up was the pledge that I would not be alone.

But what is it *not* to be alone?

Is it to live in the nuclear family? The life of the TV family itself would disprove that: Mom with her headaches and tranquilizers, provided in overabundance by the obliging family doctor; Dad wheeled back and forth to work each day like a Lazarus; Bud and Sis, a sneering, sullen pair, trapped themselves in rituals of deceit and rebellion as autocratic as the genetic chain itself. . . .

Is it to live with a partner in some matrimonial three-legged race, dragging each other through sickness and health? The final indictment of marriage in the popular mind won't be based on the ever-present likelihood that marriages might turn into nothing but grueling, monotonous, boring, and thankless ordeals—but that marriage just doesn't work. This technical failing, not the spiritual brutalization in some marriages, will be the death of the institution in America. It doesn't keep people together.

Is it to live as a member of *something*, then? Part of some endeavor—capitalist, evangelical, communal? The sporty set on Long Island with their yachts and country clubs do not look lonely. The One World Crusade kids on the steps of the public library shoutin' for Jesus don't look lonely. My old college friends living in their domes out in Arizona don't list loneliness among their privations. They are cheerful. Perhaps under the above circumstances everybody has a right, or even an obligation, to be cheerful. But all of them must, unless they're totally spaced out, feel lonely to some extent, at some time.

Perhaps it is because of our national loneliness, because we are all formerly lonely, lonely, or potentially lonely people who want company—a lot of us simply *can't* be left alone—that living alone has always been regarded as its own best curse. Living alone has always been held over us as a punishment. "Good" people, "healthy" people do not live alone. They get strange.

That strangeness is a self-fulfilling prophecy in this country. Two of the most commonly cited examples of it are Emily Dickinson and Henry Thoreau. To a nation that has traditionally revered self-reliance, these two are nevertheless considered "queer" characters.* Dickinson lived the life of an utter recluse, even resorting in later years to the device of talking to her oldest friends from where she was hidden in another room. Thoreau practiced the reclusiveness he preached in Walden, although he did so *in extremis* long after he had written about his experience at the pond, which was a short walk from Concord, skirted by railway tracks and located in a relatively populous woodland. He never lacked for company there.

We revere these two sensibilities because of the artists' works, and we have of course canonized the memories of the artists themselves because we worship the idea of the individual. But like all fanatic religions, the cult of the individual tends to elevate her or him out of reach. The possessors of these unique and influential sensibilities are no longer people; they are rated "G" for general audiences, safe for children's viewing. As such, their lives are warnings to all of us.

Without a conventional heterosexual (read: procreative) target handy nearby to thrust its head into, what motivates them is not passion at all, it would seem. No wonder that the bitter triumph of

*The literature on both Dickinson and Thoreau, with few exceptions, is notable for the lack of a clear analysis of the homoerotic elements in their works. *The Riddle of Emily Dickinson* by Rebecca Patterson puts forth the plausible theory that Dickinson's reclusiveness was the direct result of an abortive lesbian affair. Perry Miller, in his *Consciousness in Concord*, neatly shatters the myth built up by the biographers of Thoreau that he, too, had a traumatic heterosexual love affair in his youth that left him a "woman-hater." But it was the brother of the woman in question to whom Thoreau wrote his only "love poem," and not to the woman herself, as Emerson and others would have had it.

Dickinson's poems and the fierce abundance of Thoreau's journal are puzzling to us. They are contradicted by what we have learned about them, that they lived lives that never intruded on the arena of the living.

We prefer homogeneous visions, the consensus programs of the fall television network lineup. The solitary experience is a fantasy incompatible with the American dream. It is not purposeful; it is pornographic. It tampers with our notion of what is circumspect, our tightly drawn national reality, even with our minority notions of activism. That's why foreign novels like those of Jean Genêt (to his great glee, I would imagine) are still considered dirty books. And that's how and why straight society has always got its forbidden thrills from the gay experience.

None of this is to say that all our collective history (or even our collective art) is a lie. Simply that all collective history must cheat the individual. Certainly in relation to the lesbian and the gay man, history has been a cheat by making them invisible. Most Western peoples feel a great need to create their own history in the midst of living, a need which seems increasingly more urgent as the pace of life accelerates. This need is repeatedly frustrated by Western institutions, which put forth a self-serving, pseudo-history. This is how the gay experience was displaced from its position at the vital center of the Greek world by historians and why it has been threatened with extinction in the uncongenial atmosphere of the closet.

Totalitarian states are not simply a threat to individual freedoms. Before they can be that, they must annihilate the assertion of individual consciousness that homosexuality often symbolizes. Even in China, where individual consciousness is already as closely identified with revolutionary consciousness as is conceivable, where each individual *is* the collective history and the state's propaganda instrument as well, homosexuality is recognized but not condoned.

We won't, I think, be raising gay children. Everyone discovers gay consciousness in solitude, alone.

III. THE RIGHT TO SOLITUDE

Straight people suffer from their own prohibitions against the solitary life. As a matter of fact, the more "gay" straight people get, the more likely they are to suffer from it. The tyranny of the stereotyped family unit is universal.

This is all well illustrated by the "singles" phenomenon, which exists on the fringes of the gay revolution and the women's revolt. The singles scene shows what excommunication means in the straight world. The *Cosmopolitan* girl, for instance, if she were to exist, would live in a state of unremitting anxiety: in the singles world it is always Saturday night, and you'd better have a date.

The myths usually assigned to the gay world have been assigned now to the singles world. All that fucking and hollowness. Gay bars and singles bars share the same drawbacks: There is an uneasiness there, a lack of conviction that these are legitimate social institutions, that they have a human dimension to them, that communication with other people is at all possible there. The architecture of singles apartment houses betrays a similar lack of conviction that these are anything but flimsy and impermanent structures for unfinished people.

Single people are denied respectability via the conventional means of having children and owning property. The single mother suffers from the ostracism of society (she is a "failed" woman, husbandless) and from the loss of her individual freedom. The divorced man pays for his children while he is denied them. The single father and the mother who chooses not to retain the custody of her children are not recognizable types in our gallery of adults.

Need I say, any or all of these people can be lesbians or gays? And that child-rearing is not, repeat not, a lifetime's work? And that it has its place in the life of the solitary gay person?

Single people pay high taxes, suffer precarious credit ratings, are the targets of the fast sell and the "luxury" market in shoddy goods. They are somehow not expected to take out mortgages, subscribe to life insurance, or save money. Or participate in politics—what do they have at stake?

The whole list is a stock item in the women's movement, but it must also be included in the gay analysis. Being single, the larger society would have it, is a precarious, fearful state. Being gay and single must, therefore, be a horror show.

But is it?

The right to choose to live alone is a right long overdue for gay people. We have too often been forced into solitary circumstances against our will. Just as we are asserting our right to assemble, to live together in pairs, threesomes, collectives, and communes, we must

59

reassert our right to privacy. (The right to privacy is, in my opinion, the very thing that makes a lot of ordinary gay people rebel against the movement. Mistakenly, they think they have privacy, when actually they have placed themselves in the same alienated state society intended for them. Thinking they have "escaped" the penalties of homosexuality by not associating with other lesbians or gays, they have actually executed the penalties themselves.)

In the past, straight society has offered gay people three images to contend with: isolation; accommodation with the straight world (spinsterhood, bachelorhood, marriage); and the subcultural gay world. Many have chosen to be ruled by the first two images and have been duly oppressed. But the oppression resulting from the third is incalculable. While gay lives have been lived in relative isolation or "respectability," no one in actuality has lived completely in the third. For it is not the fact of the so-called gay world itself—the bars, baths, beaches—that is inhabited (only a minority of gay people frequent those "institutions"); what is inhabited is the hyperconsciousness, the fear, the awareness that in the eyes of the dominant society one is a masquerader in the "real" world who, through some inadvertent slip or another, might be unmasked and relegated to the subcultural world. The actual world of gay society which exists in small knots of emotional and economic dependency bears little resemblance to the mythical leper colony we are warned about.

Unfortunately, this myth is a barrier between the individual and her/his experience. The young woman on the edge of lesbian identity still confronts the image of salons run by predatory dykes whose altars to tribadism burn incense into spidery fingers. The young man still must contend with an image of the bars where laid out side by side like so many scented handkerchiefs in a bureau drawer exquisite pansys stand ready to waft their poisons over him. Even in post-1969 America, hip writers are still characterizing our surroundings as "Weimarian." The revisionist version of this image is the stress on "normalcy" in gay life seen on some TV shows where, as one lesbian I know put it, "they watch you eat with a fork."

In my own experience not being alone meant that there would always be women. And when there weren't women there was the assurance that it wasn't my fault. There was my mother, of course, and the prototypical mother-son mutual gratification pact to carry out. Just as surely as there was my mother, there would be a wife and, thence, a family arrayed about me, the biological and scriptural proofs of manhood. Each person around me made me a man, and I, garbed in the armor of their dependency, did battle in the world for them. This, just as surely as there was my father.

The reality, of course, wasn't that at all. The coat of mail was a prison as hot as the inside of a stove. I discovered I was gay at the very point of incineration, at the flash point.

If liberation is painstakingly undoing the chain mail links knit around you—the expectations—coming out is doing considerable violence to the straps, hinges, hooks, and rivets that connect you with the rest of the world. You sever yourself sometimes from your own history. You are unmoored, then, floating on the sure knowledge of your oppression, fueled by your anger. You can see the medieval condition of the rest of the world clearly now, with all its superstitions and its hunger for heretics.

Many people who live alone have avoided this confrontation with the self. But once it has been forced upon us, or taken on, we find we will not only survive, but that we have found the means of *being* alone the rest of our lives. This perception—one that is especially resisted by Americans—leads as a matter of course to the conviction that we will most likely *live* alone as well for the major portion of our lives.

That conviction wavers in me sometimes, but the basic perception doesn't.

THE BI-SEXUAL POTENTIAL

Laura Della Rosa

In a rationale for coalitions between women's liberation and gay activist groups, the systems that oppress both are often cited: the media, straight insecure men, religion, psychological "norms," etc. In the two movements there are common enemies to hate and attack, and a shared understanding of the joy of loving one's own sex.

However, when reading the Somerville Women's Collective book, *Our Bodies, Ourselves*, I was struck by the title and its implications. The first, that a knowledge and acceptance of our bodies is an integral part of being "ourselves," and the second, that a logical male counterpart to the book is *Their Bodies, Themselves*. Despite the obvious similarities in physical and emotional needs, the bodies of men and women are different, and are seen as setting them apart.

These impressions, shaped by my own sexual and political experiences, lead me to say that I consider myself bi-sexual, and believe that bi-sexuality is an issue that must be faced and discussed throughout the development of gay pride/power movements. The rightness of bi-sexuality strikes me from two standpoints: from the personal, to learn to deal with our learned hatred and fear of the other sex, and on a political scale, for the current gay/lesbian and women's liberation movements to achieve a basic connectedness essential to their ultimate success.

Implicit in my use of the term "bi-sexuality" is my feeling for, and experience of the inevitability, joy and beauty of gayness. But another assumption emerges—both sexes have to come to terms with each other physically, sexually, not just verbally and politically, for the honest caring and good faith that is a basis for workable and cooperative coalitions. Sexual attraction is just one aspect of human relationships, but it's a damn motivating one. There is a point when gay exclusivity says something: gay men hate women, and gay women hate men.

I use the word "hate" in the way I can feel it for men—as alienation, repulsion, mixed with the sense of hurt at the shitty feelings of failure and discomfort I've had because of them. Straight men and women hate each other too, and with good reason. The differences and "battles" between the sexes are standard American culture, with economic patterns shaping and perpetuating the framework for unrealistic and dissatisfying interaction. The issue of this hate, however, seems well within the realm of movements addressing themselves to human potential, sexual/lifestyle oppression, and a general consciousness of why we do what we do in this society.

It was in a women's consciousness-raising group that I realized my hatred of men, and the group provided me with a place to explore and share it freely. I found that one of my earliest and clearest impressions of boys was that they were dirty. Their hands were funny too, with dark hair on them, and larger than mine. In my teens, boys' hair was somehow slimy, in all places, and their strangely deepened voices and Palmolive-and-sweat smells suggested some unpredictable actions, and sexuality. Boys were always rubbing themselves, as were the men I saw. Emerging moustaches, rough skin, hairy legs—all of these were unacceptable on my body, and repulsive on theirs. The way boys would slide in "safe" in baseball was inconceivable, and exciting, even to a "tomboy" like me; when had I ever been able to throw my body around and fall in fun?

Old impressions? Hardly. In college, the men's dorms were a tense place for me with their raised toilet seats, the men's "smell" I was certain of finding, and my own inability to be comfortable in a "men's place." My reaction to men was intertwined with my reaction to their bodies, and both were distorted.

As I was attending a women's college, I soon found my comfort and best times with the dynamic and diverse women I came in contact with daily. We started theoretically—Kate Millett had said "it" was all right. Then we began combing each other's hair, massaging, leaning, and nestling. Then I slept with the woman who had always meant something "different" to me. When she moved, it all seemed right and inevitable. We went through our changes—learning and trying things out, losing our amazement at what we were and seeing each other as different women with different needs. I always said we split because her "negativity" and depression were too much for me. Later, when I was with my other woman lover, I began to love my own body and its structure. Men? They never looked stranger to me than during this second relationship—their sexuality had become foreign and irrelevant to me.

It's no news to anyone that we're taught fucked-up attitudes about our bodies and those of the opposite sex. On the other side, when do men have the unpressured, lights-on opportunity to examine and make their peace with menstrual blood, contraceptive jellies, vaginal odors and infections: women's bodies?

In my own life, a combination of mixed-sex therapy group and my current sexual involvement with my manfriend have begun a reintroduction to men, or at least to those of my general economic class and background.

In my group, several incidents stand out. When a male castration fantasy was enacted in a session, I learned that my jokes about the subject, shared with other women, were not so funny, or particularly useful. I think I got some sense, for the first time, of what a penis may mean to certain men—including men I like. In another session I screamed at and then wrestled another man in the group, using my full energy and determination to do the bastard in. In the draw that resulted, I felt less afraid of the mysterious strength I'd ascribed to men. We had sweated together and I felt we looked at each other more clearly as we sat there catching our breath and feeling our bruises.

With my manfriend, the experiences are on another level. We have watched each other masturbate, and shared fantasies, discovering that we both want to be taken and to take, as well as have affectionate sex. In a strip-tease he did for me one night I felt the soft seductiveness in him, and he's well aware of my own interest in having a penis—at least one time—for the chance to "enter" him, feel the friction, and squirt my way to orgasm. We both have been affected by standard American sexual images, and through that there is a connection between his sexuality and mine, and the chance for us to discover the "male" and "female" aspects of us both.

I don't pretend to an attitude transformation. I hate men in general when I'm pressed in the subway, when I watch Geritol "My wife, she's a wonder!" commercials, when I suffer as stewardesses perform and shuffle. I hate men in particular when I realize that it is hard for my manfriend to accept the fact that I got a good job before he did. When I see heterosexual intercourse in pornographic movies, I hate the image, and wonder if we look like that, if I look as passive and pushed around.

But loving a man, and other men, sexually, has widened my basis for relating to them, just as loving women sexually has changed my relations with women. The potential for fulfilling sex between two people of the opposite sex is a powerful stimulus to keep confronting the learned aversions and sense of strangeness. There's a lot of shit to wade through. This confrontation is a major one though, and I can't see any "liberation" without some provision for it, and recognition of its importance.

64

A BI-SEXUAL OFFERS SOME THOUGHTS ON FENCES

Jem

Fences are very important: without fences we wouldn't know where my property ends and yours begins; I might walk on your grass; you might park in my parking lot. So we put up fences—pretty little picket ones and serious barbed-wire ones, but they all mean *stop here*! Fences keep people out or they keep people in, but they almost never keep people together. Robert Frost said, "Good fences make good neighbors," but he didn't say they make good friends.

Bi-sexuals have to deal with a lot of fences every day. As a bi-sexual woman, I want to discuss three kinds of fences that I've encountered among gay women in Boulder. This is not to imply that straight people also don't set up fences for me—of course they do. But I want to write "within the family" to my gay sisters because we need each other and we can't afford these fences any more.

1)—"The grass is always greener on the other side of the fence." Some people seem to think that being bi-sexual is "easier" than making an exclusive commitment to one sex or the other. (I don't think I've ever heard a bi-sexual say this.) I personally find my lifestyle more exciting, more satisfying, more fun than being exclusively hetero- or homosexual. But it is also so complicated and more stressful. It is difficult to try to integrate the two contexts. The rewards of being able to love both women and men are far greater for me than the strains, but bi-sexuality is *not* an "easy" lifestyle.

Let me dispel once and for all the idea that being bi-sexual is safer than being homosexual. A woman who ought to know better told me she resented bi-sexuals because we had the "safety of the straight world" to fall back on. I sometimes wish that were true, but alas it is not. In this very hetero-sexist world, one gay relationship does make you gay and subject to all the penalties thereof. We lose our jobs, our housing, and our children on the basis of our sexual orientation just as frequently as exclusively homosexual people do unless, like them, we hide. (And let me assure you, friends, that hiding half one's sexual side is as damaging as hiding it all.)

Bi-sexuals face the same risks as homosexuals. The only difference is that all too often we face them alone when we are not fully accepted by gay groups which could provide support and love.

2)—"Bi-sexuals ought to get off the fence." This remark was addressed to me by a woman I've known for several years. What did she mean? Well, obviously, she sees me as *on* some fence, hetero or homo. But I *have* decided—I'm not on the fence at all. I chose both sides; I chose in my life not to build that particular fence.

William Simon said (a few World Affairs conferences ago) that he thought bi-sexuals were the only people moving from hetero to homosexual or vice-versa. I think he's wrong. I believe in transition and I can see people making choices to be exclusively one or the other, temporarily or even forever. I just don't see why it *has* to be that way. Relationships stand or fall on their own merits: if two different relationships are good, why shouldn't both last? If one fails, why should that be a sign that one is forever through with all relationships of that kind?

Some people I consider more concerned with ideology than with feelings would even say that by sleeping with a man I am "identifying with my oppressor." Although I am tempted to dismiss such a remark as merely insensitive, it reflects an attitude found among some of my gay sisters and therefore deserves an answer. First, as a feminist I do believe that the class of men has been taught to be oppressive to women, and that the class of women has been taught to be submissive to men. I also assert with pride that great numbers of strong and beautiful women are breaking those chains—they are proclaiming their freedom and their personhood. However, I do not believe that women have an exclusive claim to chain-breaking. I see men all around me struggling to overcome their conditioning, to become whole people, to deny the "macho mystique." These men are my brothers.

I do not sleep with my oppressors—male or female. I sleep with and love whole human beings—female and male. I enjoy the differences between female-female and female-male relationships, true differences, not those imposed by old role-playing. My lovers are different and I am different with each of them. I choose to love both of them—joyfully, humanly, *freely*.

3)—"Don't fence me in." Or out. I would prefer to live in a world without labels—a world in which I could just be "sexual" without any prefix. Unhappily this is not such a world, and so I must have a label—bi-sexual. Now the question is, what should that label mean? I actually heard a woman say, "Bi-sexuals are not gay" to justify excluding bi-sexual women from gay activities. Well, if "gay" means the ability to relate only to one's own sex, then we're not gay. But if it means the ability to relate joyfully to whomever one loves, regardless of sex, then we're gay and proud. The gay movement can be negative, focusing on only whom one *doesn't* sleep with.

I affirm that sense of gay liberation in which we proudly assert our right to love whomever we love, female, male, gay, straight, one, or many. Bi-sexuals are gay and we claim our place in gay liberation.

Down with fences, up with love!

BUTCH OR FEM?:
The Third World
Lesbian's Dilemma

Anonymous

Upon "coming out" or even just coming into a lesbian bar, inevitably one is confronted with the question: Are you butch or fem? Underlying this question is the assumption that one may choose to be one or the other. For the Third World lesbian this choice is, in almost every case of traditional role-playing, denied her. Since lesbians can be as vulnerable to the influence of society's prejudices and value judgments as straights can, they can become entrapped in the resulting web of limitations. This is the predicament of the Third World lesbian. In the majority of interracial lesbian relationships, the Third World woman is cast in the role of the butch. This way of perceiving her has not been limited to white lesbians alone, but has been maintained by nonwhite lesbians as well. Even in relationships between two Third World lesbians, all too often the degree to which a lesbian appears to look white determines the roles of each lesbian in the relationship. Since this situation seems to be an ordinary occurrence in the life of a Third World lesbian, I will venture to come up with some answers as to why this occurs.

Much has been written about sex and racism but relatively little has been written about *sexism* and racism. Racism and traditional sex roles deal specifically with the latter topic. According to all the cultural mythology about nonwhite people, all nonwhites are animalistic (carnal), unusually strong, and dull, as well as a million other characteristics considered undesirable. Racism has been woven so complexly into the language, attitudes and institutions of Western culture that we must constantly examine our attitudes for remnants or even large bits of this brand of prejudice. Sadly enough, although understandably, it is too easy to carry our culturally induced prejudices over into our new lifestyles.

Since Third World women have belonged primarily to a class of people who have been exploited for economic reasons to the fullest extent possible, socialization of them into an "unproductive" or rather no-market-value female would be wasteful. It seems that upon attaining affluence, the volume of workers needed subsides, releasing them to an existence of nonproductivity. Accordingly women are among the first to be phased out. However, because Third World people have always been cheap labor, the Third World women in particular would remain in demand for greatest economic profit. Consequently femininity itself, as defined by the modern nuclear family patriarchy, would not serve a very useful purpose in her life. The same is true for the white woman as her economic status decreases. Essentially the difference between the situations is that historically racism has kept the Third World woman in this unfeminine role. Therefore it follows that the character of Third World women in general is one of the perpetual butch. Among white women more economic variation facilitates role choice variation. Where traditional butch-fem role-playing exists between two women of color, the differentiation tends to go along more colored vs. less colored lines, with the butch role assigned to the less Caucasian woman. This phenomenon of race-linked sex-role-playing in lesbian relationships is another limitation that we must cast off ourselves.

SEARCH FOR WORDS

Konstantin Berlandt

There's something about a straight boy that revives innocence and simple values.

I met one the other night in Henry Africa's, a popular swinger's bar at Vallejo and Van Ness Streets. I've only been there that once. Six blocks from where I live, I always thought it looked like a pleasant place to visit. Bright lights and well-dressed people, always smiling, always having a good time. But still not my kind of place. What could I say, what is there in my life that we could small-talk together about?

But just this once I was standing at the end of the bar, drinking my orange juice and feeling very out of place, when a dark-haired young man in a red short-sleeved shirt swung in beside me. He seemed to need a place along the bar to lean against, but by gay bar habit I looked him up and down. He had nice hands and nice brown eyes that caught mine and held me till I said "hi" to escape whatever he had in mind.

"Hello," he said.

Now what? What does a gay boy say to a straight boy in a swinger's bar? I looked back at his hands.

"Is that your class ring?" I asked.

"No, it's my barmitzvah ring."

At least he wasn't a WASP on top of being straight! Maybe there was a conversation here.

"Why don't you have one?" he asked.

"I wasn't barmitzvahed. My mother never suggested it."

"Wasn't she Jewish?"

"No, she wasn't."

I was all set to tell him my family background—intermarriages, divorces—when he leaned his head back and, with a good-Joe laugh, said, "I got laid last night."

This deserved a good-Joe response, I was sure, but what is it? Do I clap him on the shoulder and shake his hand, saying, "I'll drink to that!"? Or was there hidden meaning in the use of the passive voice— got laid—had he meant fucked by another guy? The obvious suddenly needed clarification.

Psychically, he explained, "On a waterbed...by a girl... naturally."

"Naturally?" I asked, off the cuff.

"Well, not naturally," he agreed. "I'm into cunts, but I'd like to make it with a guy too." Are there no safe places left? "I think," he continued, "if you could play around with both sexes you'd have the whole world then. Wouldn't you?" He smiled. "What are you into?"

What a question! Life, sex, writing, oral copulation, Truffaut, rock 'n' roll, cab driving, dancing, masturbation, ritual, mindlessness, growing plants, looking at you. "Boys," I said definitely and defiantly.

He said his name was Andy and that he'd like to get together with me tonight. "It'll be all one way, you understand, at least at first. Is that okay?"

"Okay," I said, never one to pressure sexual encounters with preconceived demands.

He pleaded inexperience: "I've made it with two, maybe three other guys before, but I never came with any of them, you see, so I don't know really if it's for me or not."

We decided on my place and prepared to leave, but he hesitated when two of his friends came over to him. The three of them sauntered across the floor. I followed and found him talking with a pretty platinum blonde woman who was sitting on his coat.

"Listen," he turned back to me. "Will you wait here a few minutes? Then, if you see me outside the window waving at you, come out. I'm really into girls, you understand, and I'd like to see if I can get one. If I don't, I'll come back, but for a few minutes you're going to have to play second fiddle. Is that okay?"

"No," I said.

"Well, I'm being honest with you. You're going to be here anyway, aren't you?"

"I might be," I said, as he turned back to the woman. I guessed I could wait a few minutes until she turned him down. At least then he wouldn't be pining all evening for what might have been if he had only tried to get her.

Two minutes was all I had to wait before he was back to me and leading me out of the bar, down the street to his car.

We talked about sex, what-do-you-like-to-do-and-who-with—he asked the questions; I gave the answers for lack of imagining how to turn them on end.

His car was parked at a gas station, now closed, at the busy corner of Polk and Broadway. Once we were seated inside the car he asked me to unzip my pants. Right away he went down on me, with god and possibly all the pedestrians and police in the area looking on.

"Do me," he said. I did for a minute. "Don't you think we'd be more comfortable at home?" I said. Trust a straight boy for getting me fifteen years in jail for public lewdity.

At my apartment we did most of those basic sexual things faggots do together without paraphernalia besides Vaseline. He was the aggressor—the idea man—but there wasn't anything this straight boy didn't want to try.

Nevertheless, at the end of the session he insisted that once again he hadn't come; he just didn't make it as a faggot. I had thought differently, judging by the way he felt inside me and the sounds he was making as he madly pumped into me just before he had sighed heavily and fallen asleep, but he was not to be dissuaded. He was a failure, a pathetically confirmed heterosexual.

Although I invited him to drop by to try again, he declined to take down my address. "I know where you live—that's good enough," he said through his car window.

"Not necessarily for sex," I added. He didn't seem to hear me and certainly didn't understand me as he drove away from my home in the Marina to his home on Russian Hill.

Tonight when I walked past Henry Africa's I scanned the crowd through the windows to see if Andy were there. It wasn't more sex I was after but to tell him something we had left out the other night.

Throughout our conversation, his questions and my answers, I had failed to convey I thought we might be compatible as friends—not just quick tricks, strangers sharing bodies.

Although he had been somewhat cold, insensitive, and silly, there's something about a confused straight boy that begs some simple yet devastating clarification. So often, yes, sex seems to have no romance at all, but to a straight boy about to turn gay—questioning his orientation—romance is the answer. Sex can be so specific, so unflattering, so unsensual, so flat, so much twisting and turning, starting and stopping, coming and forgetting. Addictive, maybe, but not always for satisfaction delivered but for satisfaction withheld—forever promised, never revealed: I'll never do that again, unless I'm horny again.

Romance says, I'm gay. I do like it. I can't forget you.

I guess that's all I had to say.

What does a straight boy say to a gay boy in a swinger's bar after that?

ENTRIES IN A JOURNAL

Gary Alinder

This past year has been one of wandering and of a search for new identities. I went from San Francisco to Provincetown, to New York, then to Amsterdam, Paris, Italy (where I lived for two months in Positano, a small coastal town south of Naples), Tunisia, London, then to Boston, and finally I returned to San Francisco. These are excerpts from a journal I kept during those travels.

AMSTERDAM (October 1973)

Last night I dreamt I was back in the States having fled Europe in a fit of loneliness; I couldn't remember the details of my departure and I regretted what I'd done. I awoke relieved still to be here. That is the beauty of nightmares, you awake so happy it was a dream. This trip is going to be a test of my ability to cope with aloneness. I sometimes spend depressing hours wondering what I'm doing here. Being far away, it's easy to imagine oneself happy among friends at home. I am teaching myself to remember the loneliness I live with at home in order to avoid actually doing what I did in the dream.

I'm feeling more comfortable in Amsterdam . . . trying to relax and do what I want, not to feel guilty at failing to cram every moment with sightseeing or some trivial, touristy "opportunity to experience Dutch life."

I find the Dutch something like Midwestern Americans, only more sophisticated . . . the tolerance of an open red light district, for example. *Les femmes de la nuit* don't work the streets, they sit in the windows of comfy, street-level apartments, some of them flashing come-hither smiles, others blasé, reading newspapers, smoking or chatting with friends. I haven't noticed any male prostitutes.

The men of Amsterdam? Rather ordinary. Quite a few young femme types, but almost none of the exotic leather queens so typical of San Francisco. Amsterdam is a tolerant city with a large gay population, but it is not a mecca for half a continent.

One wishes there were an English-language newspaper here. Reading

73

English and American papers seems dumb when one wants to know what's going on here. Amsterdam is deceptive. One can live here so easily speaking only English, but one is shut out of so much by ignorance of the language.

All this brings up the question of language, how it divides people, how it is an expression of economic power and cultural dynamism. Certainly English is the "hot" language now, the language more people want to learn as a second language. I'm happy to have English as my native language, but the dominance of English makes it less necessary and less likely I shall master other languages. Mastering at least one other language is, I think, in principle, a good thing to do.

PARIS (November 1973)

Paris is so old, so dense, so much to know about it, it's a bit depressing. I guess when you live here that history becomes a part of the landscape, having little more significance than a tree or a lilac hedge. I feel what Gertrude Stein meant when she said that the sense of history here is not at all the same thing it is in America. Spending so much time in the old buildings of the *Quartier Latin*, I can appreciate why so many of the French love what is new.

Paris, like New York, makes me want to work. To dedicate myself to one thing, become really good at it, and accomplish something with it. Paris is a demanding city. What *does* one have to offer? One can be a streetsweeper, or one can wrench something from oneself and make it into something: work, ambition. I'm torn between exposing, flaunting, promoting myself into some kind of life actor and remaining an obsequious spectator delighting in glamor but living in obscurity. The spectator's life can be rich here, but Paris makes me want to be the actor. Ambition pierces my elaborately constructed facade of self-effacement. A year ago I read Norman Podhoretz' book *Making It*; I found it said something a certain part of me was longing to hear: ambition, even in the sacred intellectual and artistic world, is not entirely a bad thing. Paris forces me to admit my ambition. Paris tells me unequivocally how obscure I am. I am a complete outsider here. If I want to open some of those doors, I will have to do something to earn respect. I may have come a long way from the lonely Minnesota farm boy longing for an animated Paris café, but I remain nearly as obscure. All I have is what I've learned, and I wonder what that is.

The question then is, what am I to do? "Write" comes the answer. A horrible, hard, and unglamorous answer, and one I cannot fully accept. . . . Perhaps Jean Cocteau particularly interests me because he never let himself be pinned down, never was he definitely a writer, a photographer, a graphic artist, a filmmaker. He dared to express himself broadly. He had a tone, a style. He was Jean Cocteau and that was definition enough. . . .

POSITANO (December 1973-February 1974)

Two letters and a postcard from Andrea. . . . Andrea is the Italian boy I met on my last night in Florence. I'd seen him across the street. "Now that one's gay," I said to myself, and one can so seldom say that with certainty in Italy. He came over to me and started talking to me in French. I think he thought I was American, but since he doesn't speak English, he thought he'd have a better chance in French than in Italian. We walked along chatting; reluctantly I went to his apartment. He did not turn me on, no butch pretenses about him. He is a twenty-one-year-old student at the Ecole Des Beaux Arts in Florence—some of his drawings decorated his room. He grew up near Bologna, has lived in Florence two or three years. "Florence is a dead city," he kept saying, "and I am dying too." He said he was alone and needed a friend. He had already decided that I should be that friend, that I should stay with him in Florence or take him to San Francisco with me. So romantic, so naïve, as if love were born that way. In the morning he clung to me, pulled me back, hoping I would stay.

With his expressive eyes, mobile face, pixie-like movements, and his agile body, he is really an actor. He loves the drama of being alone, the mellow, cool, late winter afternoon feeling of carefully nurtured isolation and self-pity. I know it all too well. And I know his situation is difficult, but not so suicidally impossible as he wants to believe. The exaggerated masculine-feminine dichotomy in Italy is an inappropriate setting for so androgynous a being.

We spent only eight hours together and I was glad to get away. "I'm not possessive," he said, yet I feared he'd never let go. We are grotesquely unsuited for each other, considering how much space I need around me. It was a real "European experience," to be cherished as a memory, but not to be taken seriously. And now, a month later he wants to come to Positano to stay with me. . . . I've come to Positano for repose. To invite Andrea would be, I'm afraid, to invite a storm. . . .

Is there in the trashy stuff of my fantasy life the basis for some good writing? Why not interview my sexual soul, transcribe and edit the results, and see what it is? What I am interested in is the spiritual equivalent of the physical lust, the poetic electricity which is the other side of sexual electricity. And male-to-male sexual lust is the first step in an awareness of the world as a world different from the one I was shown as a child. Once one makes that break, one sees all of life from a different point of view. But first one must identify, make positive the homosexual inclination which frees one to live a different life, to dare to see.

I want to write about the slavery, glamor, illusiveness, idiocy of sexual polarity—the mythology of opposites. All of us cherish and live by weird conceptions of male and female. These illusions govern much of our lives, what we wear, whom we choose as friends, wives, lovers. So much of art is glorification of this polarity. Popular art and advertising is scarcely anything else. . . . The male-female dichotomy seems to be the most fundamental human difference. . . . I want to find out what it is I love and hate in male and female mythology. Like *yin* and *yang*, each exists only in relation to the other, and this eternal *pas de deux* is endlessly fascinating. What is the epitome of maleness now may fifty years from now be hopelessly female—yet do some fundamental expressions of this polarity ever change? Some male (and certain female) images arouse longings in me—not only lust, but memories or previews of verbally unknown times and places. I want to recreate those images and go to the places they suggest. I do not want to live in a romantic hallucination, but our "real" life is so much governed by that "unreal" life and I want in a tiny way to recreate that "unreal" life. . . .

Just read "Other Kingdom" (the E. M. Forster short story), a thrilling, concise, elegant—at times funny—perfection of a story. What poetry should be, moves fast, does so much in only about twenty-five pages. I admire Forster more day by day.

I'm feeling more and more the need for sex. Not masturbation, but the warmth and challenge of another body. I am almost thirty years old and not at home with my needs. Masturbation is, as always, pleasant, but insufficient. I sometimes want to reach out to S., to hug him, to tell him, "Come sleep with me." It's not so much sex as tenderness I want. . . . I feel myself no longer young nor innocent, drying up from lack of emotional expression. My aloofness is a necessary self-defense, but also a trap. A trap for another deeply buried me. My knowledge of life is narrow, as narrow as the boundaries within which I give and receive love.

I need a few nights a month of abandon. Someone to hold, someone with whom to create once-in-a-lifetime moments. Holding hands in the picture show. Men don't do that. I have and I love it. . . . Fear keeps me where I am. Fear of hurt and hurting. Fear of being out of control, of going beyond my experience. My world is still flat because I fear to examine my depths. . . .

Mostly these days I am feeling uncommonly contented and, for the first time, grateful. I feel blessed to have been given so much. Here in Positano I am living an easy life . . . a privileged life, and one I scarcely deserve. To whatever being it is I believe in I've been saying: "You have created a beautiful world, you have given me a glorious life within it and I am happy. . . ." Perhaps it is because I am *accepting* more of life that I am now able to enjoy it. The rebel in me lives, but I want to focus the rebellion into some concrete and polished form—a form I hope will be almost, if *not quite,* acceptable to the world as it is.

I must write about Positano. It is a romantic and mystical place. For a typically alienated American like myself, it is a revelation. Such continuity. Life is strong; you can see and feel its century-by-century progression. From where I'm sitting I look upon a shimmering sea; in the distance are the islands reputed to be the dwelling place of the sirens in the *Odyssey*. If one can be so close to powerful mythic sources thousands of years old, can one really fear the small obstacles and dangers of life?

The word "virility" occupies me. I came upon it in *The Bell Jar*; my eyes stopped. I realized it was a word that has power over me. My cock stiffened in instantaneous response.

Virility is an elusive, much-prized quality, something which only a man may have, that with which he dominates. It is a quality nearly everyone worships, yet simultaneously despises. It and the ethereal qualities thought to be its opposite are the point of *A Streetcar Named Desire,* and the reason Marlon Brando was so exquisite in it.

In the faggot world's pantheon, the god virility ranks higher than Yahweh himself. Every true faggot worships and wants what he is so sure he himself is not (I include myself in this dangerously inclusive statement). Although virility includes thoughts of a lovely cock, a nicely but moderately muscled and slightly hairy body, a "strong" face with piercing eyes, it is more than physical. It is an attitude, an air of self-possession, even a swagger. It is male pride in the glory of being male. And when done innocently and with great style, nothing is so entrancing, nothing so beautiful. When meant to intimidate, to dominate, it can be equally ugly. . . .

I'm feeling now acutely the parts of me hidden, censored by life in Italy. Here men are allowed pride in appearance, indeed a narcissism which would be suspect in the States. Men walk arm in arm. To move in an almost all-male society is normal. It is assumed when the time comes they will do their duty. The roles assigned to male and female, those ancient roles, remain not much changed. In Southern Italy they know nothing of the liberated faggot. Here they only recognize as homosexual the precious queen, the near transvestite. That's weird for me. Possibly because I'm an American and strange anyway, they don't seem to recognize me as a homosexual. I am just a male, if a bit unconventional. In a way it's a relief not to be recognized as queer; on the other hand, it suppresses an enjoyable side of my personality, one I've cultivated and found useful for years. What goes on in my mind has no relation to what can be lived here. The outrageous but ordinary things we do in Provincetown, San Francisco, New York are so out of context they can't be imagined here.

I sometimes fear that my youth is over and that I've forgotten all I vowed I'd never forget. As a child one has powerful insights. One sees with cruel clarity the vanity, the pretense of adults. One vows not to lose one's purity, not to become one of those disgusting adults. Now I wonder if I haven't indeed become one of those ugly adults. Have I unwittingly lost the passion, the clarity of childhood? What have I gained? Freedom?

HOUMT SOUK, DJERBA, TUNISIA (February 1974)

I'm sitting in the Ben Yedda square. S. has just had his shoes shined by "his" shoeshine boy, a bright, charming boy of twelve or thirteen who now is lounging in the sun, enjoying a cigarette.

Last night I talked in my broken French with a Tunisian guy of perhaps twenty-four or twenty-five. I was wandering about town at twilight, absorbing the view at the well by the crafts center. He came up to me, said "Don't you recognize me?" In truth, I did not. It turns out he had been sitting next to me in the taxi I took back from the beach a few days ago. He is Europeanized, hopes to go to Europe or America to work. His goal is to meet a man who will befriend him, including sex—which he seemed not only ready but eager for. He hopes this man will take him to live in Europe. He seems ready to work and support himself, he just wants an opportunity. He's had *"pas de chance."* Everything was set up with a Dutch man who eight days after returning to Holland was killed in an auto crash. I don't disbelieve this story, yet I don't exactly believe it. Was his friendliness all *bonne camaradarie*? Perhaps he hoped I'd be the man to take him out of Tunisia.

I am trying to find a way of writing about the sexuality here. Superficially this is a dream country for the homosexual misogynist. Men control this society; they do everything that has to be done in public, including shopping. And outside of Tunis that traditional separation remains strong. Women are not touched sexually until marriage. And having no choice, the males seek each other's company. Or is that how they really want it?

I sense that homosexuality is not exactly encouraged, but neither is it much repressed. It just *is*, but it's probably one of those cultural facts few Tunisians would brag about. The official ideology is much the same as elsewhere: before all, man desires woman, woman is man's proof of manhood. There may be men who have sex mostly or entirely with other men, but they are scarcely different from other men, so there really are no homosexuals. It is not so much a question of taste as of frequency. Also where women are hidden, the queen does not exist. In a country where the female sexpot does not exist, who would the queen model himself after? Tunisia is a poor country and sex obviously is available for money, but there are not so many obvious hustlers—it's more subtle than that. And there are plenty of handsome young Tunisian men just looking for a good fuck; if you're reasonably attractive, *you* might be it... not necessarily any money involved. A man does have his needs, after all.

LONDON (March 1974)

Last night D. and I went to the A&B, a gay pub-club, near Leicester Square... an unmarked doorway, up two flights of stairs, you wouldn't find it in a million years if you didn't know what you were looking for. Supposedly one of the oldest places in London, been there twenty

79

years or more. A friendly, late twenties-thirtyish, bourgeois, hip-artsy crowd. I've seen it all a million times before and wasn't thrilled to see it now. There we met two Canadian boys wearing nearly identical leather or leather-look jackets (not the real butch kind, but the cute style—still any leather has a bit of butch connotation). Thane was the older, the personality. I didn't get the other's name, but he was cute, had really short brushed back hair, carefully studied but charming male mannerisms—his way of smoking, for example—a facile, paper-thin butchness, touching and appealing in spite of its self-consciousness. Also there was Robert, dressed all in black, hat and tight-fitting gangster-style 1930's jacket, smoking cigarettes through a long and flashy holder, a study in style and such a queen, Scotch. There are no queens in Scotland they said, they've all come to London.

I'm feeling the need to create a butch self, would like to get some tight Levi's, so tight you can feel your cock packed in them ... autostimulation as you walk along. The coy masculinity of the boy in the bar won me over. Why can't I be more like that? Would it be as boring as I imagine? Anyway I think sex—if I ever want it again—will come to me as male, not as some ambiguous third category. . . .

ON A TRAIN FROM BRUSSELS TO LUXEMBOURG (April 1974)

My main regret in going back to the States is that all my dreams of creativity will be shattered by the impossibilities of life at home. That I'll again get lost in the draining routine of work, work, work. Or the emptiness of hanging out. Why am I not stronger, more able to make connections between what I dream and what I live? I fear too much that "reality" will intrude upon the dream and I prefer the dream.

ON AN ICELANDIC FLIGHT BETWEEN LUXEMBOURG AND NEW YORK

On arriving at the Luxembourg airport, immediately dozens of Americans. It had been months since I'd been in the presence of Americans in numbers. And I was uncomfortable. What I noticed most was self-pretense and an absence of elegance, especially among the straight kids. I was not encouraged by the prospect of being among my fellow "countrymen," bored and dismayed is more like it. On the bus to the airport the talk was all of Nixon and that he should be impeached for sure. My attitude is, I just don't care anymore. My life will go on and the mundane intrigues of that political world are beyond, and I sometimes think, below me. . . .

BOSTON (April 1974)

My thirtieth birthday and I'm supposed to have some profound and sobering thoughts. I have not. I remember a friend who cried on her twentieth birthday because she was no longer a teen-ager. Perhaps the passage from twenty-nine to thirty is not so traumatic. I've been anticipating this day for two years or more. My notion of youth and age has changed enough to vanquish most of the anguish. Youth no longer seems the only worthwhile time of life. I'm determined to make the whole thing worthwhile. Forty perhaps will not be as exciting as twenty-five, but I think it may be more satisfying . . . I'm bored with youth.

SAN FRANCISCO (May-June 1974)

Now that I've been to some of the world's great cities I've earned the right to say this is one of them. The light is gentle, the mood friendly. This is a young city, with the naïveté, the freshness of youth. Even in these days of kidnapping and random murder, the streets are more relaxed than most cities, more relaxed than London, a city renowned for its civility.

I'm sighing a lot, frustration. After these months of laziness, the effort of organizing my life seems too much to face. The agony of looking for a job, the bother of getting a place to live. Situating myself among people—so many I know, so few I feel close to. And the necessity of keeping alive the dream. From afar the dream seems full of promise. The excitement made me nervous. Up close the dream recedes and the obstacles magnify themselves. . . .

I'm determined not to lose the energy I was full of when I returned. I vow not to let my middle-class desire for a safe and predictable life overcome my perverse need of danger. I promise to sometimes walk along the edge, if only to cultivate my skill in doing so. . . . In an enclosed life one can't *take in* the world, can't appreciate the mysteries, can't imagine the awe-fullness of the universe. When I was a child, fear enclosed me, but embarrassing passions leaked through. If my life is valuable it is these uncontrollable passions I must thank. Even in the pressured moments, something touches me, needles me. A voice reaches me: "Don't be bitter, don't fear, keep moving . . ."

The lesson I am learning is not to become too attached to San Francisco, to the myth of "the beauty of life here," a myth so easy to cling to even when living in an uncreative low.

The expansive world I'd begun to know seems to be fading fast. I'm sinking into the abyss California-style. Why do I find it so difficult, such a letdown to fit myself into the routine of life in one place . . . ? Why do I so much need a transcendent fantasy about myself? I cannot accept that *this* life, this everyday struggle *is* my life.

In Europe it was clear to me that the strong energy is coming from America, not Europe, and that my place is here. I know that, but being here again is a comedown. Traveling, one has delusions of grandeur—soaking up culture, no need to face the humdrum of life as the local people live it. I was free to believe myself part of the jet set. Now I am in the middle of the grubby necessity of earning a living, and it is distressing. . . .

My life seems to be a series of hops from one surprising place to another. I'm bewildered, having no metaphor to interpret the spaces in between. I'm becoming yet another person, not having understood what I was before. It's a little dizzying. I have no strong beliefs, no ideology. I'm confounded by my inability to describe, to rationalize this newest self. Just as one skin begins to be familiar, I lose it. How to define or situate myself, that question is at the heart of my restlessness.

Part Two
Survival in a Hostile World

INTRODUCTION:
Survival in a Hostile World

Allen Young

Some gay people believe that gay liberation is unnecessary. They think that they are already liberated. Chances are they have a large income, or a unique living and working environment which brings them into contact with only certain kinds of people (other gay people, artists, etc.), or they are so "outrageous" in their behavior that they are accepted simply on the basis of an unthreatening eccentricity.

Such people are trying to ignore a broader reality that may suddenly come careening homeward. Most of us, however, already know what it means to be a faggot or a dyke or a queer in this society. Today, in America's elementary and secondary schools, the most common and the most devastating dirty name a boy can be called is "faggot." Public opinion polls have shown that despite the growth of the gay liberation movement, there continues to be widespread contempt for homosexuals in the U. S. In European countries such as England, Holland, and Sweden, where people are known to have more liberal views on sexual matters, there is an underlying hostility to homosexuality beneath the tolerant veneer. If the straight world is changing too slowly, we are changing quite rapidly. Where once not very long ago we hid, shamefully, from those who might know about our true selves, now we have learned to experience openness and even pride—but with that pride remains the awareness, the consciousness, that there is a hurtful, dangerous lurking hostility that must be dealt with—if not today, then someday. Some of that hostility is institutionalized—in the legal system, in the canons of religion and psychiatry, in the educational system and the mass media, and in the very structure of the nuclear family. Our movement has been attempting to deal with the prejudices of those institutions. But much of the hostility consists of a rather vague but pervasive sense that people don't like queers, that they are disgusted by the very thought of homosexuality. They are disgusted by our sexuality, but perhaps more important, they are threatened by the fact that often we do not behave like "real men" and "real women" in arenas *other* than the bedroom.

Ultimately, however, survival in a hostile world means viewing the world as something other than a Manichean system of gays versus straights. In such a dichotomy, we are a minority and are likely to continue to be a minority. For this reason, I have felt it was counter-productive to seek "gay power" and to use counterepithets such as the word "hets" to describe heterosexual people. A central message of gay liberation, as I see it, involves combatting *machismo* by combatting the dichotomy of the "tough guy" husband and the "little homemaker" wife. Gay liberation means undermining the things that separate and segregate people according to sex; it means putting forth the idea not of gay-versus-straight, but of our feeling that the gay potential lives within all people.

It is our goal to live in a world where people stop expressing hostility not only toward us, but also toward the gayness inside themselves. Thus, while there is truth in Martha Shelley's statement to straight people that "the function of a homosexual is to make you feel uneasy," I would also take it a step further and say that the function of a homosexual ultimately is to make you feel comfortable—with yourself, your whole self. We will survive better as gay people when straight people no longer feel the neurotic need to assert their straightness as a "higher form" of being.

Even if gay liberation is to develop such a humanistic thrust, as indeed it already has, still it must deal with the institutionalized hostility as well. And it must deal with the fact that people don't like queers. We must educate others, but we must also protect ourselves against all forms of this hostility. We cannot wait for the "normal people" of this society to be nice to us, nor can we be satisfied with mere tolerance or compassion. We have to fight back against a system of oppression that has already been developed and from which these "normal people" benefit right now. It is not enough for us to know that the shy sensitive boy who prefers art class to gym is "better" than the bully who shouts "faggot" and drives a car like a maniac, or for us to know that on some level the bully is injured, too, by this dichotomy. We have to fight back, to show our love and solidarity with the faggot, to encourage him for what he is and to stop those who would force him into a gym class or a shrink's office. Part of fighting back is to express our disdain for the bully and, most important, to render the bully powerless to do the harm he does. This is not an easy task, just as it is not an easy task to put a stop to the bullies among nations.

To me, survival begins with awareness of oppression. It must include an understanding of the joys and pleasures of gay love and gay identity (and a realistic understanding of the problems, too). It also must mean finding a way of fighting back without being overwhelmed by the towering strength of those who oppress us, and without letting the fight be an end in itself. Too often, I think, we have moved from awareness of oppression into a sense of doom, despair, and martyrdom. This is, in a sense, giving in. It often leads to utter freak-out and even suicide. Sometimes we find ourselves on the brink of freak-out or suicide, not only because queer is a nasty name to be called, but simply because we are unhappy. Too often that unhappiness comes from the feeling that we can never achieve the image of bliss that this society has presented as a model. We have to see that the presentation of that model—the happy, affluent nuclear family—is part and parcel of the arsenal used against us. If we are to survive, if we are to fight back, we cannot crave the model any longer (or try to imitate it). We must recognize it for the lie that it is, not only for gay people but for most people, especially poor people, women, blacks, Latins, native Americans, communards, small farmers, and factory workers. Neither should we give up when the alternatives we attempt seem to flounder or erupt into conflict, chaos, and even collapse. In other words, we have to keep on trucking.

There is a special relationship between the survival of gay people in a hostile environment and the survival of all people in the capitalist system. Most gay people depend on a job in order to provide the mere basics in life. A significant number of gay people—choosing work that is offbeat, perhaps disreputable, occasionally even illegal—function on the margin of the economy. (Even such fields as the theater and other artistic endeavors are on some level disreputable—average American parents would not want their son or daughter to choose such a milieu.) While "out of the closet!" is the rallying cry of the gay movement, the movement is only beginning to give some support to those gay people who are unable to be open about their gayness because of the demands of a job. This is a dilemma: the person who remains in the closet sometimes enforces gay oppression by remaining invisible, while the up-front gay can show indifference and insensitivity to the fact that people have different needs and move at different rates of speed. Civil rights legislation to protect people on the job is universally recognized as a primary goal of the gay movement. If such legislation is passed, it is likely that the gay movement will be able to assume new, broader dimensions.

Combatting stereotypes in the media, ending invisibility, fighting for fair employment practices—these efforts toward reform are needed and welcome. But gay liberation has a revolutionary dimension which should not be lost. That dimension challenges the reformist myths. Ultimately, our struggle for freedom will be shortchanged if we stop at acceptance, tolerance, and "equal rights" in a society that exploits workers, divides people according to skin color, insists on separate models of behavior for men and women, destroys the environment, and attempts to dominate smaller nations by economic and military coercion. We believe that gay liberation will have achieved little if it merely means that it's all right for a select group of white, middle-class people to "have sex" in a different way. For us, survival has to mean much more than integration into a society and lifestyle that is antithetical to our most basic yearnings.

HOW TO COME OUT WITHOUT BEING THROWN OUT

Jeanne Córdova

Some of us are beginning to realize, although we now have several proud movements (lesbian, women's, gay liberation) which speak of our pride, there is still the matter of emotional and economic survival. The political may be personal, but The Dialectics of Sex don't numb the pain of being kicked out of the house, and your landlord just doesn't think a subscription to *The Lesbian Tide* is a fair exchange for rent. And so more than half a decade after Stonewall, it is time for us to develop strategies about how to come out without being thrown out.

My thesis still is that it is better to stand in the sun than to crawl in the closet. One can offer many political reasons for making the big step ("The Invisible Minority must show itself," "We must proclaim our rights in the streets") but I offer here more personal reasons.

Closet life, just as the metaphor suggests, is cramped, dark, moldy, and isolated. In short, closet life is a drag! Surely there could be volumes written about our sisters' and brothers' schizophrenic attempts to see in the dark. Surely, if God were locked in a closet for life, she'd be sick, too. Thus for me and for many who have lived it both ways, I give no world, no society, no oppressor the right to board me up.

But the matter only begins with this assertion. The question is not whether or not to come out, but When, Where, and How to come out—with the least possible cost to ourselves. It's a skill . . . and we need to know how to take care of ourselves. Experience has shown me there are good (successful) and bad (on the self-esteem) ways to handle this oppressive but inevitable process. Usually, admitting homosexuality to one's family is the most difficult and last place to come out. Therefore, I will deal here with coming out to families, but my method can be used elsewhere.

Briefly, there are two problems: attack from without and sabotage from within. The sins of heterosexism and sexism against us need hardly be documented here, but I suggest we have not emphasized enough another more insidious enemy. None of us really needed to sit through Abnormal Psychology and hear what they thought of us, but since we did, most of us have that "knowledge" now too to deal with. I suggest, in the process of coming out, our own internalization of societal prohibitions against us are perhaps *more* self-negating than those which come from without.

When a young or old, or middle-aged faggot or dyke sits down with the big question, "To tell or not to tell?" she/he perhaps should first ask him/herself "*Why* do I want to tell my parents?" There are five basic Come Out Approaches and our own personal motivations usually play a large part in determining which we choose.

The Help Me, Help Me Syndrome is more a prostration, prostitution, or grovel than a statement and is always received as such. Prompted by self-homophobic guilt, the Help Me, Help Me Syndrome is best manifested by conversations like:

"Mom?"

"What is it, dear?"

"Oh Mom, I have to . . . I can't . . . " (tears)

"You can tell me anything darling, you know how much your father and I love you and how much . . . "

"That's why I want to tell you, I need . . . your . . . I'm afraid, I'm . . . "

Etc., Etc., This approach will doubtless result in a visit to a psychiatrist, priest, doctor, or mental institution of your choice. Very possibly you will be allowed to see one or two or all of the above because after all, you are so very, very sorry and seek The Cure. Although radical liberationists might scoff at the rarity of such an approach, sisters and brothers by the thousands who do see themselves as sick (little wonder!) have given themselves over to the enemy this way simply because they've never seen any other way.

The So There Approach, one of the most dangerous, is similarly not very successful, but has a unique loophole. Marked by extreme anger/ hatred/bitterness toward parents, which is always justified but sometimes careless, the announcement is bluntly made in the middle of a family argument which usually has nothing to do with sexual orientation.

Dad: "And I'll tell you something else, you ungrateful son (daughter) of a bitch, you never were any good, you'll never amount to anything, you're nothing . . . "

"I'll tell you what I am, I'll tell you something you can really have a migraine over . . . I'm a homosexual. Yeah, that's right—a *Queer! Fruit! Dyke! Faggot!* (so there!)"

Because the So There Approach almost always implies the corollary, And It's All Your Fault, we may be sure our parents won't miss the point.

While shoving it down their throats (for everything they've ever done to you) can be emotionally rewarding in the short run, at best it leads to being thrown out (that is, "You're no daughter/son of mine!") and at worst to incarceration in a mental institution. This time you don't get to choose because you are obviously locked in psychotic Oedipal struggle with those that love you and therefore very, very sick and therefore someone must take care of (commit) you.

The So There Approach is popular with young (high school, living at home) gays who, exposed to constant harassment and pressure, take an impulsive, quick, angry way out. Though certainly not recommended as the most successful, the danger to this approach is that the same anger and hatred which got you into this mess, if not nullified by threats of incarceration, may be violent enough to make you split before they convince you that you didn't really mean it.

The Oops Approach, while better than the previous two, will probably merit the negation its name suggests. Popular with all age groups especially before liberation days, this Freudian device was my own Armageddon.

It was one of those, "Jeanne, will you please come home and watch the kids while your father and I go to Palm Springs . . . " weekends in 1967.

Seven months lesbianized, I packed a few school books together with my lover's latest letter (to savor over the weekend) and complied.

Just as sweetly, I answered the phone the next week.

"This is your mother . . . "

"Yes, Mother . . . "

"I'm calling . . . you left . . . while you were here . . . one of your books . . . "

"Oh no, really? I guess I'll have to come out and pick it up."

"Well, that's not what I'm calling about . . . "

"Oh . . . , well?"

"Jeanne . . . there was a letter in the book."

"A letter?"

"A letter."

"(*The Letter!!! Oops!*) oh . . . a letter."

"What does this letter mean, Jeanne?"

Well, as "luck" would have it, it was one of *those* letters . . . the one about the night before . . . nitty-gritty you know. Not much room for beating around the bush. "I guess I . . . a . . . it means what it says . . . I guess."

"Jeanne, I think you'd better come out here tonight so we can have a talk."

The Oops Approach is also akin to the sisterly/brotherly sibling conversation that goes, "I just have to tell someone and I know you'll never tell Mom or Dad." And you know damn well they will.

Although good for openers, Oops is not exactly a positive statement of fact, preference, or lifestyle. Because it takes an almost apologetic (oops, I really didn't want . . .) stance, it is open to being interpreted as a Help Me, Help Me plea, rather than the backdoor statement of purpose you meant to announce. Consequently, Oops leaves us open to an endless barrage of, "I know this really isn't you . . . just a phase . . . it was *her/his* bad influence . . . " In the end, it's all the more difficult trying to convince them, "No, Mom/Dad, it really was me, *I* was the one who suggested it. . . . I really am."

And then of course, there is the Dear Mom/Dad Approach, a favorite of the, "They're in New York and I'm in California . . . so it's safe," live-away gay. Hopefully camouflaged next to their tax returns, a letter from "favorite son," bills, etc., this delivery blockbusts its way into that neat little white picketed mailbox. Mother usually opens this one only to fall apart and run to "Your Father" when she reads the words . . . "And . . . there's something else I have to tell you . . . " While seemingly safe (what can they do to me from so far away?), this approach often produces the extremes in parental reaction: (1) if you are under twenty-one, the long arm of the courts can reach you anywhere; (2) they might be on your doorstep when your lover answers the bell the next morning; and (3) you may never hear from them again. The last may seem preferable at the time (it is an effective way to get them off your back, "once and for all"), but it does not lead to understanding.

Last, but most effective (in my experience) is the Gradual or Naturalization Approach. Presupposing, as most of this does, that the goals of one's coming out are: (1) to come across honestly and proud; and (2) hope your parents will think so too one day, this approach can be used by all age groups living at home or away.

The first of four Naturalization steps entails mental preparation but no overt behavior change on your part. While preparing yourself for what might be a six-month to six-year process, act toward your parents as you always do. Send flowers, if you usually do; don't write more than twice a year if you usually don't.

Step two: Ever so innocuously in your letters or visits, drop references to Jane/John (new "friend," "roommate," "co-worker," etc.), e.g., "I bought this for you in Florida, Jane/John and I took off for a week and had a great time!" And still later ... "Jane/John and I are thinking of moving to California because the weather is better. Do you think we should live in L.A. or San Diego?" Later ... on the phone, "I'll be home for Dad's birthday next week, is it okay if Jane/John comes too?"

The principles here are to notify your parents of a new close person in your life with whom you share good times, and also to involve them in their "loving" daughter's/son's life.

It is important to avoid, at this introductory stage, being over-zealous. Casual remarks like, "Dad, Jane/John and I are having sexual problems," or, "Jane/John won't talk to me because I went away for a weekend with Susan/Jack. Now don't you think that's wrong?" will probably not solicit the desired feedback. Briefly, at this stage avoid sexual references in your conversation.

Step three: After Jane/John has been accepted, or at least properly introduced as a part of your life, initiating or participating in dinner-table conversations about feminism, the gay movement, etc., are useful ways of dropping hints. The most innocuous suburban conversation about Billie Jean King's triumph or your brother's latest faggot joke is an invitation to get out your "intellectual" perspective on that issue. There comes the flak: Intellectual conversations about male and female roles often generate more familial hostility than the terrible (but, "far-fetched") subject of homosexuality. After several months, family members will begin to accept you as a women's libber, or sexual libera-tionist, "sympathizer." Step three is completed when you hear your mother tell others, "Well, that's my daughter, Jeanne, her ideas are ... a bit different."

Step four: As your verbal affirmation of rights and freedoms for women, minorities, gays, etc., becomes pronounced, sooner or later brother David, sister Louise, or Mother/Father will ask you to "step into the kitchen for a minute."

The offensive is yours if, when asked, your answer is cast simply, "Why yes ... I thought you knew," or, "Of course ... I wasn't just talking."

Although the steps may arise differently for each of us, the important thing is affirmation rather than apology. Taken out of context and explained to a six-year-old, adult sexuality often appears gross, perverted, distasteful. Placed in context and perspective it can appear warm, desirable, and natural. Knowing our parents' already preconceived notions of homosexuality, we must be doubly sensitive and aware about introducing our lifestyle as a warm, open, natural extension of love. The best response can be expected if our coming out process seems to be motivated simply by a desire to share with them something good that is happening in our lives.

Additionally, there are three other universals of which we should be aware—race, class, and religious mores are as much or more a part of our parents' reactions as their personal feelings for their daughters or sons. Not taking care of ourselves is not noticing the different perspectives on homosexuality endemic to certain religions, races, or social classes.

Although there is a disproportionately larger number of Catholic (ex-Catholic!) lesbians, Roman Catholicism and Judaism are among the worst incubators of bad attitudes toward gayness. The more "God-fearing" one's parents are, the more deeply ingrained will be their own guilt and heterosexist bias. Naïve at nineteen, I could not understand why my Irish mother seemed less traumatized by my lifestyle choice than my Chicano father. Later, realizing the *machismic* clutch the latter had to maintain on his culturally constructed masculinity, I was in a better position to understand *his* problem. The fact my father helped raise an aggressive woman because he wanted one cannot be reconciled with his belief that a woman is "a man's soul and salvation." Gay women will find their lesbianism is upsetting to brothers and fathers not because they have sex with a woman, but because our woman-identified sexual orientation is a notice, "No man (not even you!) can bond me." Gay men, similarly, should realize they are a threat to their father's masculinity and their mother's femininity. It is helpful to recognize that when they refuse to speak to us for three years or say, "You're no daughter/son of mine!" it's not really us they're talking to! They are dealing with their own sexual identity conflicts. A certain objectivity is necessary. When they say these terrible things it is not time to jump . . . it is not the "end of the world." For most parents, this is merely a phase.

Another caution: Don't be idealistic. Do not expect them to march with you next June in the annual Christopher Street parade. Do not expect, in the first year or two, to sit down and say, "Dad, I just don't know whether she/he loves me.... How can I tell?" Number one, he doesn't know. Number two, it's not smart to expect him to show us how to love in a way he cannot.

Ninety-eight percent of parents and employers will *never* admit more than, "You're okay with me, whatever you want to do ... " Emotional outrage about the insanity of their prejudice must give way to the intellectual realization—giving us true support and affirmation means they'd have to ask their heterosexual selves, "What's wrong with me?"

THRIVING DECLOSETED
IN RURAL ACADEME*

Louie Crew

[Author's note: This article was written some four months after my
decloseting. Now, almost a year after the letter to my bosses, I can see
herein some of the marks of the oppressor still impressed upon me: most
notably the erotophobia of the piece. No longer can I say that "the use
of class time to talk about personal sexuality is deplorable to me." Today
I am disturbed by those who abuse class time by never talking about
sexuality. I feel that as gays we have much to give up-tight straight
colleagues by our being, once out of the closet, inescapably the teacher
as sexual person. Still, the article remains an honest statement and is a
moment detached from a continuing process of personal liberation. Any
pangs herein are birth pangs.]

Last November a combination of pressures led me to revise dramati-
cally my professional self-concepts. In a letter which I read to my
students, I outlined to my administrators these pressures and know-
ingly, irrevocably charted new directions:

Gentlepersons:

I wish to take this opportunity to speak clearly to explain an
unusual action which I have taken in the last five minutes of each
of my classes today. I have told my students that I am gay, and I
have tried to explain the reasons for my so saying. These reasons
are very important to me, and I would like to reiterate them.

First, I can no longer tolerate the mask of having people
assume that I am what I am not. I want honesty, with other
people, yes, but most essentially with myself. Sexuality is a part
of any person's whole personhood, hence a part of his integrity.
The use of class time to talk about personal sexuality is deplorable to me; my use of the time is merely to free people from their
logical misconception about my identity. My integrity, my

---

*Editor's note: For further information, contact the Gay Academic Union,
Box 480, Lenox Hill Station, New York 10021.

wholeness, demands clarity.

Second, all study for serious scholars is a passion, and all passion is in some vague way related to sexual passion. My passion for literature is definitely of one piece with all aspects of my identity. Any literature demands judgment based on human experience. I feel that my students have a right to know the potential biases of my judgments.

Third, I am involved deeply in some ... important research into homosexuality. ... I feel that I would be intellectually dishonest if I were to use the pronouns *they, them,* and *their* when I really meant *we, us,* and *our.* I cannot be healthy if, as a scholar, I bring one level of honesty to my research and another level of honesty to my classroom.

Fourth, sexuality is only a minor part of any person's identity. When hidden behavior is discussed, it assumes major proportion through gossip and distortion. I prefer to be open so as to minimize sexuality and to hold myself publicly accountable for my behavior. I can take no responsibility for my affections, but every responsibility for the use to which I put them.

Fifth, my many gay brothers and sisters on this campus and throughout the world need the support that can come only through leadership that is strong and healthy. I am grateful to do whatever I can, and I hope that others will not have to remain afraid and lonely so long as I chose to do. I am sensitive to the fact that the timing of anyone's coming out is immensely complicated. I am grateful that I have all along had the privilege of being of some help to such persons. I have notified campus counselors ... volunteering my services in any way that they may be useful. I have similarly notified my Bishop and my priest. ... I suspect that my main services will continue to be through articles and other scholarship.

I wish to make it very clear that this letter and the class statements which prompted it are not intended to be a radical confrontation. I am thoroughly committed to the assignment I have accepted here, and I am giving my fullest energies to the institution, which has my great loyalty and respect. I am not asking for any special treatment, only this brief opportunity to make it quite clear who I am. Most assuredly any dangers rightly or wrongly associated with a gay identity are hereby greatly minimized. I ask only to be judged on the quality of my work, not on factors over which none of us has control.

Finally, I wish to thank all of you for making my stay here thus far one that has been immensely enjoyable and productive. I thank you for the faith that you have shown in me, and I hope through service and work to justify your trust.

Warmly and professionally,
Louie Crew, Associate Professor

This letter was never officially answered. One dean, in confidence, admired my "courage." All others continued to treat me pleasantly, and I have not been notified of being fired, as I would have had to be by the first of February, according to faculty statutes for first-year people without tenure.

It is gratifying to report that the euphoria of that first day of revision has been at least partially sustained in many of the consequences. In my classroom, I speak from a clearer, if narrower base of authority; hence my students more freely negotiate my comments as they pick and choose in the charting of their own literary judgments. For example, I now offer as an insider my critique of Somerset Maugham's preference for heroes and anti-heroes who never share themselves openly, who never decloset, who, like Maugham himself, endure stoically, sterilely. (Cf. Noel Coward's similar gay indictment in *Song at Twilight*.) Likewise, I now possess an outsider's detachment in evaluating literary heterosexual conflicts. I no longer have to translate into my experience and ignore what is lost in translation. All of us who are gay have been living in straight families all along, and we know the truth about loveless families, about unwanted babies, about careless birth control, about a marriage license as an excuse for legalized rape, about a whole host of crimes against the human spirit in which we have not been directly involved, except often as victims. We do not have to go along with straight writers who make special pleadings for straights who are inauthentic.

As a teacher of black literature, I have often been frustrated by my black students when they tell me that they do not need to read most black literature, that a man like James Baldwin, for example, writes only to tell whites about the black experience, an experience they claim already to know all about. When I have told them that Baldwin speaks to me as a man, not as a white man, many students have said that I muddle only from my white experience. Perhaps I do. But now I can say what I really mean, that Baldwin speaks to me as a gay brother, that I read myself more readily into a book like *Go Tell It On the Mountain* than I read my students into it!

The real importance of this revision of my gay identity in the classroom is not any claim to greater accuracy for my judgments, but the claim to making those judgments more negotiable and accessible as buffers for the students' growth. Most of my students will hopefully never again invest me with the undesirable role of being spokesman and deliverer of their cultural values. Rather, my classes become vehicles of healthy suspicion, mandates that they weigh all issues and be prepared to defend their positions.

Student response is always difficult to measure. I have always enjoyed high class attendance without requiring it; yet it has risen even higher since my coming out. The first quarter this year I had several visitors almost daily, in addition to those on roll. My department chairperson, who has never specifically mentioned the letter, has told me that she is pleased with my work, specifically with the good response that she is getting from students. For my part, I know that I continue rarely to lose a pair of eyes in discussions. I know too that I like this attention more than ever now that I am not worried about their finding out about "the real me." Also, I get enough mixed feedback to know that they are neither mesmerized nor otherwise intimidated.

Equally positive has been my continued freedom of mobility on campus. In fact, I am freer. I now fearlessly, even righteously, charge my colleagues—particularly librarians, historians, psychologists, but also fellow teachers of literature—with their blatant neglect of gays, not only of those in their classrooms, but also those who ought to be in their textbooks, or on their committees making decisions affecting sexual understanding, etc. For example, one historian here has written the definitive work on lynching, and yet knows nothing of the historic persecution of gays, whether by Justinian or by Hitler. Silent for thirty-six years, I am now discovering my voice, my identity, my wholeness. In fact, I am not even sure that I would still say, as I did in the original letter, that sexuality is a "minor part of a person's identity." As I have been asked to speak to classes in numerous other departments (including philosophy [ethics], psychology, physical education, and religion) on our campus and elsewhere, I have become aware of how major a part sexuality is for all of us in the academy. In these forums I am constantly having to counter the stereotypes that straights have about gay people, primarily because we gays have never been allowed to be visible, or even to write the major accounts of our experience. I have had the pleasure of affirming, celebrating gay diversity. Moreover, I have been free to speak out on behalf of specific gays persecuted by the academy. One gay student dismissed in a witch hunt eight years ago, charged with being "a moral danger," is about to be readmitted because certain administrators would be quite happy if I did not get my right to review his confidential folder so that I can properly advise him. Similar memoranda throughout the bureaucratic land need to be rooted out, and all dishonorable discharges need to be reversed. Even closeted faculty here have rejoiced with twinkling eyes to see me bring the aid they were powerless to bring to this student.

Not all results have been positive. Many have been mixed, as in the case of the talented student who dropped my course in creative writing because he said I "talked about gayness too much." How does one measure "too much"? Did my teachers who were parents draw too many literary generalities from their socially acceptable experiences of sexuality? Am I really talking about sexuality merely to mention my "lover" rather than my "friend"? Maybe it is a mark of my oppression that I never questioned the rights of my straight teachers to allude openly to straight roles? Did my literary textbooks through the doctorate—which never gave a positive view to, rarely gave any view to gay experience—cheat me and my straight classmates of an experience of the world as it really is, with one out of every six of us having had homosexual experience? Am I talking "too much" when I'm the only openly gay professor most of my present students will ever have, when I give less than five minutes out of every fifty to anything directly relating to the gay experience? Clearly one student felt this much was "too much." I wonder how much my professors would have respected me had I dropped a course saying that they talked about straight identity too much; yet strangely I do respect this student. He told me to my face what he felt.

Equally mixed has become the "blessing" of being The Campus Homosexual. By the stingiest straight sociological estimate, I have at least 160 brothers and sisters on this campus of close to 2,000 souls. Their tight closet doors are a partial measure of my vulnerability. Being conspicuous is not new to me. In the past I have been highly visible as Louie the Actor, Louie the Writer, Louie the Choir Member, Louie the Seamster, Louie the Jogger. . . . Now, in the public mind these roles

100

have all been subsumed under Louie the Queer. A nice queer, perhaps, but a queer nevertheless. I am often exhausted by taking on this role, by the internalized pressure to feel a credit to my race, my tribe. Still, I consciously fight to preserve, to integrate all other roles and dimensions of my identity while my colleagues and students come to terms with their own homophobia.

Homophobia is indeed the problem. One colleague shared with me the fact that he had overheard some of my students saying that they felt they would be penalized if they told me what they really felt about gay people. This colleague cautiously suggested that their fears were rational. I countered, "Would you think to lower my grade for what I think about heterosexuality?" "Of course not, but that's different!" he exclaimed. Is it? Why? Fortunately I was able to take the matter directly to my classes and reaffirm their freedom. The game they were really playing was projection, in that, doubting their own ability to be fair to sissies, they projected their own inadequacies upon me. "How," they rationalized, "can you be fair to us if we can't be fair to you?"

I have had to expose similar homophobia in many academic social contacts with my students. Always a gregarious person, I noticed shortly after coming out that fewer students spoke when greeted in public, that many looked nervously about when I stopped to chat in the student center. I called this behavior to the attention of my classes so that I might explain that I really don't like embarrassing people, that I have no desire to have my students maligned by their peers' thinking that they have something going with the teacher, etc., but also explained that my only alternative is to go to the back of the bus. I refuse. I shall keep on being as friendly as I have always been, even if this means I must sit by those who do not want me, that I must share my oppression until there is indeed no back of the bus.

I have been very fortunate in being loved through all of this by a very great man. I have also been fortunate in having already known a good bit about my strength before I ever dared to make this move of coming out. More than ever I respect my brothers and sisters who have either come out or been forced out without such preparation. Those straights who complain about the gays still hiding, a complaint I hear daily, would better spend their energies making their own families places safe for gay members to come out in. Each person must work on her or his own timetable. To those of you still in the closet, if my experience says anything to me it is the greater awareness I have of how much we have to contribute to this culture. When we come out, we not only start revisions for ourselves, but also for our straight brothers and sisters. If we keep our heads about us, we may yet make the world a safer and happier, healthier and more knowledgeable place in which to live.

One of my student friends who already knew, told me last November that she had heard about my "confession." "But it wasn't a confession," I said; "rather a profession." "But why in Georgia and in 1973?" she asked. "Because I live in central Georgia and in 1973; I have no other time or place in which to work out my own salvation."

OUT IN THE WORKPLACE *

Don Mager

Being out at work erases all fear of "being found out" and some of the fear of being fired without redress. It brings to a halt the oppression of being treated as someone whom you are not (lesbians being asked when they will get married, etc.). For myself, being out at work means a new and very tangible freedom to deal seriously and competently with the people who come through my office each week, because I am not distracted by fears and intimidations. If the *gay power* button on my shirt upsets someone, I can choose to turn the conversation to a discussion of gay liberation and gay oppression. Formerly, when a person at work "suspected" that I might be queer, an elaborate game of testing was initiated, throughout which I felt intimidated by the uncertainty of what that person would say or do if she or he concluded I was in fact queer. Now, I am in the position to initiate the discussion, and to some extent I can define the terms of the discussion. For me this discussion is never of my private life and emotions, but of the politics of sexism and homophobia; thus, from what had been an environment of intimidation and uncertainty, I now find my job to be a place where I feel pride and self-determination. If this is not a tangible increase in personal freedom, then I don't know what is. But make no mistake, because I am out in one work environment and therefore feel an increase in my personal freedom, in no way does this make me as a gay person free in this society—no way! Even so, the increase in freedom is important, and because I know so well both the former intimidation and now the freedom, I desperately want my closeted coworkers to share this freedom too. Somehow I believe that my coming out will crack open a closet door here and there so that some of this freedom will spread beyond my single small office and reach into theirs.

I work in one office environment. Other gays work in other

*Editors' note: For continuing information on this subject, we recommend the magazine *Gay People in the Labor Force*, P.O. Box 5826, Middle City Station, Philadelphia, Pa. 19103.

environments. But the politics of coming out is the same everywhere. We need to grow strong in ways of coming out which destroy the straights' control over the politics of confrontation. We must choose to be triumphant in verbal confrontation; this means we must identify ourselves not as isolated individuals but as members of a movement and an ideology which has more validity and persuasiveness and human decency than the typically irrational and prejudiced sexism of most straights. Finally, we must come out in all environments where closeted gays will see us, so that they can begin to understand the self-liberation that coming out can bring, and thus redefine their own options and open up their own closet doors. Open gay people are strong women and men, let's make no mistake; we have taken real risks with our lives and learned in the process how to stand tall. The politics of coming out is nothing more nor less than the spreading of this gay strength to all gays everywhere, not because closet gays are weak, for surely to come out sexually is itself a remarkable act of self-assertion, but because public coming out is a conscious political activity which expresses a person's identity with gay comrades in contrast to sexual coming out which is a private act.

BUNDLES OF TWIGS
IN NEW HAMPSHIRE:
A High School Teacher's
Report *

Robert LaRiviere

An acquaintance of mine once said that homophobia is the national ailment of the United States; after teaching for a year in a New Hampshire high school, I now know that, at least in this rural community, it is much too true. From the first week of school I was branded as a faggot, and, since I don't consider myself to be particularly effeminate, I was curious to discover why I was labeled derogatorily (for this was the intent) so early in my teaching career. (I was fresh out of college.) I found out that on the first day of school some of my students had checked out my car, a Plymouth Duster. Obviously, any real man would not be caught dead owning a car whose engine size was a whimpering 198 cubic inches! Also, since I had answered "no" when they asked if I had played sports in high school or college, I was undeniably a pansy in their minds. Although I was somewhat surprised by such primitive mentalities, I pressed onward, confident that I could do my part for society by enlightening 120 teen-agers. I soon learned that these assumptions made by my students about me were serious intimations of an age-old malady running rampant—the age-old malady of homophobia.

My eleventh-grade class consisted primarily of the football and basketball players; their preoccupation with the whole *macho* trip was amazing in its awesome power. Anyone who didn't play varsity sports or hunt deer was immediately at a disadvantage when dealing with these students. Obviously, they thought, anyone who would want to teach English was a queer, anyway. I realized immediately that my first job would be to make an attempt at some sort of sensitizing; to make my students aware and sympathetic to individuals and their differences. The problem was so acute, and the damage was so extensive, that I didn't know where to begin.

We started with the obvious question of what determines manhood

*Editors' note: For further information, contact the Gay Teacher's Caucus, c/o Friedman, 831 Carroll Street, Brooklyn, New York 11215.

105

and womanhood. No one even touched upon the subjects of responsibility, gentleness, or personal ethics. One student's ultimate explanation of Man and Woman was, "The man *must* be more important: he's the one who always gets on top when they fuck!" The amazing thing about this comment was that none of the girls in the class found any errors in that boy's comment. None of them found it necessary to defend themselves against this obvious attack on the importance of women.

The student who had voiced this comment was the most extreme case of homophobia. He was constantly expounding upon his sexual prowess, and was always trying to seduce his female classmates with tales of the endless pleasure that lay waiting at the end of what he considered to be his gigantic penis. Any time the subject of love arose in class discussions, however, he suddenly became painfully silent. He was finally suspended from school for urinating on a seventh-grader in the lavatory. When questioned about his motives for this act, he simply said, "Because faggots turn my stomach."

I was becoming increasingly more despondent over the massive obsession with the distinction between "fags" and "men." There was mounting hostility between myself and several of my male students; on several occasions this hostility erupted into major confrontations. I was a faggot because I gave homework on Fridays, I was a faggot if I kept anyone after school; a student's father was a faggot if he didn't let him have the car on Saturdays. In short, the term was used to denote contempt for any undesirable person.

This is the manifestation which most frightened me. It scared me because it illustrated an obstacle which was impervious to any form of reason. How can you instill respect and sensitivity, or any sort of practical ethics, when something as harmless as homosexuality is viewed in such a light?

Homophobia wasn't the only form of oppression I encountered here; all the other age-old prejudices had found themselves a place of nourishment as well. A tenth-grade student of mine ran into more than her share of prejudice and aggression when she moved here from New York City. Having lived in the city for most of her life, she is naturally more sophisticated and aware than her classmates in New Hampshire: she is fortunate enough to be able to talk and think much more openly about subjects, having been exposed to so much more in New York. She is literally an outcast in this New Hampshire school. She is, as far as many of her female classmates are concerned, a "slut" because she can talk about the subject of sex without blushing and without stumbling along with such phrases as "well . . . uh . . . you know . . . " But not only is she a "slut," she is also Jewish, the supreme degradation. In my classes, the subject of "Jew" comes up almost as frequently as "faggot" does. The students—always the males—talk about "Jewsday" coming after Monday, and "Jewn" coming after May. One of the protagonists in a novel we were studying became known in the class as "Jewlia."

This girl from New York came to me after class one day and asked if I would allow her to spend the next three weeks in the school library. We had started the novel *1984*, and Becky was extremely disgusted with the anti-Jewish sentiment forced upon the novel's characters by the government of Big Brother. She objected very strongly to the fact that the supreme traitor, the supreme enemy of the state, was a character named Emmanuel Goldstein. What infuriated her beyond words was that most of her classmates had totally missed George Orwell's intention; they were, instead, very amused at the whole idea of Emmanuel the Jew. Becky, in requesting to be allowed to stay in the library until we finished the novel, mentioned to me that until she moved to New Hampshire, she had never thought of herself as being inferior or unworthy of respect. She finally, after much persuasion by me, decided to remain in class, and was able to contribute much to the education of my students.

Another interesting incident involving *1984* occurred in my other tenth-grade class. A student came to me and said that her father had forbidden her to read the novel because of its "immoral qualities." She was extremely reticent to explain what her father had meant by this term, but I finally discovered that her father objected to the sexual references made in the novel. There was a grand total of two sexual incidents, both of which were very sketchy and implicit, but her father had apparently been infuriated by the mention of the word "climax." Since there is a recently-made school policy which allows students to read alternative literature if their parents object strongly to any assigned book, I had no choice but to concede. She ended up studying *A Tale of Two Cities* and writing a book report on it for her final project. What infuriated me most about this incident was that her father, who had read the book before condemning it, completely missed the value of the book. The ironic and frightening point was that this girl's father was doing exactly what was being done in the supposedly fictitious world of *1984*, in which Big Brother forbade sexual activity, under penalty of death. Big Brother's rationale for doing so was that sexual activity makes people "too human," and hence, too hard to dominate.

During an "Open House" organized by the school I came to appreciate the extent to which my students' values have been shaped by their parents. The Open House was organized to allow parents to meet with teachers and to become acquainted with the courses of study their children would pursue through the year. After speaking to the father of one of my students, I happened to hear him talking to another parent in the corridor outside my classroom. He was angry that I would be teaching *The Great Gatsby*, instead of grammar, to his son. "God knows," he said, "only pansies read books like that!"

I was infuriated by this comment, but I was also, strangely, somewhat relieved. I was angered for the obvious reasons, but was relieved because I now realized that it wasn't myself who had been the total failure. I had become extremely depressed over the insurmountable obstacles of ignorance I had encountered, but I now saw that, no matter how hard I tried, one year of my efforts would not even make a dent in the sixteen years of home education my students had been given by their parents.

When I was studying Thomas Hardy's *Return of the Native* with a class, I had to give them a weekly vocabulary list, because of the unfamiliarity of many of the words in the novel. In the first chapter of the book, the word "faggot" is used. I had been sort of half hoping that the students would miss the word while reading, but I knew that this was inconceivable. I wrote the word on the board, and defined it in the context of the novel as a bundle of twigs which is burned as fuel. I even mentioned how this definition was the source of the contemporary definition so dear to their hearts—that in the Middle Ages faggots, like witches, were burned to death. From that moment on, the boys were obsessed with calling each other "bundles of twigs." There was even an occasion where, during a break in one of the interscholastic basketball games, some of my students began calling members of the opposing team a "bundle of twigs," much to the confusion of the other team.

I even had a student write a Creative Writing composition using Egdon Heath—the locale of Hardy's novel—as a setting. The composition concerned the annual bonfire which the novel's characters held on Hallowe'en. It turned out, however, that the townspeople weren't burning peat moss or twigs, but were burning Fred F. Aggot, the village idiot and queer. Under different circumstances I would have been amused, but the writer of this story was definitely not sympathetic, so the story took on a very ominous quality for me.

108

One of my students recently "discovered" the famous case of Christine Jorgensen and mentioned it in class one day. Most of the other students found it infinitely repulsive that anyone would not be satisfied with his or her sexuality. I tried, unsuccessfully, to explain the difference between sex and gender, but no one was convinced that George Jorgensen had done what was right. Obviously, my students agreed, Mr. Jorgensen was nothing but a faggot, anyway; by having a sex-change operation, he could now wear women's clothing without ridicule. My students found it very "gross," as they put it, that any man would want to be castrated. As far as they were concerned, all human worth and all human values were based upon the procreative organs.

There is an eighth-grade student in my school who is a good example of the analogous relationship drawn by many people between competitive sports and so-called "manhood." Wayne is a very frail, delicate-looking boy who has been repeatedly harassed because of his appearance. Although he is not a student of mine, I see him regularly when I monitor the students eating lunch in the cafeteria. The problem of harassment by other eighth-graders, and by eleventh- and twelfth-graders as well, had become so acute that he was finally allowed to eat his lunch in the principal's office. On several occasions, I have seen a group of boys walk to his table, sit beside him and across from him, and bombard him with myriad insults and insinuations. When I confronted these students to find out their reason for this harassment, they told me that Wayne skipped gym class because he doesn't like to be forced to play sports with his classmates. Since he is not athletically inclined, he is constantly laughed at by the others. The other students found out that Wayne goes to the art room and paints, instead of going to gym class. They found this to be reason enough to call him "faggot." He was driven to tears on several occasions because of these insults which, at his age, were unthinkable. If he begins to believe he is a faggot because he paints, how can he ever come to any true realization of his own sexuality, heterosexual or otherwise?

I cannot help but think that all of these manifestations of homophobia are merely rationalizations on the part of many of the students. I am sure that there are many of them who are confused about their own sexual identity. Because they have been conditioned from every angle to believe that any sort of sexual activity deviant from the norm is sick and obscene, they must, I suppose, react with affected hostility to the subconscious drives and questions they must be experiencing. This is a serious problem, and it's not getting any better. If these

109

adolescents continue to believe the stereotypes and irrational fears of their parents, how can they ever see the truth? How can those who are different ever reconcile themselves with the community and still retain their own sense of self-worth?

As a gay teacher I am faced with a situation which not only offends myself as a teacher, but myself as an individual as well. Because of this oppression in the schools, it is impossible for any student who may be gay to find sympathetic people who can guide him or her. I would be a very likely person to help these students, but obviously, at this time, it would be impossible for any interaction of this kind between myself and a student. It would take an immense amount of courage for a student to expose his or her homosexuality: most students, I would assume, would not have the self-conviction to expose themselves to so much hostility and aggression. As for a gay teacher such as myself, there is no question but that I would be immediately dismissed were I to reveal the fact that I am gay.

The atmosphere in this state is hardly conducive to gay liberation for teachers, or anyone else for that matter. The infamous governor of New Hampshire, Meldrim Thompson, was interviewed about his responses to the Gay Students' Organization which had recently been formed at the University of New Hampshire. In addition to his standard remarks about "sickies" and "fruits," he stated that he would close down the G.S.O. on the grounds that he was afraid that it would attract homosexuals from all over the country to invade the New Hampshire university system, including three state colleges. Governor Thompson's remarks are so steeped in superstition and idiocy that they defy explanation. If I were to publicly reveal my homosexuality, I would probably be barred from talking to any male students, and the local playgrounds would probably be patrolled to ensure that I don't offer any candy bars to the little boys who play there. That is, of course, if I were even allowed to remain in the state!

The obvious fallacy in this type of logic is that there are probably many heterosexual teachers who secretly lust after their female students, and this applies also to the women who admire their husky young male students. Yet, no one ever questions the morality and good judgment of these teachers. I obviously do not spend my nights in fantasies of debauching my students, although I do enjoy admiring them in class. Because of the atmosphere of the school, and the state in general, however, I find myself becoming paranoid if I do admire these boys for their bodies. Yet, I hear my male colleagues in the teachers' lounge rambling on about the endowments of the senior cheerleaders.

I have been visited in my apartment on many occasions by a sixteen-year-old boy who lives in town and attends the school in which I teach. He is not a student of mine, but I know him in school because he spends so much time with two female students of mine who are apparently infatuated with me, and who regularly come after class to chat. Joshua has been visiting very frequently, and I can't help but believe that he has recognized me as, if not gay, at least sympathetic to homosexuality. He is obviously troubled and, because of his slight build, his lisp, and his glasses, he has been beaten up several times, both in and out of school.

Many times, when we talked in my apartment, he seemed to be trying to steer our conversations to the subject of homosexuality; there was some indistinct quality in his choice of words and his discussions which made me think that he was trying to tell me that he is very unsure about his homosexuality, and is asking for help. He is always telling me about how he trusts me, and is always inviting me to go hiking or mountain climbing with him. I have always been too busy to go with him on the weekends he has chosen to go, but I keep assuring him that I will go with him sometime.

I feel so badly for him because he is so insecure and relatively friendless, but my fear for my job prevents me from really opening up to him. I also have the feeling that, were I to expose myself fully, he would react very negatively and defensively; he has exhibited to me several times the same sort of homophobic logic that my other students have shown. Until I feel more secure about my job and community, I cannot deal with him in a totally honest manner.

I am sure that much of what I have stated would be abhorred by many heterosexual teachers and by parents. I am obviously not attempting to "proselytize," that is, to "promote" homosexuality, but I could very easily be accused of it if the above paragraphs were to be misinterpreted. My primary goal is to sensitize the majority to the fact that the stereotypes and false accusations must be erased if we are to survive without cutting each other's throats. Being a teacher, I am able to see very clearly the myths that continue to be perpetrated and nourished. These myths of Man and Woman, Masculinity and Femininity are obviously harmful, especially to adolescents, for they have not yet had the chance to determine their own conditions or their own sense of values. Many of them are still clinging to what has been forced into them through so many sources for so many years. Until adults can refrain from allowing their children such narrow conditions to live by, we will continue to breed neurotic, prejudiced, unhappy people, both homosexual and heterosexual.

HOOKERS:
Queer Fish *

Catherine Nossa

Picture prostitution as an amorphous animal peering out from a dense Rousseau-like forest that is filled with angry denizens, a sea of angry faces. The animal is amorphous because it has been manipulated through history to exemplify either the most exalted in sexual expression (the vestal "virgins" of Persia and Greece) or the most condemned (Christianity's "fallen woman"). And just as present society is outraged by this "freak" which it has created, so is the freak itself angered by the ignorance and ugly images which insist on handy answers and smother its attempts at self-definition and change. Prostitution has yet to emerge from the severe shame and self-doubt which homosexuality, by striking contrast, is finally casting off.

My own experience as a gay person *and* a prostitute has made me painfully aware of the disparity between the shame and suffocation hanging over my working life, and the pride and liberation of my (personal) sex life.

A prostitutional relationship is hardly comparable to the blissful ideal that a homosexual relationship holds out to me, but it does share with my homosexuality a very gut-felt right to the freedom and privacy of a relationship that is freely entered into.

Female prostitutes who keep tabs on their image in academia are well aware of the highly imaginative and varied psychoanalytic categories that are offered them in their quest for a self-concept: nymphomania, frigidity, overdependency, underdependency, masochism, sadism, retardation, oral fixation, anal fixation, incest, agoraphobia (fear of being out on the streets) (sic), and all-around lack of character. (Male prostitutes have not yet been recognized as existing [much less as having a self-concept] by psychoanalysts because relatively few psychoanalysts have felt a need to seek them out.) These theories about female prostitutes make a lot of sense to those who believe women should be

*Editors' note: For more information, there are two organizations of prostitutes (not exclusively gay). COYOTE, P.O. Box 26354, San Francisco, Cal. 94126 (415) 441-8118; and PONY, Box 900, Madison Square Station, New York 10010.

113

chaste and possessed (literally, owned), but unfortunately the theories just don't ring true—to my own experience or to that of other prostitutes I know—any more than the numerous scientific disquisitions on homosexuals ring true.

My own particular entrance into "the life" was the culmination of a gradual awareness of the poorly paid prostituting of myself (waitressing, etc.) that I had done for quite a while under a respectable and socially acceptable rubric. So, high-paying prostitution was a natural step in the course of my search for a means of support that is flexible enough to leave me with the time and energy to do the things that are important to me.

The very perceptive writings of Kate Millett,* Elizabeth Fisher,† and Kathie Sarachild†† were influential in erasing for me the enigma of sex-for-pay and illuminating the continuity of prostitution with other lifestyles open to women in this social structure.

The point at which I started countering strange men who approached me for dates with, "Yes—for a price" was, in a sense, a natural outgrowth of the grooming in make-up, poise, clothing, and conversation that was an integral part of my upbringing. This was the first time that all my training was able to serve a useful purpose for me, rather than just getting me into hot water and hang-ups. And, typically enough, the only real financial advantage that a bachelor's degree has brought me is the "right" to demand much higher pay in prostitution than "less educated" women get for the same performance, a performance that any high school cheerleader could improvise with her eyes closed.

What is demeaning about prostitution, for me, is the phoniness that the protocol forces me into. In the cult of "See What A Sexual Person I Am" (the practice of which is hardly limited to sex-for-pay), both participants must keep up a front of ecstatic horniness, and any relaxation prior to ejaculation is chalked up as a loss—of time, tumescence, and manliness. From what I can gather, the object of the game is to race to the finish line with a minimum of distraction and detour.

*"Prostitution: A Quartet for Female Voices," in Woman In Sexist Society, Vivian Gornick and Barbara K. Moran, eds. New York: Basic Books, Inc., 1971, pp. 21-69.
†"Hustlers All: A Speculation," in Aphra, vol. 2, no. 2 (Spring 1971), pp. 2-14.
††"Notes on the Prostitution Conference," Woman's World, vol. 1, no. 4, pp. 12-15. (The conference was sponsored by four feminist groups in December 1971.)

114

Allowing oneself to lose interest in reaching the finish disqualifies all previous and following affection.

The depressing side of prostitution is the isolation and lack of unity and support among prostitutes. Organizations such as COYOTE (Call Off Your Old Tired Ethics) in San Francisco and PONY (Prostitutes of New York) are doing a lot to bring unity and self-pride in those cities, but there are a lot of wondering prostitutes in the cities between them. The frustrating lack of openness among prostitutes (including myself) is strikingly similar to the scared silences among homosexuals before the gay movement.

I also feel I've paid a very strong emotional price because of the degrading image of prostitutes that I do battle with every time it rears its head, usually through offhand comments about "whores" that unknowing persons make in my presence, and through carefully constructed monographs on *the* psyche of *the* prostitute.

I don't feel that prostitution in itself is degrading or exploitative, as long as the arrangement is seen and approached as an exchange of services (financial for sexual) by each of the persons involved. It certainly is no more degrading than sex therapy is degrading, especially since the two professions, in actual practice, are almost indistinguishable. The difference between them, according to a woman I know who has worked both jobs simultaneously, is that one is legal and respectable; the other is high-paying. This thinness of veiling between the two comes as no surprise to me because my own experience with customers has convinced me that they patronize prostitutes for the sake of their psyches rather than their genitals. Believe me, when a man makes an appointment three days in advance to see me at one in the afternoon, it's *not* because he's horny. I have no truck with the convenient conceit that men have an inborn biological urge toward sex and that it is woman's duty and definition to accommodate it.

Many (mostly gay) female prostitutes occasionally combine lesbianism with their profession, either by performing lesbian acts with another prostitute for a male customer, or through having female customers themselves. Many people see these arrangements as an exploitation of homosexuality, but my perception of the first, the trio (I haven't been in one) is that it is no more than a businesslike agreement between the two prostitutes to make their lovemaking *look* spontaneous, whether they are actually lovers in off hours or not (many are). It strikes me as being as exploitative as two actresses ooh-ing and

115

aah-ing over Maxwell House coffee in front of a TV camera; they are obviously doing it for the purpose of earning money; the pleasure of drinking the coffee is secondary. Even the most gullible TV viewer knows this, and in the case of the trio arrangement, every customer knows that he is paying for a performance and not the real thing. (Genêt's *The Balcony*—about life in a brothel and life in Western civilization—gives a stunningly crystallized view of performances like this.)

The second instance of the combination of lesbianism and prostitution, that of having lesbian customers, is also outside of my own experience at this point; I know only that I would welcome the opportunity to experience it, and would consider it exploitative or degrading only if the customer approached it that way.

Prostitution is a work-a-day job that is sometimes enjoyable and sometimes not, but one which many women and men pick simply because it's about the highest-paying job for a woman—and for most men—in this society (it can be $50 to $100 an hour). It is a vital means of support for a great many homosexuals and deserves to be accepted by their community as legitimate.

I apologize for not having given male prostitutes equal treatment in this article, but I feel less qualified to represent them than to represent all other female prostitutes.

Many persons who are painfully aware of the flippant remarks that straights make about gays, are at the same time completely insensitive to their own flippancies about prostitutes. Listen!

HUSTLER:
A Boy for All Seasons

An Interview Between a
Hustler and His Customer

(Below is an interview that involved John—a seventeen-year-old, white, former hustler; Phillip—his twenty-eight-year-old, white customer and friend; two people from *Fag Rag*—Andy and Louis.)

Louis: How long have you been hanging around The Block?

Phillip: I've been hiring hustlers on The Block for about three or four years. But there are really two areas: The Marlborough—Commonwealth Ave. area, and the most important area for me would be around St. James Street—the Greyhound Bus Terminal.

Louis: What were the circumstances under which you first became involved with the Greyhound area or The Block?

Phillip: I went down one night because I was lonely, and it had been about five years since I had had any sexual relationship. I determined somehow that there are hustlers hanging around the Marlborough Street—Arlington Street area and one summer night I walked down there around 8:00 and I walked by this teen-age kid. I stopped about ten feet beyond him and just stood there. He came up to me and asked if I had any spare change. I said sure, how much do you need, and he said fifteen dollars. I asked if he'd come back to my place for that and he said he would. We were both very nervous because it was my first time and it was close to his first time. He was from New York City and he was seventeen years old. I've never seen him since then.

Louis: And you John?

John: I've been hanging around The Block for about the past nine months. The reason why I went down there was because I was always a horny kid. I could get paid for something I dug doing. I went down to make money. Christmas was coming up soon and I just thought money was the answer.

You can get anything from five dollars to probably thirty dollars there. Like for five dollars somebody would pick me up and they might feel my body, you know, caress my body. And I'll sit there and say, Oh I really dig it, and he'll give me five dollars or maybe five more because I dug it. For ten dollars you might go home with him, you might get into a 69 thing. For more, you might go into it a little bit deeper. Like he might want you to fuck him or he might want to fuck you. There's more money involved there. See, the more time, the more money. That's the idea, time is money.

Phillip: The lowest I've ever been asked for is two dollars which was for an all-night session with a kid from Providence, Rhode Island. The most I've ever been asked is thirty-five dollars, again for an all-night session. In my experience, I've never gotten what I've paid for, or rather what you get isn't proportional to the price. The quality doesn't depend on the price. The typical prices are either ten dollars, fifteen dollars, or twenty dollars; most typical is fifteen dollars and mostly that involves oral sex—mutual type thing, caressing, kissing. Frequently, these deals are by appointment, they're not random meetings.

Louis: What is the general age range of hustlers that you know of?

John: Probably between fifteen and twenty-four.

Andy: Most of your customers are, say, older than in their twenties?

John: Yes, most of them are probably from thirty and over. I've had one or two customers that were in their early twenties. Those are the customers you like cause they're not too old and they kind of appeal to you sexually, plus you're getting paid for it.

Louis: Is there any sort of racial preponderance of customers?

John: Most of them are white—white Irishmen.

Louis: Do black people have any trouble either as hustlers or as customers?

John: I've noticed as customers they don't seem to make out cause nobody wants to go with some big black guy—he's afraid the black guy's going to beat him or something. And black hustlers don't get off very good cause most of them are into ripping off.

Louis: Could you describe some of the customers you've had in the past?

John: I've run into a lot of fairly successful professional men. A lot of them are nice to me cause, I don't know, I used to con everybody. That's the whole idea of hustling—not just going and doing your thing and coming back. You get them involved in almost like an imaginary life of your own. I told this one guy I had a jones—a habit. For about a couple of weeks he gave me about thirty dollars a day. Cause he believes me. They're very gullible. I tell them what they want.

Phillip: Given my preference, I like teen-age kids, very good looking ones. But I don't think that's a completely exclusive desire. The reason I got into the teen-age kid scene was that I wasn't aware there was anything else. Once into it I liked it and stayed with it. But I didn't go there looking for teen-age kids—I went looking there for anybody.

Andy: Do you choose a customer the same way a customer would choose you? Is there also a selection process?

John: Yes, like I'll get in the car and it depends on how that person talks to me. It depends on the type of clothes they're wearing and how they present themselves. I'm out there for a reason, they're out there for a reason. They're out there to get satisfied, I'm out there to make money. I'm not going to go with some shmuck that says he's going to give me twenty dollars and throws me out of the car, which happens a lot—it's happened twice to me and I don't like it. It's not that the money bothers me, it's just that it irritates me that somebody would do it to me.

Phillip: When I meet a new hustler on the street, new for me, first I always try to get recommendations from other hustlers I know or from other customers. If I ask another hustler, it's mostly about safety—to tell if the guy is a genuine hustler or if he's just out to rob me. And sometimes the hustler can tell if the guy's any good sexually, because I'm sure the hustlers interact with one another physically. One of the

119

first questions I ask is, are you gay or straight or bi—what do you think of yourself as? If they say they're bi it usually means they're really straight but they're willing to compromise, they are willing to do what the customer's interested in, at least they're open to negotiation. The bi ones are the ones who tend to be the most flexible in a way. I used to pick up almost anybody. I've become much more selective and I'm only interested now in two different types of people. One are those that I really will enjoy a sexual relationship with, which means to me some sort of mutual relationship. Secondly is somebody I have a desire to get to know after talking to them, to break down the barriers between us and to see what they're like. And hiring them's the only way I can find out.

Andy: Do you find that hustlers, generally speaking, are sexually responsive or mostly just sort of passive?

Phillip: Most of them are pretty responsive with me . . . they enjoy sex.

John: There's something funny when it comes to hustlers. When they're away from the scene, or The Block, they're themselves. On the street they're totally different. I've taken hustlers home myself—they might need a place to stay, or they look like they haven't eaten for days. You get to know the people and you kind of care a little bit. Like if I was hungry I'd want someone to care about me. Most hustlers are very lonely, most of them come from broken homes. Myself, I come from a kind of broken home, I guess. Most hustlers claim that they're straight. There's something actually wrong with being gay in their eyes. Actually what they're doing isn't being gay—they're prostitutes and they are just trying to make a living.

Louis: Could you tell me about any particularly good experiences that you've had?

Phillip: There have been a lot of good experiences. Most of them have been good or I wouldn't have pursued this. The good experiences make .ne pursue it and also the excitement of the bad experiences. It's sort of interesting to be chased around the block by a couple of guys with knives—when you always win. And I've never lost. After my first loss maybe I'll change my mind on that. I've met really good people whom I think I've been able to help. And I've enjoyed being of help to people.

Like the kid from Providence. He wanted two bucks to spend the night with somebody. What he really wanted was a place to spend the night. That's a little thing but it's good to be able to do little things for people. I don't get much chance to do that because ... nobody ever asks.

Louis: Have you had bad experiences?

Phillip: There are a couple of different kinds of bad experiences. One is really rotten people who have a belligerent attitude and take the attitude that I'm exploiting them. They're really cold, hard to get to know. The other bad stuff is the physical violence, and I've had all sorts of neat experiences of that. I've been attacked with a broken whiskey bottle, a metal pipe, a gun, two razor blades, probably about thirty or forty knives and two sets of fists. Most of the violence is on Marlborough Street and Comm. Ave. and a little bit around Greyhound, but Greyhound is much safer. I've never had any trouble in my apartment—I think somebody who was just interested in just robbing you would do it sooner, I mean, why wait till he gets there?

Louis: Is that what it's all about—robbing you?

Phillip: Yeah. Maybe once or twice somebody attacked me with other motivation—there was once some people who were really down on fags. One had the whiskey bottle and one had the club. They chased me up Marlborough Street for three blocks. They weren't hustlers—they were just hanging around bothering gay people.

Andy: Did you ever have any problems?

John: I've been robbed a number of times by other hustlers. You see, with hustlers there's a big problem with drugs, junk mostly. And it's getting so they don't even want to go out and hustle. Now they just step in the car and they put a knife in your side and they say, your money or your life.

I have a friend who had a very bad experience. He got beat up badly, his eyes were just a mess. He's very bitchy now, ever since he got beat up. He starts arguments with you, he's very flip with his answers. All he cares about is himself, which of course you can't blame him for.

Louis: Have you ever been harassed by the police?

Phillip: Yes I have, but only superficially. Only in the sense of telling me to move on when I've been hanging around looking for people. But they've arrested hustlers I was about to hire, though. That's really annoyed me.

Louis: Have you ever been harassed by the police?

John: I've never been harassed on The Block cause I don't let the police see me. That's hard to explain. I see everybody else but sometimes they don't see me. Like, I watch. Find out how many police there are around, why they're around. Kind of like case the joint before I go in there. Something I do for my own protection. I've never been busted. There have been people down there for three nights who have been busted. There are people who have been down there for three years and they've never been busted.

Louis: What are the hazards of disease from the point of view of the customer?

Phillip: I've had about two hundred different hustlers over three years and the only thing I've ever gotten is the crabs—once. I've never had syphilis or gonorrhea. I don't think many hustlers are diseased. I've brought hustlers back a lot who've had crabs. And I keep a supply of A200 on hand to cure them before we have sex, that's all.

John: I must have caught venereal disease two dozen times. Every week I was in the clinic and they were sick of looking at me cause I'd walk in and they'd say, Oh man, you're here again!

Andy: Do you cruise in other places where it's presumably free? Like the esplanade, the Fenway, the bars, the baths, or something like that?

Phillip: I guess I don't do any real traditional cruising, not really. You could say that I'm discriminating in who I want to meet, but really . . . I don't meet anybody at those places. And I'd certainly be open to talking and getting to know, at least on a conversational level, anyone at all who would want to talk. But it just doesn't happen . . . I think the cruising scene is a lot easier for people who are a lot more outgoing than me. I'm trying to meet other people besides Greyhound hustlers. The big attraction to going there is that I get what I'm looking for and I'm willing to pay for that, although it's not really all that easy to find what you're looking for at times, like the summer.

Louis: And you say that even sometimes when you do find somebody, that you're not always satisfied with what you get.

Phillip: Yeah. Most of the people I've dealt with I've been dissatisfied with. You get what you pay for in the sense of the deal negotiated in the street, and I try to negotiate pretty explicit deals because I've had bad experiences when things were assumed in the street. But I haven't liked what I've found in them intellectually, spiritually. They haven't interested me, they've just bored me. I guess I'm looking for somebody I can love.

Louis: Do you ever go to other gay social functions or bars, and what happens when you do?

Phillip: Yes, I go to several gay meetings. Like GML meetings—I go quite regularly. And I've been to a few community center meetings. I've been to most of the bars in the city. I go fairly often to either Sporters or The Other Side. I sometimes meet people whom I know, whom I've met as hustlers or as customers of hustlers, or whom I've met at GML. I've never met anybody new in a bar so the bar scene has never been a place for me to meet people. I assume that's the case for a lot of people—people are shy, it's hard for people to meet in any social environment I think.

That's something good about the street—it's easy to meet. A customer is never embarrassed to go up to a hustler and ask him if he'll go with him, cause it's very rare that he's turned down on the basis of the customer being too ugly. That's happened once with me. But ordinarily, that's ridiculous—most hustlers will deal with almost anybody. So there's no danger of rejection on the street which there is in a bar. And I'm sort of nervous to go up and talk to people and be rejected. But it's happened on the street. The Block is a cruising area as well as a hustling area, and I've had some bad times there with people who were cruising who were sort of unfriendly. And that sort of made me all the more want to hire a hustler.

John: I go to The Other Side mostly and Jacques. I just go in and I might order a drink or something or somebody might send me over a drink and I usually send one back. I'm usually just in there for a few minutes and I see if there's anything in there that I'm interested in. If there is, I talk to him, if there isn't, I don't. I don't stay in the bars very often.

Louis: Do you ever go to gay social functions?

John: No I haven't. It's probably always too busy on The Block. Hustling begins to be your life after a while. I'm afraid to miss something if I go to a meeting that's not in the downtown area, if you can understand that. Like I find myself going down to The Block—I don't hustle but I still go down there, because I want to know who's around and why and what is going on. It's like a disease. Once you get the money it's like a big magnet . . . and you're a piece of metal, it's dragging you to it.

LESBIAN MOTHER *

Jeanne Perreault

Last year my daughter, in second grade, mentioned casually at dinner, "Today we were talking about what we wanted to be when we grow up. I told Mrs. S. that it is a secret, but that I wanted to be free when I grew up so I am going to be a lesbian just like my mom. I figured I could trust her."

Jennifer's trust instincts were okay that day, for her teacher responded that people should be free to do what they want to do. Lucky kid.

There are three important aspects to this incident:

1. The family life that Jennifer experiences was satisfying enough for her to want to imitate it. She sees lesbianism as both pleasant and possible. It is one alternative open to her.

2. She, at age seven, experiences and is limited by the secrecy that is part of our daily lives. She didn't know that most of the kids in her class had probably never heard the word "lesbian." Jennifer assumed that they would understand the word and would ridicule her: consequently she measured her knowledge of Mrs. S. and decided that this person could accept and respect her comments.

3. Had Jennifer been mistaken about Mrs. S. a terrible scene would have ensued. The teacher would notify the principal who would have social workers called in. Our home would be inspected. I'd be told to change my life or see my child placed in an institution. This happens to lesbian mothers. They are in danger from schools, families, ex-husbands, "concerned neighbors." (Remember that lesbianism is not "illegal.")

As Jennifer grows older she grows more "discreet," that is, more afraid. She has not yet asked me to be more cautious, but I expect that

*Editors' note: For further information contact Lesbian Mothers National Defense Fund, 2446 Lorentz Place North, Seattle, Washington 98109.

will come.

People often say, "You aren't giving your daughter any free choice. You are indoctrinating her into a lesbian lifestyle."

"Damn them," I think, then I take a deep breath, grit my teeth and begin. "Look at the world around you. How many ads, stories, TV shows do you see that acknowledge the existence of lesbianism? My kid lives in that world too. The only place in her life that she sees anything to do with lesbianism, with women loving women, is in her home. I wish I could know for sure that the good loving Jennifer sees around her would influence her to choose to be with women."

Sure—I'm providing as much of a nonsexist alternative to her as I can. I get books, make up stories, bring people home, all women-oriented, all attempting to show humanness under the sex roles. It doesn't begin to balance the weight of the straight male-dominated world around her.

Lots of lesbian mothers are unwilling to share their relationships with their kids. This may be because these women have bought the lies themselves, are ashamed of loving women and don't want to "corrupt" their kids. Or it may be that the fear of discovery is so great that children are excluded from the love between two women. Kids talk. It's hard to stop them. Much safer to hide, sneak around, deny one's relationships, than to risk one's security/livelihood/children. Much easier than it is to build a trust and understanding with the kids.

Or the possibility that our children will turn on us and spit the "sickie-pervert" line in our faces stops us from really sharing ourselves with them. Teen-agers are generally expected to reject the lifestyle of their parents. They usually do, for a while. But when this happens the straight family has tradition, culture, and God on its side. They *know* they're right and the kid is wrong. The lesbian mother has nothing but her own feelings to go on. Rejection is a constant specter. To risk it from our kids is too much for those of us who do not have a deep good feeling about ourselves and a supportive lesbian community to cushion us.

After some hassling with myself and other lesbian feminists, mostly around wanting to protect Jennifer from the real world (my thoughts went something like this—she's too young to understand; she'll have her whole life to face these problems; she won't be able to deal with the conflict between her home and the rest of the world), I realized that if she doesn't get a strong sense of my values she'll be left vulnerable to the male world values that will teach her contempt and loathing for me

126

as a lesbian. I have told her, gradually, and in ways that she could grasp, about the ways that straight families work and about male domination, economic control, and ego gratification; and I have pointed out to her the innumerable injustices and insults to women in books and on TV. I have talked about the lies that the male world tells about women loving women. Her reactions were a shocked disbelief at first and then a gradual understanding of how male supremacy is in Big Trouble when women get together and that's why they hate us.

She'll need every particle of this knowledge to resist the insidious and constant pressure from the straight world; to reject the lewd remarks and looks of her friends; to keep her sense that lesbianism is good, real, and alive.

Wishing that Jennifer wouldn't have to fight the world around her is futile. They have drawn the lines; she either goes down or fights it. I just want to make sure she's got three good weapons: a sense of her own good selfness; knowledge about what she is up against; and good women with her.

FAGGOT FATHER*

Don Mager

I suspect that the problems of faggot fathers and lesbian mothers are rather different, just as the problems of divorced fathers are different from those of divorced mothers. Sexism as the social and economic structure of our country with its patriarchal foundations is nowhere more oppressive than in the assumptions it makes about parental roles and expectations of adult behavior toward children. Thus, any situation which breaks through the constriction of the nuclear family brings down upon the "deviant" parents the wrath, or indignation, or alarm, or disgust, or discomfort of society. This reaction is most often expressed by close friends and relatives.

As a faggot and a father I have experienced this process exquisitely, for in my case I have almost a sociologist's "classic" test case. I was closet gay and a father, now I am openly gay and a father. Basically my fatherhood has not changed, my activities and attitudes toward my children, my behavior—all, I assume, are pretty much the same as they have been in the past. But people's attitudes toward my fitness to be a parent have altered, in some cases drastically, in some cases subtly. One friend, who in the past had repeatedly told me how he admired my nonauthoritarian, patient, and very physical ways with my children, now interrogates me in his letters as to whether I can possibly provide the proper "role model." He is especially concerned, he says, since my children are both boys, and even goes so far as to say it would not be as worrisome if they had been girls!! He asks, wouldn't it be best *for them* (!) if I let them live exclusively with their mother—in hopes that she might remarry and thus fill their need for a father.

But to step back from my immediate case, I think it is important to ask, What is a faggot father? Many people seem to see this as a contradiction of terms. As I see it, a faggot father is not simply a faggot who has at some point fathered a child, but more significantly, he is a man whose sexual orientation is gay and whose daily life includes an active participation in the lives of his children. For me the term "father" is not just a legal label but a description of an active, ongoing relationship,

*Editors' note: For further information contact Gay Fathers Unlimited, 625 Post Street, Box 283, San Francisco, Calif. 94109.

specifically involved in the day-to-day living and growing experience of his children. His is not merely a formal relationship as provider and protector, in the patriarchal sense.

A faggot father, in my sense of the term, is therefore likely to be separated or divorced from his child's mother. In fact, I think that this separation is almost inevitable in being a faggot father. And the real pain of faggot fatherhood comes out of this almost inevitable situation. This is the pain of trying to work out an individual solution to a very difficult problem, i.e., the sharing of children between separated (or divorced) parents. This individual solution for the father must be worked out by trial and much error, by fumbling and uncertainty, with very little understanding from friends and relatives—often, even from his gay friends. His struggle (and that of many single parents) may even take place in an environment of low tolerance for children. Many adults who have not lived intimately with children have a low tolerance for them. (Certainly one thing that a breakdown of the heterosexist nuclear family pattern would make possible is a *real* choice for people as to whether they want to spend a portion of their adult lives raising children or not, and women must have this choice as easily available to them as men—hence the importance of legalized abortion.)

For a short while, I lived in a group-living situation with other gays, and discovered that their low tolerance really meant that my children's presence was a nuisance to the other members of the household. I respect their right to a lifestyle without children, and I admire their candor in being able to affirm this choice of lifestyle without a sense of guilt or apology; and yet for me it meant pain. To have my children at my house meant to place a burden on my fellow housemates—an uncomfortable situation to say the least.

Another aspect of the pain a faggot father experiences is in terms of his discovery of his isolation. None of the sympathy that wells up to support a mother going through separation or divorce comes to a father—or, rather, very little does. Instead, one hears time and again remarks such as: "You must be relieved not to have your kids around all the time"; or, "How does it feel to be a free 'man' again?"; or, "It must be great to have so much free time again." The attitude of others is that I should provide financial security for my children (child support, alimony, or a college fund) as the best way to appease my guilt for having wrecked their chances of growing up in a "harmonious nuclear family." In answer to this, I say, I have no guilt, and I chose to be a father because I wanted the experience of fatherhood which to me is an active, ongoing relationship with my children, not a financial settlement of some sort.

But this particular attitude is even structured into our legal system. It is very difficult for a man (even a widower) to go on ADC (Aid to Dependent Children) and thus to choose to raise his children actively, especially younger children, providing them with a home life. Instead he is urged to continue his job and hire a maid-babysitter to raise his children for him; or better yet, and most often, he is urged to remarry. Furthermore, in most states there is no provision for joint custody of children between divorced parents. Thus, the faggot father must face a situation in which the state rules through its courts that his children can no longer remain with him; this is true even where both parents willingly want joint custody and have no contest over who should "get the kids."

So the faggot father, if he persevered through the dense bigotries which define men as generally inadequate for the raising of children, must work out an individual solution. There are no models. There are few people with experiences to turn to for advice, and so the pain is ever-present. I have sought out older faggot fathers, only to find that the typical solution which has been arranged by men who faced this problem ten, fifteen, or twenty years ago is to maintain the front of a heterosexist nuclear family, often with separate bedrooms for husband and wife, where each has a separate sexual lifestyle. Often for the faggot, this means one-night-stands in neighboring cities. The couple's friends have no suspicion of irregularity, and often the children, now in adolescence or college, have never been told. Have middle-aged lesbian mothers settled for this kind of facade and closet too? I understand why men over the years have chosen this solution, and in some cases the understanding which has been reached between spouses is truly admirable; neither member of the couple abuses or uses the other, and an amicable household prevails; but for me and the openly gay faggot fathers of my generation, this cannot be a model.

How nice it would be to sit down over coffee one morning a week with another faggot father to talk about potty training, temper tantrums, Marlowe's new song he made up, Rainer's beginning to string words together, the new outfits I'm sewing for them, etcetera. These small everyday things fill my head, they are real, they are a big part of the ever-presentness and ever-excitement of a life with young children, and they scream to be shared. I find it unhappy always to have to share my reactions and surprises with women—not that I don't enjoy

130

swapping child-talk with women, I do; but there is, even in the rapport of such conversations, an isolation that I feel.

Finally, I think, this pain has another aspect; it will be there as long as the children live part-time with me, i.e., until they reach their late teens and establish independent lives. Increasingly, there will be confrontations with "straight" adults who will be strangers to me, but will be important to the lives of my children. What sort of subtle oppression will confront them, which in some cases I must simply watch and try to help them comprehend, knowing that their pain is because of my choices? I chose to have children, but they did not choose me to be their father.

Faggot fathers are a minority within the gay community. So much so that in many places they rarely meet other faggot fathers, forcing each to seek solutions to his problems in isolation. And often the isolation leads to failure. For instance, while still in my closet, I watched a faggot father who wanted to continue his ongoing and active relationship with his three children after coming out into an open domestic life with his formerly closeted lover. This resulted in an eruption of tension between himself and his wife, and for three months she left the city. He quit his job at a factory and he and his lover took over entirely the care of the children. When the mother returned, the three adults talked things out, and what finally resulted was a self-denial of the father's own worth as a human being—a kind of capitulation and denial of the validity of his gay relationship. From the point of view of "straight" society, the outcome was happy, for in the end the parents reconciled themselves to each other and moved to another city, leaving the "troublesome" lover behind. But from the point of view of the two men, so much courage to attempt their open life together led only to capitulation, inner self-denial, and perhaps even self-hate. I do not mean to portray the mother as villainous; her needs were real, and her confusions were great. But unlike "straight" society, I do not see the outcome as happy, but as pain-filled and tragic—for all three adults, and certainly for all three children as well.

I am sure that some of the isolation and pain of the faggot father corresponds to that of the lesbian mother. The two types of gay parent have much support to share between them as they are able to come together in shared dialogue; but there is a difference as well. Many a lesbian mother chooses motherhood with full knowledge that she intends to raise her child by herself, with no man in the picture at all. Other lesbian mothers are likely to be separated or divorced from men who willingly settle for a nonrelationship with their children, i.e., they are willing to settle for paying child support, or for some other legally sanctioned solution.

By contrast, no faggot father can choose to have children (at least not until adoption laws are changed) without being involved in a relationship with a woman. Thus no faggot father has the option of raising his children by himself, except in the very rare cases where a divorce settlement has granted him full custody, or where the child's mother is dead.

What can I say about solutions? What suggestions can I make to other faggot fathers? Not very much. My experience is young, limited, and still very much in a trial-and-error stage. About the pain, I can say that two things seem obvious. Faggot fathers getting together would help, especially during the rough early days of coming out and perhaps separating from the children's mother. Such meetings would break down the isolation, would bring the feeling of self-confidence, and would open up alternatives which a person alone might not think of. Second, gays in general should be more open and understanding of the special problems of gay parents (both faggot and lesbian). Children are not, after all, pets or toys, and I have grown weary of the attitude of some of my gay friends that it is cute that I have children—cute, but not very important.

The last thing that must be said, and perhaps the only generalization that I can draw about solutions for the faggot father, is this: In most cases he will not have the option of raising his children by himself, but rather will have to work out a shared relationship with the child's mother. This means that he will have to confront and work through all the typical notions of nuclear family and reject them. He must listen to her and understand what his former patterns of behavior were, especially patterns of male dominance and sexism, because until he understands how his behavior has been oppressive to her, he cannot ask with much validity for understanding and cooperation from her in working out solutions to *his* oppression. If he expects to have his children part-time at his home, whether as a single man, as a member of a group-living collective, or as a partner with his lover, he must also recognize and rejoice in the options his child's mother may elect. She may take a male (or female) lover, she may remarry, she may join a collective, she may live with in-laws. Thus, with the fact of part-time parenthood comes also the likelihood that his children will grow up in diverse and multiple relationships with adults, in place of the single relationships of one mother and one father within the nuclear family. This solution, different in each instance of faggot fatherhood, I find truly to be a radical alternative to the nuclear family.

But because each solution will be unique, a high level of openness and receptiveness to all other adults involved, as well as to the children, is mandatory.

Especially, I think, faggot fathers may be the ones to provide new alternative models of fatherhood, wherein men can express their love in ways other than the traditional roles, and in which physical affection and daily shared experiences are a major part. The struggle of gay parents is thus very much a part of the struggle of all gays, and the isolation they experience must be bridged by childless gays as well as by the gay parents themselves.

POSTSCRIPT: This article was originally published in June 1973. I would like to add a few words to what I said about solutions, based on discoveries I've made since then and which I could not have foreseen then. At the time I wrote the article my relationship with my lover was new, and I was uncertain how he would involve himself with my children. He has gone through many changes in working out a comfortable understanding of his relationship to the kids, because he knew from the outset that he did not want to assume the role of surrogate parent. In the process of discussing his ambivalent feelings, I discovered a wealth of support from him for me and my choices. I think gay couples should never underestimate the strength of their relationships, and I think both lesbian mothers and faggot fathers should realize that often the sympathy and support and love they so deeply desire may be available from the very person (or persons) who share their lives, if only they will allow themselves to open up and listen. My lover is one of the true blessings in my life as a faggot father. Second, after the tensions of the separation abated, my former wife and I discovered slowly that we had a lot of support and care we could give each other. After all, we share our lives with the same two youngsters and therefore the vitality they bring to me is the same vitality they bring to her. Separated or divorced parents sharing children between them should not underestimate the strength and support they can give to each other, once they work past feelings of villain-and-victim, feelings of competition, etcetera. Third, I am beginning to learn how to discuss and act out my confusions and excitements with my children themselves. Although they are four and three in age, I am continually amazed at how much

133

they comprehend of what I as a candid person can share of my life with them. Gay parents must never underestimate the power of candor and openness with their children. Gay parents who closet their sexuality from their children, or who disguise their activities in gay groups, or who keep their gay friends away from their children are only asking for trouble. Finally, in terms of very specific solutions, I have found a day care center, which my children attend part-time. The center is a co-op, so parents put in hours working with the children; this allows me to experience my children in an environment with other children and other parents. The center is partly staffed (both full-time and part-time staff) by several gay women and men. This provides me in particular an environment wherein I feel comfortable and relaxed. And the center is attended by children of several lesbian mothers as well as children of polygamously bi-sexual parents; in fact, the majority of children come from either dual-households or homes with single parents. Thus, my children discover not oddity about their lives but shared experiences between themselves and their friends.

THE LIFE AND DEATH OF A GAY PRISONER

Edward E. Loftin and Join Hands

MAY 22

Dear JOIN HANDS,*

I am a prisoner at Folsom prison, I don't have any family or friends on the outside. I have been in prison "4" years and never received a letter from the free world.

A little about myself. I am white/M.–5'5" tall, 118 lb., Brown hair, hazel eyes. I was raised in Georgia, and I am also "GAY" and I am 30 years old (but don't look it, that is what people tell me). I hope you can find another gay person who would like to write to me.

SEPTEMBER 19

Dear Jerry, †

Just received your first letter today. . . . I am an artist also, but I can't get too much practice in this place, I borrowed a couple of felt pens to draw you this envelope. I tried to get into the Hobby Shop here, so that I can sell some of my pen and ink drawings, "BUT" the first thing the Hobby man asked was "If I had the money to buy art supplies with" so that knocked me out of the hobby shop.

Jerry suggests that he collect as much of his art work as he can, because when he is released he needs exposure for his work. All that is presently available of Eddie's art work are a few envelopes and cards; since his death the authorities have denied the existence of the larger works that Eddie talks about bringing with him on his release. We are hoping that they haven't been stolen and are making efforts to see that Eddie's art works are released.

OCTOBER 5

. . . I hope that you can find the time to come and visit me, I never

*A gay-prisoner support group.
†A member of Join Hands.

135

had a visit in prison. It sure would be wonderful to set and talk to a friend that can understand my feeling. . . .

OCTOBER 11

Jerry, see if you can get a copy of the MCC Cross Currents (Fall, 1973) of San Francisco. If you can, look on page 19 and you will see one of my drawings—it isn't much but it does have a lot of meaning in it.

You want to know about me. Well, that is my hardest subject to write about. But I will fill you in a little about why I am in Prison and I am not ashame about why I am in Prison. I was working for a man for three weeks without pay, and also living with him. The last day I was with him I asked him for my pay (which I did have coming to me) and he wouldn't give it to me, so I robbed him, which I only got $8.00.

Eddie's case is not unusual. Although the prison authorities stereo-type the criminal as someone who is vicious, hardened, or depraved, most prisoners, gay or otherwise, are accused of crimes against property or victimless crimes rather than violent crimes against people. When unemployment in the country rises, so does the number of people in prison.

Five years is a lot to pay for eight dollars, but in our criminal justice system it's not what you steal but who you are. Being poor was one half of Eddie's "crime." Nationally, 50% of those convicted of robbery are sent to prison, but only 14% of those convicted of tax fraud ever do time. We've all seen how corporate "crime in the suites" or political espionage can be paid off with token prison sentences and minor fines.

OCTOBER 17

Jerry, did you receive the card?? I drawed a card last week—(it was a thinking of you card)—let me know if you received it. . . . Well, just about anything is Cool to put on paper, just as long as you don't run down the place, you can be as blunt as you want to, I do have an open mind. Do you have a friend or lover? and if so does he approve of you writing to me? Myself I don't have a lover. (this is not a hint) (smile.) Do you go to the Bars or Baths? I have heard a lot about the baths and bars, but never been to either one. All these things don't mean anything in terms of our friendship, I am just curious.

OCTOBER 19

Yes, I do a lot of reading, there is not much of a choice of books in

136

this place, especially where I am living now, I do have 24 hours in which to read, because I am in my cell all day and night. In fact, I haven't been out of this building since January 15th of this year. I wrote to the Prison library, to see if they could get a book for me (THE LIGHT FROM THE SECOND STORY WINDOW by ??). Guess what the library officer told me. *"We don't carry those kind of books"* That statement shows where these peoples' minds are at. . . .

In the outside society the silence about homosexuality is starting to break down. Prison officials still exercise their power to suppress gay ideas. By interfering with gay publications, books, and films and banning gay organizations they seek to prevent the growth of gay identity and pride. Gay prisoners are thirsty for contact and exchange with the outside. The arrival of a gay newspaper is a major event. It is passed from hand to hand as long as it can be read. For Eddie the knowledge of a gay community outside was a source of self-respect and strength.

. . . You ask about my family, (that I don't know) I was in a foster home until I was 12 years old, I ran away when I was 12 and travelled all over the east coast until I was 16. Then I was in and out of jail from 16 until now. Well, I will have to finish this letter in the dark, the lights just went out. . . . The worst part of doing time is when the lights go out, it's just lonely at that time, especially when one is alone (know what I mean?)

My program just came on the earphones, I guess the radio man is on the ball. The program is country music of yesteryear for 4 straight hours. . . .

Yes, my parole board interview is creeping up on me, and I am nervis as a chicken in a frying pan, for the last couple of days I have been chewing my fingernails off and walking the cell floor, I've been really worrying myself half sick, *–I WANT OUT.*

NOVEMBER 9

You are right about the SEGREGATION of gays. I am segregated myself since January 15th of this year. There used to be a gay Organization in Folsom, it started June 26, 1971, and lasted until July 22, '71. The administration did "not" like it. There is not much to smile about in this prison. There is one thing that makes me smile and that is your letters, they really make me feel wonderful.

NOVEMBER 10

I just got some *"bad"* news, I did *not* get a *parole.* The parole board sent me a letter stating that they wanted me to go to *Vacaville* for about '6' months to take some test, and they also said I *would* get a parole *"if"* Vacaville sees that I could make it on the outside, *so,* I *could* get out around March or April. I think you know why the parole board didn't give me a parole, they *"do"* think that *"ALL"* gay people are sick and need to be in a Hospital. There was (7) gays that went to the parole board, and out of the (7) only one made parole and that is because he has been locked up for 9½ years. The other (6) gays got *1* or *2* years. That is a *"Hell"* of a average. I hope you don't mind tears on this letter, "I am crying." . . . Everyone that I know, even the officers and councelor thought I would get a parole. The true reason is I am *"GAY"* and *proud* of it.

When the indeterminate sentence started it was supposed to be a humanitarian reform that tailored the punishment to the particular prisoner's progress. A judge didn't give a statutory sentence like 2 yrs. 6 mos., but instead an open-ended one like 1 to 5 yrs. or 5 yrs. to life.

The Parole Board (California Adult Authority for Men, California's Women's Board for Terms & Paroles, California Youth Authority) was set up to decide when a prisoner was "rehabilitated." Since its members are appointed by the governor, it has degenerated into a panel of white, male, ex-guards, police and FBI agents who use it as another form of controlling prisoners and further punishing them. In the case of gay people, all the Parole Board does is point to their sexual preferences as lack of rehabilitation. This was the other *half of Eddie's "crime."*

In late 1971, 70% of all male prisoners coming before the parole board were getting parole dates for release. Now only 10% are. The policy changes were the result of a drive by the California Department of Corrections and the Reagan administration to get funding for two new maximum security prisons. High prison population is one of their best playing cards.

They still haven't gotten all the funding they want but in the meantime what happened to Eddie Loftin is the result of their playing with the lives of the prisoners in their custody.

NOVEMBER 18

I received your no. 4 letter in the prison hospital, in which I have been since Tuesday morning the 13th. I had a fall in my cell and hit my

138

head on the sink and I have a mild concussion. I don't know how long I will be in the hospital. The Doctor wants to give me a brain wave, sure hope they let me out soon, this is one place I hate. . . .

I received the Brother paper yesterday and it is what I wanted, I have read it twice and plan to read it again. On page 10 (GAY MEN IN PRISON) the petition for gay rights, we in Folsom were wondering when something like this would start rolling for us. I have "not" received Gay Sunshine as of this writing. A friend told me that he got *his* last week. . . .

Jerry, don't worry I will never *"give up"*, even if it means I will have to spend the rest of my life in this prison.

The petition Eddie talks about was written by JOIN HANDS and INSIDE/OUT, based on the complaints and suggestions of the gay male prisoners that they work with. It was signed by close to 15,000 supporters in the community, women and men, gay and non-gay.

Specifically the petition demands an end to the "extra" punishment inflicted on gay prisoners such as: illegal denial of parole because of sexual lifestyle, forced segregation at the prison's whim, denial of access to a prison education, job training, reading materials, and recreation.

Representatives of the gay community arrived for a confirmed appointment at the offices of the California Department of Corrections (CDC) in order to present the petition signatures in December·of last year. They were met by armed guards, denied entrance, and not allowed to present the petitions. It became clear that appealing to the CDC to change itself was useless. Many of our sisters and brothers in prison have known that for a long time. We will have to do much more than petition.

DECEMBER 13

Have you read about the "big" lock up, four of the biggest prisons locked up for about (5) days, and they tightened up on us quite a lot, but that won't solve anything, there will still be killings. Just like they done me, when I got out of the Hospital the officials put me on the same floor with all my *enemies*. I wrote an attorney (Mr John Wahl) of San Francisco, and explain all of this to him, so "if" anything happens to me, you will know why, also will Mr. Wahl. It is really cold in these cells, the sun is out and it is still cold, well, that is December for you.

The lock-up Eddie refers to represents a change in "correctional" policy from rehabilitation and training to security and control. It was preceded by a carefully planned series of stories in the press about sex, drugs and violence among prisoners. The California Department of Corrections (CDC) portrayed prisoners as wild animals running amok and offered their lock-up as a necessary step to control the violence. In its aftermath many prisons have reduced or suspended vocational and recreational programs, instituted more rigid rules concerning visiting and correspondence rights, and created new schedules for meals and exercise.

Just recently they banned outside organizations which had offered prisoners classes, counseling and other aid. All to minimize the contact prisoners have with each other and with the outside world.

UNDATED LETTER: CHRISTMAS

No, I can't tell you why the prison people put me on this floor, but I can tell you this, if I leave my cell I will be hurt, or maybe worse, another way to put it. These people want a new prison and as long as [there is] violence, they will get what they want, and they don't mind losing one of *my kind*. . . .

There are all sorts of *oral satisfaction* in here (smile) but I don't have a cell partner as of yet, anyway the prison officials pass out a bag of hard candy at Christmas so at the present time the candy will have to do.

But it is prison by its very nature that creates violence. Certain kinds—rapes and gang stabbings—are ignored or even encouraged by the authorities. Racial antagonisms are played up to keep people isolated and suspicious, and gays are often used as scapegoats. Violence provides a justification for repressive treatment of prisoners. But repression like the lock-up is the system's response to the political resistance of prisoners. They punish the many for the alleged actions of a few and respond to specific acts of defiance with generalized terror and repression. In an ironic turnaround, violence is then the justification the CDC uses in its budgetary drive for more guards, modern military-type weapons and equipment, and new prisons.

JANUARY 14

You ask me how I am relating to you in my mind, Jerry. As you know there are a lot of meanings of the word Love, and the Love I have for you is friendship and I do think you are a beautiful person and a wonderful gay brother, and Jerry, the love of my heart is a gay brother by the name of Doug—I was with him for 4 years and I can't forget his love, I don't know where he is at now and I haven't seen him in 5 years, 6 months, and 18 days. I met him at the Ohio Prison, he made a parole and when I got out eight months later I heard he was in California, so I jump parole and came to Calif. to look for him. . . . So Jerry, my love for you is not in the world of fantasy, it is friendship.

. . . If a good looking man would be sent to this prison and he was not a homosexual, he would be by the time he left prison and the reason would be his looks. Another reason is weakness, if a man comes into prison scared and weak, then the pressure bullies will get him trapped in a spot where he has two choices—one—break the code that no inmate wants to do (rat or inform), that may cost him his life. —two—give in and become a homosexual, either way he loses. Now the guys who are not forced into becoming homosexual are the guys who run in groups or gangs. The guys who are big and strong or old and dried up. And there are one other kind of guys and they are the gay guys who want to have sex and as you know, you can't force the willing.

The main reason I ask you not to send money is, a gay brother in prison really doesn't need any money for two reasons—one—among us gays in prison we have a saying, anytime we need money or anything (Get off your gold mine that you sit on and get what you need) —two—if you did send me money I would probably lose it when the bullys take it away from me, so I'd rather get off my gold mine and get a pack or two of cigarettes, then I will come out ahead. The gay newspapers you send me mean much more to me than money.

. . . Yes, I am finally taking a class in English, in my cell. I can't go to the prison school because I am still locked up in the Adjustment Center and I will be in lock up until I get transferred to Vacaville.

We don't want to romanticize prisoners: they are people with the same possibilities as other people, but with far fewer choices. And selling yourself for "canteen" favors is one of the few social options available to gays in prison. Others include keeping your sexuality a secret and taking your chances on the main line, getting onto a segregated gay unit like P-Wing at Vacaville, or taking an "old man" for protection. While women's and gay liberation have made some real changes in the society at large, they have not yet penetrated far into prison. There, sex takes on super-importance as one of the only areas available for release of the volatile feelings of being locked up, and

141

follows all the oppressive patterns known as sexism.

Sexual relations among prisoners are officially prohibited but unofficially condoned and very widespread. If two men form a mutual loving relationship they face the constant threat of forced separation. Guards and prison officials become expert at using sex, just as they use race; with promises, threats, rumors or transfers they can try to manipulate inmates and stir up antagonisms whenever prisoner unity threatens their control.

JANUARY 29

I think I just found a half of my "Doug." Yes, I think the angel of love put a fool arrow in my heart again, this time like all the other times since I left Doug it will probably end as fast as it began. I'm not going to put my hopes too high, altho he does look like he's going out of his way to please me. He even bought a TV so that if I desired to move into his cell we could watch TV. . . .

An officer came to my cell to give me lunch and he saw a couple of nude pictures I had of men on my wall and he got red in the face and dropped my tray of food, and today when he passed out lunch, he made another officer give me my food (smile)—(he is a new officer) give him a few months and he will learn.

I may be getting out of lock up tomorrow and be put on the main yard. This is the only way I can get with the other half of my Doug. (smile) He wants me to move in his cell, I hope they will let me!

Yours with much Gay Love,

"Little Eddie"

This was the end of the correspondence. Jerry's last letter to Folsom was returned to him with one word scrawled on the envelope: Deceased. But the story of Eddie Loftin has no end; there are many unanswered questions about his death, which is attributed to a heart attack. A recent court ruling allows the prisoner's attorney to review his prison file. This could tell us what reasons they gave for denying parole, his medical reports, and why he was moved from one cell to another. Eddie's attorney, John Wahl, a member of Metropolitan Community Church, was denied this access. The prison authorities obviously have no desire to see the truth known. This is not surprising. Whether Eddie should have been out by March 30, and whether his death at the age of 30 was actually a "heart attack," whatever an impartial autopsy might

142

reveal, the real responsibility for his death is on their hands, and they know it.

Eddie Loftin is buried in an unmarked grave. At present, the best way we can pay our respects is to let the outrage of our community be known. Not only for Eddie, but because what happened to him has happened to many of "our kind" and it must stop. It is an election year and more candidates than ever are realizing their need for the gay community's new strength. Under a new regime in Sacramento, there is a chance for changing the laws, officials, and intolerable conditions that led to Eddie Loftin's death.

If any change does come about, it is based in our acting as a cohesive force, as a community. There are several gay organizations in California that have been working to protest these conditions and to lend support to our sisters and brothers behind bars. JOIN HANDS urges all concerned people to take this time to find out what these groups are doing and discover what each of us can do with them.

JOIN HANDS has existed since 1972 to bring together members of the "free" community with gay prisoners through correspondence and visiting. We feel this one-to-one communication is valuable to both correspondents, and also offer a course through Lavender U in San Francisco where those writing to prisoners can get together to talk over their experience. We now receive over 20 letters per week from prisoners all over the country; interested people are always needed to answer them. Referrals are made to other agencies, to women's correspondence groups, and to gay organizations elsewhere. Requests for information, letters or contributions to continue this work can be made to JOIN HANDS, P.O. Box 42242, S.F. 94142.

METROPOLITAN COMMUNITY CHURCH of San Francisco is a church with a primary outreach to the homophile community. The church's Prison Ministry, however, is a national organization corresponding and visiting with and assisting both male and female inmates, both gay and straight. Its efforts to be allowed into prisons to minister as a church are now before the Federal District Court. Address correspondence to MCC Prison Ministry, P.O. Box 99369, Station O, S.F., California 94109.

The PRISON, PAROLE AND PROBATION PROJECT of the Los Angeles Gay Community Services Center has been active in correspondence, legal and job counseling to parolees, and is a fully accredited

143

social service agency. Their address is 1614 Wilshire Blvd., Los Angeles, California.

Also involved in this kind of work is the GOLDEN GATE GAY LIBERATION HOUSE, 934 Page Street, San Francisco 94117, and the FORTUNE SOCIETY, 29 East 22 Street, New York, N.Y. 10010.

GAY COUPLES AND
STRAIGHT LAW

Tom Hurley

I.

A man and a woman fall in love. They get married, have children. The husband and wife take care of their children, feeding, clothing, educating them, loving them. The relationship is so familiar we hardly stop to notice it.

Another relationship is more noticeable: two women or two men fall in love. They get married, adopt children or retain custody of their own from previous marriages, feeding, clothing, educating them, loving them. This relationship gives pause to most people, gay or straight. Such relationships do, however, occur—now—in this society.

But if gay couples, with or without children, want the protection of the law over their unions, they have to perform legal acrobatics straight couples never dream of. No marriage statute in this country forbids the marriage of two people of the same sex, but legal custom and usage have held that the intent of the law is for marriage to be a contract between two people of the opposite sex. The Washington State Court of Appeals, for example, upheld in 1974 a lower court decision that denial of a marriage license to two gays is neither unconstitutional nor discriminatory. The Court's opinion was based on the argument that marriage is primarily for the procreation and education of children. Apparently the judges weren't aware of the fact that many straight couples marry without the intention of having children. Or that gay couples can raise children as well as the straight family next door.

In spite of what the courts have said, gay couples are still seeking to have their unions ratified by law. The first such marriage took place on June 12, 1970, when the Rev. Troy D. Perry married two Los Angeles women who had a *de facto* common-law marriage. Under California law, a religious ceremony alone and not a license is needed to validate a common-law marriage.

Consider also the case of Jack Baker and Mike McConnell, who began fighting for gay civil rights several years ago when Baker became president of the student body at the University of Minnesota. Baker and McConnell applied for a marriage license in 1970, but authorities denied the application. Appeals through the state court system were defeated, and a final appeal was dismissed by the Supreme Court. The couple finally solved their problem with the law by a two-step process. Making use of the relatively uncomplicated Minnesota adoption laws, McConnell first adopted Baker, thus binding the two legally. Baker took as his new name Pat Lyn McConnell. Then Mike McConnell drove to a Minnesota town well out of the range of the Minneapolis media and took out a marriage license. In one space he filled in his own name; in the only other space left—that for the woman—he wrote down the name of his spouse: Pat Lyn McConnell. And so they were legally married. Local authorities now recognize the marriage as valid, but both the Veterans' Administration, to whom Baker applied for a change in status on account of his spouse, and the Internal Revenue Service, are challenging the union. According to Baker, he and his lover are eagerly awaiting the new court contests. They are also presently seeking to become foster parents.

Baker, now a lawyer, and McConnell possessed the energy and determination to enter test cases that would radically alter the law. Baker sums up their approach this way: "If you're concerned about the movement—whatever that is—there's a duty to get yourself into the most controversial position you can, and then put out a press release. You get things changed very quickly that way." Baker has little patience with lawyers who counsel their clients to seek ways *around* the law.

Not all gay couples feel up to putting their lives under the legal spotlight, but many gay couples still feel a need to solemnize their relationships with legal contracts. A Boston couple, for example, wrote a chapter in the history of gay life versus straight law, a chapter that involved a circumvention of the law rather than a head-on collision.

Bob Jones and Harry Freeman presented themselves to Richard Rubino, the Boston lawyer who has made a name for himself by defending gay people. What they wanted was a legal relationship that would bind them together as an ordinary marriage does, but would allow them to avoid a confrontation with city hall. Rubino did three things: (1) He drew up a mutual contract combining a partnership agreement and an ante-nuptial agreement (the latter making stipulations about what would happen if the pair were to desire a "divorce"). The mutual contract made each partner liable for the other's debts and dealt very specifically with the property they shared; (2) He drew up mutual wills, making each the other's executor and sole heir; and (3) He arranged for a legal name change that involved a hyphenation of their last names.

To be sure, there are some differences between this arrangement and the usual marriage contract: the legal relationship was tailored to Jones and Freeman's particular needs; they could end their contract easily while the divorce of a straight couple would require lengthy legal procedures. But, explains Rubino, the contract gives the pair what they asked for: legal as well as moral obligations. "It's not quite the same as marriage, but it's as close to the same as we can get now," Rubino comments.

Whether a gay couple are legally bound together or not, other legal problems, depending on the nature of their relationship, may arise. Wills and insurance policies, for example. While talking with Rubino about wills, for example, the specter of Alice B. Toklas arose in my mind. She was left destitute because the family of Gertrude Stein prevented her from sharing in her lover's estate by contesting Stein's will. But Rubino's attitude in dealing with a family challenge to a gay person's will is optimistic. The basic legal argument in the contest of a will is that the person was not "of sound mind" when making out the will. If a family could not prove this, they could not successfully challenge the document. Rubino feels that the will he drew up for the Freeman-Jones would withstand a family challenge. A couple's homosexuality, he would argue, is certainly not evidence of mental instability and is simply not relevant to a case of this kind. More importantly, says Rubino, objecting to the introduction of a client's sexual preference into a civil case has worked for him: the courts have refused to consider the matter relevant.

Books about gay life often present us with one story after another about the legal hassles of couples: Look, for example, at the chapter on "Lifestyle" in Del Martin and Phyllis Lyon's *Lesbian/Woman* (Bantam, 1972). These disturbing stories are culled from the authors' own experiences and those of their sisters. But while the horror stories are true, Richard Rubino emphasizes that in many cases they need not have occurred. Civil cases involving gay couples, if handled by a sympathetic lawyer and tactfully presented, can be successful. The rule is to be pragmatic, to determine what strategy to use in each particular case.

Claire Shanahan of Boston agrees. Most gay couples, she feels, stop short of legal confrontation anyway. If they do go ahead, they proceed carefully and slowly, and they get what they want. Claire had her insurance policies made out to her lover, Linda Lachman, describing her relationship to Linda simply as "friend." The insurance company did not object and even stated specifically that the policy was hers and she could name whomever she pleased as beneficiary. The company might have been a little uneasy had it known that the policy holder and beneficiary were gay lovers, but Claire feels Linda and she got exactly what they wanted without a lot of fuss. Her medical coverage, however, specifies familial relationships, thus providing for her children but excluding her lover. This bothers Claire for obvious reasons, but she remains philosophical while keeping her eye on the Massachusetts State House for legal changes favorable to gays. Her approach, in the meantime, is to "walk very softly, and don't carry too big a stick."

Hospital rules do not have the force of law, but if a lover becomes seriously ill and enters a hospital, doctors may restrict visits to members of the immediate family. This separates lovers at a crucial time. An *ad hoc* group of the Homophile Community Health Service of Boston, according to Paula Bennett of Lesbian Mothers, is now talking about getting lovers spouses' rights. But while awaiting changes of this kind, people solve the problem in various ways. Rubino says one solution is to have the sick lover grant "power of attorney" to the other. This tactic, of course, depends on the condition of the patient—he or she must be able to write—but if the power is granted, no hospital authority can deny access to the sickroom. Claire Shanahan's approach was a bit more direct: when Linda was in the hospital, Claire simply explained to the nurses that she was Linda's "sister." It worked.

So this much becomes clear. If two women or two men desire to live together as a couple, the legal aspects of their action—whether they involve marriage, wills, name changes (or other legal questions like property and taxation not touched on here)—can be handled in either of two ways: the couple, as openly gay people, can fight a long, difficult war that may involve many defeats before it produces a victory; or they can avoid directly confronting the law and seek less dramatic but effective solutions. In either case, people should consult a sympathetic lawyer who will fight what fights are needed, make what arrangements are necessary, in the manner most appropriate to the desired ends. In fact, says Rubino, more and more gay people are coming to him about civil questions rather than criminal cases: "It's a healthy sign of the gay community getting its head together."

On his part, Rubino vows that when a case must go to court, he will "educate the courts about individual clients and what is going on in the world today, especially with gay people in the United States." The courts, as legal arms of straight society, certainly need that education.

The American Civil Liberties Union is also trying to educate the courts. The ACLU's "National Project on Sexual Privacy" declares as its purpose "to coordinate a national effort to remove all laws which proscribe private consensual sexual activity among adults and to eliminate discriminatory practices which flow from the existence of such laws." A legal docket prepared by the project shows that a good number of cases completed or in progress during 1974 pertained to the lives of gay couples. The docket should thicken as more gay couples attempt to make the law serve their own needs.

A larger question, however, is whether gays should be getting involved in the institution of marriage at all. Reverend Don McGaw, director of Boston's Homophile Community Health Service, thinks that "gay marriage is beating a dead horse." He argues that "if we have to [have gay marriage], it's because we haven't yet figured out other ways to get what we want legally." But the fact remains that at this stage in gay history, many gay people believe that a marriage relationship is the best way for two people in love to build a life together.

II.

The law, reflecting the society that creates it, does not approve of gay love. The courts have usually found a gay household, whether male or female, unsuitable for raising children. Martin and Lyon's *Lesbian/Woman* pointed out the difficulties gay women, particularly women who live with their lovers, have had in maintaining custody of their children from previous marriages. In one case, a woman was denied custody and allowed visitation rights only in the presence of her child's father—this on the basis of a psychiatrist's testimony that although the woman was a stable, sensitive person, a heterosexual environment was preferable for a growing child. But *Lesbian/Woman* records another case: a woman openly declared her love for another woman; the husband's lawyer could find nothing in her background to prove her unsuitable as a parent; the woman won unrestricted custody of her children.

Martin and Lyon were quick to point out that the first case was far more the rule than the second, but the situation just a few years after the publication of their book appears to be changing. Women in

149

Transition, a Philadelphia group that helps divorced and separated women, is currently investigating custody and visitation rights of gay mothers. Favorable precedents are hard to come by, but a 1974 Washington state decision may give the group the argument they need. A Tacoma judge not only granted a lesbian permanent custody of her three children but did so without preventing her from living with her lover. The court's decision was based on testimony by a sociologist, on the viewing of a movie called "Sandy and Madeleine's Family"* and on a social worker's investigation of the family environment. Nothing in the woman's background, the judge declared, made her unfit to have custody of her children.

But one legal precedent does not mean a sudden change in the attitudes of society. The courts need to be educated, case by case, before they will reject the widespread view that homosexuality is a necessary bar to child custody. Richard Rubino explains that although a woman in a child custody case is usually presumed to be fit, the presumption reverses itself when the mother is a lesbian. But Rubino would argue in court (armed with statistics) that gay people who bring up children no more affect the sexual preference of their offspring than do straight parents. From that point, Rubino moves to the question of what is best for the child, given the individual circumstances of each case. He also asks questions like: do the parents want a court fight? How sympathetic has the judge been in the past? Usually, Rubino notes, custody cases can be worked out before the formal court appearance. In any case, he recommends that a client neither confirm nor deny his or her gayness. If the non-gay party raises the issue, Rubino feels confident he can persuade the court of its irrelevance.

Gay couples are also adopting children with increasing frequency. In fact, adoption agencies are seeking gay parents for the large number of gay children who have severe problems living with their straight families. Of course, not all the authorities have hopped on the bandwagon; some have even tried to pull its wheels off. In the state of Washington, the head of the Department of Social and Health Services tried in 1974 to prevent gays from becoming foster parents by changing adoption regulations. The proposed rules specified, among other things, that "foster parents shall be persons who have satisfactory, stable interpersonal relationships, free of chronic conflict both within and without

---

*Available from Multi-Media Resource Center, 540 Powell, San Francisco, California 94108.

the family group and who are without severe problems in their sexual orientation." After continued pressure from gay groups, the wording was modified, omitting "severe problems in their sexual orientation" but retaining phrases that could be used against gay people. Gay Oregonians have run into similar problems with that state's Department of Human Resources.

But there have been victories, too. A Philadelphia lesbian couple are now foster parents for a fifteen-year-old transvestite boy. The boy had been shunted from the streets to straight foster families and back again. Although the judge was not aware of the couple's sexual preference, the adoption agency knew that the two women were gay and found them fully qualified to care for the youth. In Minnesota, Jack Baker and Mike McConnell, those indefatigable gay challengers of the law, have applied with several agencies to adopt a child. In New York City, the National Gay Task Force announced, in June 1974, a program to find homes for gay children. NGTF will search out mature gay people who want to help troubled younger gays and will then recommend the prospective parents to cooperating local agencies.

Boston's Homophile Community Health Service experimented with such a program but abandoned the effort in 1973. Director Don McGaw explains that the service had trouble finding couples who were: (1) financially sound; (2) together a long time; (3) not up-tight about dealing with a gay teen-ager; and (4) aware that they would not be "parents"—since McGaw feels that the parent-child relationship is inappropriate to adolescence. Unhappy with the idea of the nuclear family, McGaw would prefer a foster house made up of several gay adolescents, two gay adult men, and two gay adult women. Significantly, however, he found no problem with the state agencies, who were very willing to place gay young people with gay foster parents.

Whatever their life plans, gay people are now demanding that the law serve *their* needs as it does straights. Gay couples who want marriages and children are figuring out ways to change the law or get around it. The efforts of gay couples help themselves and other gay couples, but they also make it easier for all gays to obtain equal justice under law. The courts, like society itself, must realize that we are here, and we are not going to be adjudicated away.

LESBIANS AND THE LAW

Karla Dobinski

Somehow we all know that lesbianism is illegal . . . We can feel the LAW lurking out there somewhere waiting for us all to step too far out of the closet.

But exactly what laws are there? How do they affect us? Why is the State so concerned with our way of loving? Are those laws ever going to be changed?

The following article will discuss the difficulty of finding information about lesbians and the laws; some statutory laws about sodomy and marriage; some problems in housing, employment, the military, and professional organizations; the situation of lesbians once in the legal system; and what's ahead for lesbians and the law.

This is by no means an in-depth report—there's tons of research to be done, and a lot more to be said about every one of the areas mentioned herein. It seems important, however, to go once over the whole area lightly, to get a sense of how our lives are being chilled by the State's cold hands.

First of all, remember that lesbians usually rank as only a footnote in most studies, records, and statistics; probably because lesbianism has not been as visible to the straight world as male homosexuality (or maybe they just weren't looking). "Homosexuals," after all, are men. Even the Wolfenden Report, which in 1957 in England studied homosexuality and recommended that laws against it be abolished, spoke only of men. Legend has it that when English laws against homosexuality were written in the late 1800's, Queen Victoria said there would be no need to apply them to women because "English women would never do such a thing."

STATUTORY LAW

Although most state legislatures have made laws regulating sex and marriage, many statutes do not directly mention lesbianism or homosexuality except when talking about corruption of minors. Some sexual

152

laws, however, do prohibit "unnatural acts," specifically oral sex. Of course, most courts have made it clear that those laws are not to be used against good heterosexuals: Their real intent is to prohibit homosexuality. The courts thereby continue a practice of applying the same laws differently to different persons.

Homosexual acts may result in long prison sentences in all but eight states—Illinois, Connecticut, Colorado, Oregon, Hawaii, Delaware, Ohio, and North Dakota. Countries which have no anti-gay laws include France, Italy, Belgium, Holland, Denmark, Switzerland, Sweden, Great Britain, West Germany, and Canada. Repression of homosexuality is prevalent in Cuba, Communist China, and Russia.

Sometimes the laws against homosexual sodomy are not valid for lesbians. For instance, in 1939 in Georgia, a sister of ours named Thompson was arrested for violating a sodomy statute. But the judge released her from jail, saying that as loathsome as the act may seem, two women cannot commit sodomy. He said the legislature meant the anti-sodomy laws only for men.

But then, in 1967 in Michigan, a sister named Julie Livermore was sentenced to five years (and served three) in a house of detention for being caught by state troopers while camping with her lover. There the judge ruled that "gross indecency" between two women was certainly punishable.

Even if the state doesn't use direct laws against lesbianism, police will often arrest someone on vagrancy or loitering charges when they can't prove a specific crime. There's also the devious device called entrapment, whereby a disguised police person suggests unlawful acts to you, and if you don't refuse, they arrest you. Entrapment is a favorite device for harassing women who may be prostitutes or persons who may be gay.

There have been, to my knowledge, no cases directly challenging the constitutionality of laws against lesbianism, and the U.S. Supreme Court still insists that it has a right to rule on the sexuality of its citizens. But the first steps toward such a case were taken by six persons in Los Angeles in June 1974, when they all "confessed" to the crime of oral copulation and surrendered themselves to the Los Angeles Police Department. The "Felons Six" included two L.A. lesbians. The law enforcement officials refused to arrest them, in an attempt to preclude a constitutionality test. The last word on the situation is that the Felons Six are going to court—to protest the negligence of the police for not arresting them, and thus the constitutionality of

California's anti-gay law.

There are several possible reasons why lesbians haven't often used the courts—it takes large amounts of money to hire a lawyer and pay court costs, and there are relatively few lawyers who will sympathetically and effectively handle a lesbian case. In addition, cases are dealt with on the narrowest legal principles—for instance, even if the whole situation arose because the woman was a lesbian, the judge will deal only with a narrower question, such as "was she actually disturbing the peace?" Thus, the case becomes totally irrelevant to the lesbian issue.

WHY WE CAN'T MARRY

All marriage statutes are based on three main justifications. First, since the State has replaced the old ecclesiastical courts and has assumed the responsibility of pushing a Judeo-Christian ethic toward sex, sex is valid only for procreation. That is, sex for pleasure is not only unrecognized, it is specifically outlawed. Thus the State has blessed only those of the human race who, regardless of love, make a contract to live together and produce kids. But mainly because of the overpopulation dilemma, and the recognition that sex for pleasure is healthy, this argument has lost validity. Also, the State does allow persons who are too old to produce children or who are sterile to get married.

A second reason for heterosexual marriage statutes is the sexist nuclear family, the basic unit of capitalism. One breadwinner and one homemaker, who will do free labor, and lots of little consumers is an ideal structure for capitalism. Any form of communal living or bread-winning messes up the system, causing less consumption, thus less demand, less production, etcetera. For instance: a luxury item like a dishwasher is generally used to full capacity if twenty-five people are sharing it. But because capitalists separate and group people into small living units, a dishwasher generally services only four or five persons. Thus, five more dishwashers are bought to meet the needs of the other small units, and the economic system grows. Capitalism always needs expanding markets.

A third reason involves the State's assumption that it can regulate morality. This practice of course is dangerous, arbitrary, and subjective: Unsubstantiated fears and misconceptions evolve into statutes and then the statutes give rise to further unsubstantiated fears and misconceptions—a very vicious cycle. Puritan morality ignores thriving cultures

154

from the Grecian to the Mohave Indian, where homosexuality has been an accepted lifestyle.

Thus there is no justifiable explanation for the anti-gay laws against marriage. The laws were tested in 1973 in Kentucky, where the Court of Appeals held there is no constitutional sanction or protection of the right of marriage for persons of the same sex. The court said the two women applicants were incapable of marriage as it is defined, i.e., a relationship between a man and a woman for the primary purpose of sanctified procreation. That decision was based in part on an earlier 1971 Minnesota decision which denied a legally sanctioned union between two men because, the opinion read, "what they propose is not a marriage." In effect, the courts were denying marriages to the couples simply because "that's the way it's always been."

SO WHY GET MARRIED?

Why would two lesbians want to get married anyway? As long as they can live together as friends, why cause trouble? An obvious response is that people should have basic rights. If two women want to become married, why not? Laws prohibiting same-sex marriages are in violation of the individual's right to privacy, due process, and equal protection.

In addition, the State offers great inducements for people who marry. Among these blessings are the right to file a joint income tax return and pay less money to the government, the right to deduct estate taxes, the right to inherit from a spouse if no will was prepared, the privilege not to testify in court against a spouse, the right to sue and collect for injuries to a minor child, and the right to visit a spouse in jail or hospital when only immediate family are allowed. There are also "couple" rates for transportation, insurance, and entertainment.

LESBIAN MOTHERS

The straight homophobic society pressures many lesbians into repressing their lesbian feelings and getting married to men. Sometimes there are children involved. Thus, when a woman has finally come to terms with her lesbianism, she not only has a marriage to pull away from, she also has children whom she may want to keep. The grueling divorce proceedings allow a judge to rummage through her personal life. If a woman is a lesbian, the divorce will probably be granted to the husband on grounds of cruel and inhuman treatment by the wife, or perhaps on grounds of fraud, and then the marriage could also be annulled. If there are children, lesbianism may be an issue which causes the woman to lose custody of them. The label "unfit mother" has usually been immediately attached to a woman who is lesbian. (The question of why, after fifteen years of marriage and children, she should suddenly become an unfit mother has never been answered satisfactorily.)

But child custody is a growing issue. Although most courts still "grant" the children to the straight parent, there have been some important exceptions. Perhaps the most exciting case is that of Eunice Brown and Arlene Smith, in Flint, Michigan. The case arose when a policeman discovered their lifestyle when he came to their house for a different reason. After a long court battle involving three different lawyers, the women were finally permitted in October 1973 to have their eight children remain with them.

There are other cases, however, where the lesbian is allowed to keep her kids but not her lover. In San Jose, California, in 1973, a woman was allowed to raise her children, but her lover was forbidden to come to the home unless the children were off visiting their father or were in school.

And there are still many other cases where women are denied the right even to have their children near them because of "moral depravity." In March 1973, in Georgia, a lesbian mother named Ruth had her nine-year-old daughter taken away from her and handed over to the child's sixty-five-year-old grandparents. Even the child's father had wanted her to remain with Ruth, but the court directly interfered and gave the child away.

A case still being litigated (since 1972) in Seattle involves two middle-class housewives who are lesbian mothers. The custody issue has been expanded to presenting evidence from expert witnesses on lesbianism to educate the judge. The lawyers there are also hitting the primary question of the stress affecting the children when they are taken away from those who love them. The mothers in the case—Sandra Schuster and Madeleine Isaacson—are featured in a movie about the situation called "Sandy and Madeleine's Family."*

In a related development, gay foster parents are being licensed by

*Available from Multi-Media Resource Center, 540 Powell, San Francisco, California 94108.

several states. In a 1974 Seattle, Washington, juvenile court proceeding, a gay dependent child (male) was placed with a gay foster parent.

DOES YOUR BOSS KNOW YOU'RE GAY?

Most working lesbians are under the constant concern that their employer or supervisor will learn about their lifestyle and fire them, often on some other contrived grounds, since it is "slanderous" to call someone a lesbian. But even if you can prove that you were fired for lesbianism, court cases are expensive and risky. In 1972, Peggy Burton, a schoolteacher in Portland, Oregon, was fired for being gay. After a long court battle and appeal, the State allowed her to keep her job and have back pay. The judge said the statute under which she was fired was too vague, because it referred to morality in a very general and overly broad way and was therefore unconstitutional. (One can guess what might have happened with a more specific statute. In other words, if lesbianism had been defined as a brand of immorality, the judge would have ruled differently.)

The constitutional requirement of "due process" has been interpreted to mean that a person cannot be fired from a job unless a violation of a requirement related to that job has occurred. That is, you can't be fired just for being a lesbian—the boss has to show that your lesbianism is directly detrimental to your job. This interpretation has cast a shadow over gay women who work with other persons—doctors, teachers, psychologists, counselors—because the State could probably decide that lesbianism, as a "disease," is a valid reason for firing someone.

But seeing lesbianism as an automatic mental sickness is a concept slowly being chipped away. In early December 1973, some twenty million homosexuals were instantly "cured" when the American Psychiatric Association declared that homosexuality *per se* is no longer a sickness; that instead, it is a valid expression of sexuality. (They set up a new category on their sicklist called "sexual-orientation disturbance" which unfortunately perpetuates much of society's psychological oppression.) The APA decision is an improvement, however, and is expected to have some impact on the way the law and other American institutions (Ann Landers, for instance) regard gay persons. At an APA convention in Detroit, May 1974, a lesbian activist told the shrinks: "By deciding what is sane and what is pathological, you decide who has

157

civil rights and who does not; who may be employed and who may not; who may love, and who may not."*

A Washington, D.C., court has recently outlawed the automatic firing of homosexuals who work for the Federal Civil Service Commission. The court said homosexuality did not directly interfere with the person's job. In March 1974, the Wisconsin Supreme Court upheld the firing of a male homosexual working with young retarded boys, on the grounds that the gay man did not fulfill the proper male role model expected of him. During the oral argument, one justice implied there is a distinction between a homosexual working with income tax returns for the Department of Taxation and one working with small children in a state home. Again, the case reflects the misconception of homosexuals as child molesters.

Thus schoolteachers, doctors, social workers, etc., have an added burden of showing that their lesbianism is not detrimental to their jobs, that it is not a "disease" to be caught by innocent children. The state has determined that it alone will decide who will teach, cure, or help its children, based, in part, on the person's sexuality.

The State's preoccupation with homosexuality has resulted in witch hunts and paranoia-engendering periods in professional circles. This persecution is especially high in the military where a woman can be dishonorably discharged for lesbianism. The real insidiousness here lies in the forced psychological trauma and paranoia, the hidden meetings, the fear of surveillance, and the hesitancy to trust anyone at all in the micro-world of the military.

Lesbian lawyers? A survey last year of state bar associations (you must belong to one in order to practice law) showed that many states do not allow open homosexuals to become lawyers. In 1975, a resolution was pending before the American Bar Association, however, which supports the right of gay persons to be lawyers. There are at least two relatively open lesbian lawyers in the country, and countless others justifiably waiting for the weather to change before coming out of their closets.

*Eds.: For further information on the APA resolution on homosexuality (December 15, 1973), a press release and rationale paper is available from the APA, Division of Public Affairs, 1700 18 Street NW, Washington, D.C. 20009.

WHAT'S AHEAD FOR LESBIANS AND THE LAW?

Will the blindfolded woman who holds the scales of justice ever recognize and protect her lesbian sisters? Things could go both ways, and probably will: A backlash and a liberal acceptance could be concurrent in the future of lesbian liberation.

On the one hand, the State is beginning to recognize that lesbians do exist, and sees us as a threat. The number of arrests of lesbians is growing. A survey by Kinsey showed that until 1952 (when the survey was published) there had been no outright arrests of lesbians. But a 1969 article in *The New York Times* showed that ten gay women were arrested in 1968, and that forty-nine had been picked up in the first half of 1969, all on charges of loitering. (I present these figures only to show the relative increase; their absolute accuracy is difficult to determine.)

I couldn't find any more statistics on lesbian arrests, but the trend is obvious. An on-the-street backlash is also arising. The "crunch" came in 1973 for many lesbians in Ann Arbor, Michigan, when they were questioned by the F.B.I. about the gay liberation movement. In Madison, Wisconsin, in 1973, a private security force compiled information about fifty community persons, then bragged to local businessmen that they could reveal each person's political beliefs, sexual habits, and "whether she was a lesbian." Also, in the small city of Wukesha, Wisconsin, a John Doe investigation, sparked by the apparent suicide of a male hospital administrator, is sweeping up a circle of closeted homosexuals.

On the other hand, ordinances banning discrimination on the grounds of sexual preference are passing in city governments throughout the country. The disposition of these proposals has varied greatly. For instance, in Seattle, Washington, the issue got hardly any publicity and was passed as a matter of course. Such ordinances have also been passed in Ann Arbor, Washington, D.C., Denver, and San Francisco.

But in New York and Boulder the opposition from the Catholic Church, fire departments, and reactionary citizens defeated the ordinance proposal. And then, in Madison, a typical governmental ploy is occurring—the proposed ordinance is being reshuffled on bureaucratic paper piles and it will take over a year from the first time it was publicly introduced for it to be acted upon. (The Madison Gay Caucus is working with the Equal Opportunities Commission, and therefore has added other classifications to the list, such as age, economic status, marital status, and being handicapped.)

But note well that the passage of an ordinance may not be the end of troubles. Ann Arbor lesbians filed a complaint under their ordinance following severe harassment in a local bar. The Human Rights Commission dismissed the complaint and refused to act to help the lesbians gain equal treatment. Continued support and pressure is needed, and a rule on the books is but a small first step.

Several state-level government committees and commissions have come out with proposals to repeal the laws against all victimless crimes, such as homosexuality or prostitution. Unfortunately, many of these liberal types still consider homosexuality harmful—they just think we ought to be cured instead of punished.

And, another glimmer of hope: A justice on the Wisconsin Supreme Court, in February 1974, said that expression of homosexuality might be considered under constitutionally protected free speech standards—but, he was quick to add (playing on Justice Holmes' restrictions on shouting fire in a crowded theater), it would still be wrong to "shout queer or lesbian in a kindergarten."

This article merely sketches the fronts on which we must begin a serious struggle. It is a very necessary struggle, the first step of which is education about our present situation. Many of our sisters have a lot to lose by visibility before major gains are made in the public arena. Many sisters' lives are being, and will continue to be, restricted—if not directly obstructed—by the State, unless we begin to organize effectively. We need to support each other; we need to feel the presence of other lesbians when we confront the State in the many areas outlined above.

There are plenty of laws against lesbians. What's needed are more lesbians against the laws.

POCKET LEGAL GUIDE
FOR GAY PEOPLE

Chicago Gay People's
Legal Committee

Editors' note: The following was originally published in 1973 as a pocket-sized legal guide for gay people in Chicago. Several lawyers and gay activists were involved in the project. Though much of the information is oriented toward people living in Chicago and subject to Illinois law, the basic ideas contained in it remain valid for most locales. We are reproducing the text of the pamphlet here with the idea that the information is helpful and that other local groups may wish to develop a similar pamphlet for use in their communities. Following this legal guide is a brief list of gay-oriented legal projects. In addition, local gay organizations can usually refer gay people to sympathetic lawyers.

Of the many problems gay women and men can face, some of the worst involve the police and legal system. The Chicago Gay People's Legal Committee has been helping gay people with legal problems for the past two years; the following tips and information are based on first-hand experience we have had working on dozens of cases.

We hope you will never have to use this information yourself. But we do want you to know about these things and be able to deal with police and legal situations if and when they come up. For additional information, for counseling, or for the names of a couple of good attorneys, call the Committee. We suggest that you keep this booklet, or at least make yourself a card such as this and keep it in your wallet:

GAY PEOPLE'S LEGAL COMMITTEE

Call for: Information
             Advice
             Legal Defense
Phone: (312) 750-2590
After 7 p.m. & weekends

SOME GENERAL ADVICE

Point 1. If you are going cruising, or to other such community activities, we suggest you never take employment cards or identification with you, and never take personal phone directories. It is possible that if you were ever stopped and detained, or arrested, that:

    a. the cops might call your employer,
    b. they might make copies of your phone directory,
    c. they might keep such information permanently.

Of course, all three such possibilities would be illegal, but they happen.

Point 2. If you are ever detained by a police officer, you are not supposed to have your personal effects searched nor your auto or home, unless you have been put under arrest and told that the search pertains to the arrest. The most an officer can do to you is to frisk you for possible weapons (which amounts to being groped or patted down). Of course, if a cop shows up at your place with a search warrant, he can snoop around, but he should have a valid warrant that specifies the person and place to be searched.

But note: if a cop is vicious or threatening, don't argue your rights with him. At least get his name and badge number and (if possible) the names of any witness to such an incident.

ARREST

If you are confronted with a situation involving policemen, don't talk to the cop about what happened. If you are put under arrest, don't have conversations with anyone at the police station, even if the people there are friendly. Also, don't argue the facts of an alleged crime with cops. The information you supply could be used against you in court.

BEING BOOKED

The police can legally ask you your name, address, age, where you were going, and that's all. But they will also ask you where you work, who your roommates are, and possibly other such personal information. You do not have to tell them such information and we strongly suggest that you don't. Tell them you would like to talk to your lawyer before supplying such information (even if you don't have a lawyer).

Also, the police can take all of your personal effects from you while you are detained. When they take things from you, remember carefully what they take, and ask for these things when you are bailed out. The only items they may legally keep are things which they claim are evidence. After you have been booked, you have the right to make phone calls until you get someone who can bail you out or until you reach a lawyer. While you are waiting, mug shots and fingerprints will be taken and you will wait in a cell for a few hours.

CO-DEFENDANTS

If you are arrested with another or other persons, get their names and addresses for later (legal) contact. It's for your own benefit and theirs to keep in touch with the person(s) who will stand trial with you. It helps if you can have the same attorney. Remember, if your co-defendant is not ready to stand trial, you have to wait as well. Courts will usually not separate the cases of co-defendants.

BAIL

Bail is what you have to pay to get out of jail until your case comes up in court. In Illinois the usual misdemeanor bail is $100, or 10% of the formal bail charge. Chicago misdemeanor bail is usually $25. You can bail yourself out, if you have that much cash on you. The police department does not honor checks. Probably you will have to have a friend come to the station where you are being held with the bail cash. The only other way of getting out is by receiving a personal recognizance bond (see below).

Note: For all practical purposes, bail bondsmen no longer exist in Illinois, although they still do business in many other states. Also note: you get your money back after your trial in court has been completed and you have been found either not guilty or received supervision (which is neither guilty nor innocent). At this time you will get 90% of your money back.

PERSONAL RECOGNIZANCE BONDS

This is the way to get out of jail without paying money and without having to call anyone for bail. This is a good solution for the problem

163

some gay people face, that is, not wanting to tell anyone that they have been arrested. You will have to sit in jail until morning to get such a bond set for you.

Personal recognizance bonds are issued by a judge and the decision of who can get one is his. Usually if you have a job, are a local resident, are in jail for the first time, etc., you have a better chance of getting one than if you are unemployed, an out-of-towner, or have a previous record.

If the judge doesn't suggest personal recognizance to you, you should suggest it to him—it's worth the try, and it's likely to work.

LAWYERS

When you are out of jail and need to get a lawyer to go to court with you, be careful of what you buy in terms of legal help. We have found that most lawyers in Chicago charge at least $500 for defending the typical gay case. For that kind of money, you should be critical and discerning. We've found that for $500 they don't do very much.

THE GAY PEOPLE'S LEGAL COMMITTEE REFERRAL SERVICE

One of the major tasks of the Committee is finding gay people good, low-cost legal service. Although we are a strictly volunteer group which does not solicit business for any lawyer, we do know good lawyers who are not anti-gay and who charge low fees. We are interested in finding a good lawyer for any gay person who calls, based on the charges involved and the needs of the person.

Note: if you don't have any money for a lawyer, there are only a couple of things you can do.

1. You can call the Legal Committee. We will try to find you a lawyer who is both good and cheap.

2. You can go to court alone. This is risky of course since you don't know what you are going to be up against.

3. You can go to the public defender's office, or find the one working the court that day. Their services are free. Yet going to them usually is hazardous for a gay person. If we had heard of any good public defenders, we would tell anyone who asked. So

far, we have only heard bad things.

Also note: we have been told that some of the big-time, high-fee lawyers who do a lot of gay cases will occasionally do a free or budget case. If you try one, tell us how it went; we want to believe it's possible.

COURT APPEARANCES

You must appear in court every time your case comes up. If you have hired a lawyer, the lawyer should go with you each time. But we strongly suggest that you also go with someone else, especially someone who is gay.

We have seen the effects the courtroom has on gay defendants. It is a straight straight scene, and it can make the innocent feel guilty. So go with a friend, go with a sister, go with a member of the Legal Committee (we are glad to go), but don't go alone. On cases that we work on, we make sure a Committee member makes every court appearance a defendant must appear for; we have found such a policy to be of great help to the persons involved, and even the cases have been helped by a little team spirit.

Note: if for any reason you miss a scheduled court appearance, your bail bond will be canceled and after a month, an arrest warrant will be issued against you. If you have missed an appearance, make sure you have your lawyer get your bond reinstated.

WHEN IN COURT

When you are in court and the bargaining begins between your lawyer and the state's attorney, make sure you know what is going on. Don't let the lawyer "handle everything" to the point where you no longer understand what is going on. Ask questions, even if you think they are a little elementary; talk things over with your friend in court; and don't let the lawyer run your case based on his or her convenience rather than your own good. For example, in many cases the state's attorney will offer an attorney a "deal" which is an informal arrange- ment where some of the charges or penalties are dropped so that the case can be quickly disposed of. Although sometimes this "plea- bargaining," as they call it, can be a good thing for a defendant, it can also be no deal at all. In other words it is possible that a lawyer will settle for a so-called deal when the defendant is not even guilty and has a good chance of *winning* in court. In such a situation a lawyer may actually be going against your own best interests for the sake of caution or just laziness, or worse, not trying harder "because that's all a queer deserves anyway."

Now it is our experience that most gay cases are settled in an informal manner, in which plea-bargaining takes place, and where the merits and facts of the case are never argued in court. Although we have known such a settlement to be a good thing in some instances, we have also seen perfectly innocent gay defendants talked into such a settlement by lawyers who won't go farther than what is easiest for them. Let's be honest: anything good (like justice and constitutional rights) doesn't come easy. If gays keep taking the easy way out of their legal dilemmas, then justice for us will consist of what other people think is good for us. Most legal professionals think gay people are like children; if they are easy on us in court, it is because they hate to see children suffer. Outrageous? But true.

Note: if you are ever in a jam in court, in terms of having a rough time with the way your case is going, ask for a jury trial. It's your right to ask for a jury trial; it might help. And if you change your mind later, then you don't have to go through with having a jury trial, but can just have a bench trial.

SENTENCES AND FINES

Most gay arrests end up either with small fines (under $200) or more likely, with a funny kind of sentence which isn't a sentence, called "supervision." *Very* few gay misdemeanor cases end up with jail sentences. Fines frequently include the bail money you put up.

SUPERVISION

This is the court's way of saying you are neither guilty nor innocent. Instead, after your lawyer enters a technical plea of not guilty, you are given a set amount of time to be "good" in (usually six months to a year). By being "good" we mean you can't get arrested again during that specific period of time. Lawyers like this supervision setup very much because it is rather easy to obtain for gay cases and requires no courtroom arguing. However, the fact that the case may be based on an illegal arrest, or that the arresting officer mistreated the defendant or violated constitutional rights, is no longer an issue after supervision has been accepted. At the end of the term of supervision, the case is technically dismissed.

EXPUNGEMENT

It is possible to have your arrest record cleared after you have successfully finished your supervision period. There is a rather small fee involved in it and any lawyer can do it for you. What the lawyer charges, in addition to the court fee, is variable. Some lawyers will charge you very little to expunge your record. One qualification: expungement is available only to persons who have been arrested for the first time, and only to those who are not found guilty (that is, have their cases dismissed or are acquitted). If you received probation, which is different from supervision, or if you had to pay a fine, then you cannot have your record expunged.

THESE ARE THE LAWS WE ARE USUALLY ARRESTED UNDER:

11-14 PROSTITUTION

a) any person who performs, offers to perform, or agrees to perform any of the following acts for money commits an act of prostitution:
  1) an act of sexual intercourse;
  2) an act of deviate sexual conduct.

b) Penalty—a person convicted of prostitution shall be fined not to exceed $200 or imprisonment in a penal institution other than the penitentiary for a period not to exceed one year, or both.

The Illinois prostitution statute includes solicitation to commit prostitution, and the initial offer need not even come from the prostitute. All the police need is a verbal "promise" from you—not necessarily even a physical act—to arrest you under this statute.

11-9 PUBLIC INDECENCY

Any person of age 17 or upwards who performs any of the following acts in a public place commits a public indecency:

a) an act of sexual intercourse;

b) an act of deviate sexual conduct (any act of sexual gratification involving the sex organs of one person and the mouth or anus of another);

c) a lewd exposure of the body done with intent to arouse or satisfy the sexual desire of the person;

d) a lewd fondling or caress of the body of another person of either sex.

"Public place" for the purposes of this section means any place where the conduct may reasonably be expected to be viewed by others.

A person convicted of public indecency shall be fined not more than $500 or imprisoned in a penal institution other than the penitentiary for a period of not more than one year, or both.

LIST OF LEGAL PROJECTS

Sexual Privacy Project
American Civil Liberties Union
22 East 40th Street
New York, N. Y. 10016
(212) 725-1222

Lambda Legal Defense and
Education Fund, Inc.
30 Grove Street
New York, N. Y. 10014

Gay Caucus
National Lawyers Guild
c/o Gerald A. Gerash
Majestic Bldg., Suite 412
209-16th Street
Denver, Colorado 80202
(303) 266-1354

Chicago Gay People's Legal
Committee
913 Fullerton
Chicago, Illinois 60614
(312) 750-2590

Gay Law Students
Peoples College of Law
2228 West Seventh Street
Los Angeles, California 90057
(213) 388-8171

Part Three
Creating Community and Helping Ourselves

INTRODUCTION:
Creating Community and Helping Ourselves

Karla Jay

In the preceding section of this anthology, our sisters and brothers wrote about the plight of being a minority group in a hostile world. Outrage at straight society is only a first step toward gay liberation, although it is a useful and necessary one. For if our justified hatred of our oppressors leads only to tearing down their society, their values, and their traditions, and if our creative energies are lost in such an endeavor, then we will have defeated ourselves in the end.

And so, it is not enough to complain about oppression or even to combat various aspects of that oppression; we must, in addition, create alternatives and a culture of our own. We must build our own community, one in which we will be able not only to survive but to thrive. This process has already started. Lesbians, in particular, have started to create an Amazon culture, one not based on male ideologies or constructs, but one which comes from our experience and which appeals to our way of life, our sense of humor, our needs. In the last few years, lesbians have created women's music networks, in which we have produced and distributed our own records. Women's Waxwork Productions in New York, Lima Bean Records in Washington, D.C., and Olivia Records in Los Angeles are examples of music companies owned and operated by women. We have also begun to create our own literature with novels such as *Rubyfruit Jungle* by Rita Mae Brown, which was published by Daughters, Inc., a woman-owned-and-operated publishing company in Plainfield, Vermont. Other women-owned-and-operated companies, such as Diana Press in Baltimore, Maryland, and Violet Press in New York City have given lesbians books which male-run publishing houses would not produce. We have also created our own theater, videotapes, movies, and histories. We have also created physical environments where lesbians can feel free to be whatever they want to be—coffee houses, country retreats, women's centers, rap groups. Thus, we are slowly developing alternatives to the dark, gloomy, overpriced bars which are part of our oppression.

Gay men have also created their own culture, but it seems to me that

171

theirs is not developing as rapidly, perhaps because gay men already have a culture based on "camp," and therefore they haven't felt the need of a separate or new culture as much as women. This opinion, however, does not intend to demean the very real efforts gay men have made toward publishing their own newspapers, creating their own rap groups, and making their own music.

In addition to culture, gay people are also starting to take care of one another. The importance of this fact cannot be overestimated. For years, both gay men and women were forced to avoid therapy completely or to take a chance on a homophobic shrink who might try to cure us at best or lobotomize us at worst. Now there are gay counseling services in many cities across the country where gay people are helping one another with problems.

We are also providing physical help for one another. For years, gay men in particular often did not take care of venereal diseases because of the hostility of the straight medical establishment toward oral or anal symptoms of these diseases. In other cases, gay men got inadequate help because they were not checked out in these areas at all. Now we have our own health centers where we can take care of venereal as well as other diseases without the fear of any social or moral stigma.

Women are also helping one another with medical problems. Several self-help or woman-run clinics are scattered across the country where lesbians can receive adequate gynecological and other medical treatment, without the oppression of straight male doctors prying into our sex lives. And both gay men and women are trying to care for some of our more difficult community problems—drugs and alcohol.

However, we have by no means created a utopia—not yet anyway! The road to building a community is not a smooth one and there are many problems we have not yet solved or even adequately dealt with. Among these problems are how gay men and women relate to one another, how white and black gays relate to one another, and relations across the generation gap. Perhaps the discussion of these problems in this section will be a first step toward realization of the problems of others within our community, and realization of the fact that we will never be free until we are *all* free.

172

CAN MEN AND WOMEN
WORK TOGETHER?

A Forum

Editors' note: Gay liberation is a complex and difficult-to-define movement. People work for gay liberation—for the freedom of gay people—in many different ways inside and outside organizations. This book is a part of the gay liberation movement; it was put together by a woman and a man working together. The editors recognize, however, that their experience of working together does not reflect the overall reality of the movement, nor is our working together meant to be "exemplary." Quite the contrary, we recognize and support the existence of an independent lesbian movement. We also recognize that for many gay men, unfortunately, the struggle of women is a negative, threatening force. For us, the concept of gay liberation means nothing without an affirmation of the values of the feminist movement. But while there is an independent lesbian movement, there is also a sector of the gay movement which attempts to unite men and women under a gay banner. This attempt at unity is made by both men and women, and its validity is often hotly debated, both by people who work together and by those who are separatists.

Because of the relevance of this issue, we felt that it was crucial for us to bring a discussion of gay male/female relations into the book. Therefore, one day in 1974, the editors of this book sat down to discuss this topic with Morty Manford and Rose Jordan, two movement activists. The discussion took place on the floor of Rose Jordan's living room on the Lower East Side of Manhattan.

Before we present a transcript of that discussion, we should point out two things. First, although we attempted to assemble four people holding divergent viewpoints, we certainly realize that *all* viewpoints on this issue cannot be voiced by only four people. We also understand and would like to point out to readers that it was philosophically impossible for us to have included a pure "dyke separatist" in this discussion, since such a lesbian would not talk with men at all.

Secondly, we would like to point out that in some ways the dialogue became a living example or working model of some of the problems gay men and women (and all people in general) have working with one another. First, we have difficulty in really listening to what other people are saying. Then, even when we are listening, there is a communication problem which often causes the listener to misinterpret what the speaker

173

is trying to say. Finally, the speakers' opposing points of view usually led to pandemonium rather than to an understanding of another person's viewpoint or to any sort of agreement. Thus, the philosophical question of whether men and women *should* work together often became a question of whether they *can*.

ALLEN: In my experience, I first went to a Gay Liberation Front meeting and there were both women and men there. Then very soon thereafter, the women began vocally criticizing the men for male chauvinism, and there were arguments about it. Before too long most of the women left, and Radicalesbians was formed, and the men had to deal with the fact that these criticisms were being made. We had to learn and to respond, and some people learned more than others; some people responded better than others.

KARLA: Some people never learned!

ROSE: I don't know if I should say this, but I guess I will. Gay liberation always reminds me of "people." You know: "the Jewish people," "the black people." It's always men and *their* women. And I think a lot of the objection that a lot of women had in GLF was that once again it was gay men and their women. It's almost like if you don't have a straight husband, you have a gay husband or brothers or uncles or nephews. And it seems as if women can't find their own place.

I have no objections to gay men. (Obviously I don't because they're here.) And I've worked with them in Identity House [a counseling center] and other places. But the thing that I'm kind of concerned about is that to me the work "gay" means "with men", and the word "lesbian" means "with women". Women have no pride, no dignity, no history, and if we keep connecting in political ways with men in the same groups, we will never have a history because we'll never start one. And that's my objection to working with men. I don't mean that we shouldn't connect with them in any other way, but I mean politically we should have our own groups, and they should have their own groups. And we should come together in certain ways.

MORTY: You know, I think that the different groups within a community are ultimately going to have to affirm their unique interests, their unique concerns, and pursue them. But we're faced with an interesting phenomenon here with the gay movement and the

174

women's movement. Because these are two movements that historically are developing concurrently, with the women's movement preceding the gay movement. In the long run, we have to work together as gay people, and I use the word "gay" in terms of both homosexual women and homosexual men. At the same time I recognize that the feminist identity, while it involves a lot of the same things that the gay liberation movement involves, demands certain sensitivities amongst women.

ROSE: You know, before the women's movement, it seemed to me that lesbians had no identity as women. They didn't consider themselves women. They were gay. It is almost as if, I don't know, we were set apart from the other females in the world, that we were different in some way. We had a community that the straight women didn't have, although if you examine it very carefully, we have the same community—that is, if we do a gay thing, it's men and women, and they do a straight thing, it's men and women. To me, gay liberation is terribly heterosexual in that symbolism. I'm trying to get away from being straight. I don't want to have to be a heterosexual homosexual.

MORTY: But to a great degree, you as a lesbian must deal with a lot of the same problems that I as a gay male must deal with.

ROSE: No, I have less problems than you do, because straight society seems to be more threatened by a male, a man who is behaving as if he's a woman, because if you're going to have sex with a man, according to straight society, somebody's got to be the woman, okay? It's very anti-woman actually: Homophobia is anti-woman to begin with. It's just that whatever men do is more noticeable to the male population. Women don't really count for very much. If they really took us seriously for a change, we'd get into much more trouble than we get into now. So if you take it from a feminist viewpoint, you'll see that you should really be on our side. You should be more feminist-oriented than gay-oriented.

ALLEN: Now you're touching on a crucial point. It has to do with the diminished importance of women in society that more attention is paid to the male homosexual, perhaps, as in legal stuff, and even in the religious laws. Like in Jewish law, there are all kinds of strictures against male homosexuality, and female homosexuality isn't even mentioned.

175

MORTY: What we're really talking about is the common ground that I think both movements have. Because in each situation we're saying roles must go to hell. Just because I am a genital male does not mean I have to have sex with only genital females, and because you are a genital female, you should have sex only with genital males. And then behavior, and so on and so on. An enormous amount of the anti-gay comments that are hurled my way are anti-female. You know, "You're a sissy!" "You're acting like a woman."

KARLA: I think the real point is that we have a common core of oppression, which is roles. Both women's liberation and gay liberation are fighting against roles, and the oppression that roles put on all human beings, straight or gay, and that we are fighting against the laws, which potentially affect all gay people, and could be used to oppress gay women as well as men. But the problem comes at the point where women's liberation differs from gay liberation, and the fact that we women have two oppressions (as women and as lesbians). Gay liberation often doesn't effectively deal with our oppression as women, which is our major oppression when we go out to look for a job and when we face the world in general. I mean somebody looks at me first as a woman. And gay liberation has failed to deal with the problems of women.

ROSE: I don't feel gay liberation *can* deal with the problems of women, because they're dealing with the problems of men, first and foremost, and women, if they're gay, homosexual. The thing that kind of annoys me is that the words that are used signify sexuality. Now, there's a whole lesbian community out there that does not look upon themselves as first being sexual beings, but as persons. And that whether they have sex or not doesn't diminish the fact that they are lesbians at all, whereas it seems as if gay men, or some gay men (I don't know if it's all of them) seem to always stipulate homo-*sex*-u-al-ity—it's always an action that you do.

KARLA: They're sexual labels which lesbians don't really like.

MORTY: We have to make a distinction here between the commonness between the two movements in terms of role-playing, as distinguished from the lesbian and gay male sensibilities, sexuality and unique problems. On the one hand, both movements are trying to broaden the roles that we function in—you know, saying that roles really can't delineate a person's behavior. But on the other hand, the lesbian sensuality and the gay male sensuality and sensibility, and the harassment and the condemnation and the theft of culture *is* something we do have in common. You as a lesbian are condemned for being sick—up until the recent American Psychiatric Association change in nomenclature—just as I was. But as a woman you're not. Okay, here we've found some common ground.

ROSE: I'm condemned worse for being a woman.

MORTY: In different ways, yes.

ALLEN: I'd like to point something out just from my personal experience. When I first came to GLF meetings, this was not a subject that I thought about. I mean I was just too concerned about the whole idea of coming out of the closet. I didn't really imagine that there would be a conflict between lesbians and male homosexuals. Well, the first conflict that I really observed was over the question of the dances. What was happening basically was that the men were incredibly outnumbering the women at the dances—so much so that the women were uncomfortable. There were also some men at these dances who were actually hassling women—you know, feeling them up and things like that. And so the women complained about the dances and eventually made demands for some money so that they could organize their own dances. And a lot of the men were very hostile to this idea. And I think those men didn't understand that one of the reasons that more men came to these dances is not because there is more male homosexuality in this society (I don't really believe that there is more male homosexuality) but because men in this society, because they are men, have an incredible mobility. Men come out into the street, men have an established night life, and men can go walking around in the streets at two in the morning, or four in the morning, which women can't do. Now I don't know whether or not lesbians or women would develop that sort of so-called free sexuality that the gay male world has anyway.

ROSE: We're not even talking about sexuality, you know, we're talking about personhood first. And the reason I think the women were upset over the dances was not the sexuality per se. I mean you can have fifty women in a room and seven men, and it'll be male-dominated. Because it's the attitude the men have about their manhood, within the context and framework of where the women are.

MORTY: Rose, understanding that there are many differences between gay women and gay men, would you agree that there are some things that gay women have in common with gay men which you don't have in common with heterosexual men?

ROSE: Yes, when I said before that I didn't feel that lesbians should be working politically in the same organization, let's say, with gay men, I didn't mean that we didn't have something in common on a certain level. I meant there should be separate organizations so women can learn how to do things. Women don't feel that they know how to do things. The women's movement said that. The lesbians are saying it even more. If you keep connecting with men, the way straight women connect with their men, if you keep doing this, you never will be on your own or feel your own strengths. It doesn't mean to say that we are not harassed as lesbians, that we're not harassed because we're "homosexual." That isn't true; we are. And we know that we have something as a common bond because of that because we know that the reason you're harassed is anti-woman. But this other thing that happens when we don't have an identity. . . . You have an identity as a man, remember, first in the society. You deviated from it, that's true (more power to you), but you had an identity to begin with. Women do not have an identity. We are still trying to make one.

KARLA: I don't think lesbians would question that we have things in common with gay men, but the problem of gay women and gay men working together as I see it is that we have a list of priorities. Let's take lesbians as a group. Can we work with straight women?

ROSE: We have problems with that.

KARLA: Right! Next we ask whether we can work with gay men. And if we talk about human liberation, then straight men are at the end of the spectrum.

ROSE: Way at the end!

178

KARLA: It's not a clearcut, black/white issue. It's a very gray thing. Gay women come first, but we don't even know as lesbians whether we can work with our straight sisters, because whereas we have our womanhood in common with straight women, I think culturally we probably have more in common with gay people—certain kinds of gay humor, a kind of lifestyle that we don't share with straight women who are locked in nuclear family relationships.

ALLEN: I have mixed reactions to what you said before about male domination. That was something that confused me about the accusations that came out in GLF. When I first came to GLF meetings, I felt that the women were generally more together than the men. The women who spoke at the meetings—I suppose I could mention names, but maybe I shouldn't—their faces and their names are coming to my mind right now.

KARLA: Do you know why? Because there were so few women that when the women spoke you noticed them. There was a monotonous sea of men and they did most of the speaking.

ROSE: And then they'd turn around and say, "Oh, a woman can speak! She's together." They'd applaud. That's a nice compliment, but it's not a compliment in a funny way. The applause was condescending.

KARLA: The problem of the whole GLF was that people were condescending and bending over backwards to try to deal with people's problems, but people were really relating not to people but to labels. They'd say, "Let's have a lesbian, a black lesbian, a transvestite, and a preoperative transsexual, etcetera." The thing about working together is that we weren't really relating to others' needs, we were relating to our conception of how we thought *we* should treat them.

ALLEN: One thing I've noticed, just to sort of jump ahead from that period to this period, is that at the present time, just in terms of what we actually have, is that we have some organizations that are mixed and some organizations that are predominantly male, some publications that are mixed, some publications that are all lesbian, some publications that are all male—there's a little bit of everything going on.

179

ROSE: The thing that discourages me, that's glaringly noticeable, is that any organization in which there are men—the National Gay Task Force, GLF, whatever the hell it happens to be—seems to be more effective. But only because there are men in it, and men have entree to places that women don't. So that a lot of women say, "Look, if we want to get anything done for ourselves, we're going to have to join the men." It's like straight women saying you have to get married.

KARLA: Look at the Gay Academic Union, for example. If you had a gay academic union that was women only, how many people would you have, because how many women are prominent in academia?

ROSE: That's the point. So a lot of lesbians get discouraged. They say to me or to you or whoever it is, "Don't talk like that; we can't have a separate organization. We won't get anywhere." And I say, "Well, maybe we won't, but at least we'll be talking to each other and we're going to be trying. It'll give us some sense of ourselves."

ALLEN: Well, a lot of gay people want to work in the Democratic Party because they feel they won't get anywhere in a gay organization. But I think one of the things gay men have to do is that any gay male organization or publication should be open to women. I don't believe that gay men should establish a publication or an organization that is closed.

KARLA: But *Fag Rag* doesn't include women.

ALLEN: But I argue with them against it. I wouldn't approve of a straight organization that excluded gay people.

ROSE: I don't think it's wrong particularly. Let's put it this way. I'm getting upset with the bar scene because aside from the fact that they charge too much for drinks and they're very raunchy and shitty—aside from all that stuff—because of the women's movement (that raid of the Oak Room and McSorley's) in which the women said, "You can't keep us out," now the men are saying, "You can't keep us out." Okay? So now they want to come into the women's bars. And I'd like to exclude them, because again we're going to have the same hassles.

KARLA: Women excluding men is different from men excluding women. It's exactly what Allen is trying to say. Because men excluding women reinforces our oppression. We don't oppress gay males as they do us, so we should be able to exclude them, but they should not exclude us.

ALLEN: There were two parts to what I was trying to say. One is that gay men's organizations and publications should always be open to women, but that we should also respect the right of women's organizations and publications to be exclusionary, that we should not pressure the women to join men.

There always seem to be gay women who want to work with the men, and those women should be welcome. But there are women who don't, for a lot of reasons that you've mentioned, and I think that needs to be respected.

ROSE: The thing that disturbs me is that the women who want to work with the men (again, it's like heterosexual women)—we lose those women and we need those women. There has to be a way, I don't know how, of having them split their energy.

KARLA: It's hard. I admire the women who can work with the men. I can't, because even a group today, when people have had their consciousness raised to some extent by the media (you hope), they're still saying, "girl" and "chick," and I just haven't got the strength personally to say "woman" every time a man says "girl." But I certainly admire those women who have that kind of energy, and I feel that women should certainly have the opportunity to work with men. But I think because of the very mechanics of groups, every time women go into a mixed group they have to fight for fifty percent of the power, so that women aren't put in a subservient position, and they have to educate the men. There's so much energy expended every time a new group is formed because groups never learn from previous groups' mistakes, so those errors just keep on being repeated. And so although I admire nonseparatism, I understand why the majority of lesbians choose to work in separate groups. And I've found mostly that the places where you find women working with men are primarily small campus groups in colleges where there aren't enough people to have separate lesbian groups.

ROSE: Sometimes they rally around each other for a specific issue, which is okay.

MORTY: Here's a point. As a gay male I certainly respect any gay woman who says we want to have an all-woman's dance, an all-woman's function, an all-woman's organization, and I would never try to intrude myself on such a group. It's like today at the Firehouse. It's a facility that's used by the Gay Activists Alliance. It's also made available to Lesbian Feminist Liberation, which is an all-woman's group. We had a freedom bus that traveled around the city recently. We're all fighting for civil rights legislation in the city, so here was an action where members of both groups decided that we're all interested in seeing this bill pass, and that we're all going to go out in the bus together. And I think at this point as a gay male I have to pretty much take direction from the women as to when they want to cooperate.

KARLA: I think gay people have a much better chance of working together on specific issues rather than in large umbrella-type groups that have no specific purpose. However, I think there's a whole other issue that we haven't even touched on. We're talking only about groups. Can gay men and gay women work together? But there's a question of individuals. And I think that's the other side of the coin. I think that a lot of women have shut themselves off, and a lot of gay men too, to working individually with gay men, or even talking to gay men at all, and they've shut off the entire gay male race. Now I've had a lot of bad experiences with gay men, but I've had a lot of bad experiences with lesbians too. But I think that there are individual gay men whom people can trust, and women have to let themselves be a little more open to see which gay men they can make alliances with (for we will need alliances if we are ever going to change society), and which gay men won't be oppressive to us.

ROSE: Now wait a minute. This smacks, to me, of the arguments that we used to have when I belonged to the New York Radical Feminists, which is, well, not a straight group, but comparatively so. When the women were saying things like, "Yes, men are bad, but my husband is nice. And if I have a good relationship with my husband, the world is rosy and pink and cloudy and everything else, and you can fuck off. And I'm not going to work as hard as I'm supposed to." I think some people get into a trap, saying, "Well, I have a friend. His name is Morty and he's a nice guy, and we have a good relationship, and so you shut up about that man-hating stuff, you know."

KARLA: You're talking about a primary relationship in which a woman talks about her husband and that kind of relationship in which you're usually sexually involved.

ROSE: No, no, because they're not sexually involved with their fathers. They're not sexually involved with the Senator they like. It's all a thing of "*that* man is all right," you see. I know that deep down I am convinced that these two men also, that their consciousness is not so high that we can be that open with each other completely, the way I could with a woman whose consciousness is as high as mine. That's what I'm trying to say. So that I can trust Morty and I can trust Allen. And I can trust Brad Wilson whom I've known for three million years and love very much. But there's a part I cannot trust at all, because there are certain priorities that he's got, secret agendas that he has as a man in this society, that exclude me.

KARLA: I don't feel that way. I feel that Allen, as a person, has been more supportive to me and better to me than a lot of women, who theoretically should have been better able to understand me. But I also understand, on another level, that no matter how close Allen and I can ever be, that should a war come in which men start fighting against women, or something like that, I certainly know which side I'm going to be on, and I'm not going to be fighting with the men shooting women.

ALLEN: I listened to the two of you discussing that, you know, feeling very meek.

KARLA: You look very meek.

ALLEN: And sort of trying to make an analogy with how I feel about straight people; I have straight friends that I feel very close to. And I have some gay friends who are not my friends anymore, or I thought were my friends, and it turns out I have a lot of bad feeling, and I don't care to see them anymore. I saw an old friend (I'll call him Billy) at a conference recently, someone whom I lived with and worked with in New York. He sort of practically recruited me in New York. And we just got into conflict with each other, and developed a real dislike for each other. Yet, this conference was filled with straight people, and there was a straight atmosphere there. Billy was there, and I didn't feel that good about seeing Billy, but there was a certain sense in which I felt that when push comes to shove, somehow, even though I actually preferred to have conversations and to be with some of my straight friends at this gathering, there was some level on which I'm really closer to Billy than I am to those straight people. So I sort of see what you mean. On a human level, I really preferred the company of those straight friends, but on some other level, there is that understanding that Billy as a gay person is somebody that I'm really closer to.

MORTY: I would disagree that we could make these statements categorically. When it comes down to a subjective relationship of trust and confidence, then each one of us has to judge for ourselves. However, I do agree with the point you're making when you're talking about functioning on a political level, in terms of the movement. We have to find the greatest common denominator amongst ourselves, and I fully respect and appreciate the felt need that women have expressed to work together as women in situations without men.

ALLEN: Can I throw something entirely out of left field into this—something really different?

ROSE: Why not?

ALLEN: I heard—maybe this isn't good to do because it's not a personal thing from me—but on a couple of occasions I've heard gay men (and not particularly gay men involved with the movement, but just kind of other gay men) express a distaste for lesbians because of their perceived "butchness" or toughness, the fact that these men (I don't know whether it's a stereotype or something) seem to be afraid of lesbians because lesbians seem to them to be sort of tough. First of all, I wonder if you as lesbians have felt this from gay men, and if there's a counterpart to that where lesbians feel that these gay men are sort of trivial, silly, passive, inoffensive.

KARLA: Well, you know I had that from a gay male roommate of mine. He used to phone his friends and say, "Oh, Mary, these two butches are oppressing me, and I'm just an oppressed femme here with these two butch women. What am I going to do?" And he used that as an excuse never to deal with his male chauvinism, never to do the dishes, never to do anything. He pretended that he was the oppressed woman to get out of doing anything around the house. And it was just in his mind that we were both butches. Obviously we couldn't *both* be butches and live together if he knew anything about stereotypes.

ROSE: I have a feeling that a lot of these gay men are threatened by strong women. They like a woman to be what a woman is supposed to be. It's okay for a gay woman to be gay, but gay men want to see that they're kind of like what women are supposed to be—sort of passive and quiet and things like that. I had an incident at the One Potato. Four of us women went in there to have drinks, just before the dinner hour, but it was very empty. We were just sitting there at a table near the window. Somebody said a joke, and we were laughing, having a good time. And some leather-jacketed creep came past the table. (I must mention that at the bar these men were giggling and screaming and carrying on; it was just something awful. We paid no attention to them and they paid no attention to us.) This leather-jacketed guy passed by and said, "Why don't you bitches shut your mouths?" I said, "Hey, who do you think you're talking to?" And he said, "You're just a bunch of women, that's all." I said, "The men at the bar are giggling." Then he said, "They can do that 'cause they're men." So I said, "I think I'll kill you on the spot if you don't stop it." The women felt intimidated by what I did also. And the waiter came over and said they needed the table for dinner. I just looked at him and said, "I'd like to have another drink." And he said, "Well, we need the table for dinner." I asked, "Are you telling me to leave? I want another drink, and you get it, or get the manager here, and he'll get it, but I don't think you should throw us out. . . . "

MORTY: You're raising two points now. One is about people with different roles—

ROSE: No, that's not the point I'm raising. I think there are an awful lot of gay men that are threatened by strong lesbians. They don't really like women, you see. That may not be you and it may not be Allen.

KARLA: I think the other side of the coin is what happened at the Gay Pride march last year, when a transvestite called us "dirty dykes" and said, "I'm a better woman than you are!" In other words, we are women who don't fit into women's set roles, whereas they dress like very dainty women, as transvestites tend to, so that they feel they are "more women" than we are, that we aren't playing the role as well as they do.

MORTY: In an analogous situation, there's this guy, whom I've never met personally before, who approached me and said he resented me because he had perceived me as being, you know, butch, virile, whatever; he felt that this was an affront to his somewhat more passive carriage. There can be that resentment simply on the basis of roles. Now when you talk about someone who's saying, "Well, because you're a woman you cannot have another drink in this place, or just keep quiet; it's okay for the men to behave that way," you're talking again about two different things—people who first can't deal with the role of other people (or the role they perceive) and the other thing, which is a resentment of women. Certainly, it would be dishonest for any man in this culture to deny sexist feelings. It would be dishonest of any heterosexual to deny homophobic feelings, or any white to deny racist feelings. And those are all things that we have to come to grips with.

ROSE: The point I was really making was that it seems to me that you could take any individual gay male and find out that he may not feel this way, or he's coping with it, or he's struggling with it, or whatever. We were talking about "should men and women work together," and the only reason I'm bringing up these "isolated cases" (we'll call them "isolated cases"—though they're really not very isolated) is that when you multiply that incident by the hundreds, in an organization like GAA or GLF or XYZ or National Gay Task Force, or whatever it happens to be, I do believe that a lot of the men in these organizations harbor these hidden feelings. And it only took a kind of *macho* creep like the guy in the leather jacket to voice it.

KARLA: Let me comment on something. You said, "*macho* creep," and I think the stereotype of gay men that turns off gay women is not the so-called effeminateness of gay men so much as the supermasculine type of gay man, which I think to gay women symbolizes the gay man who rejects women because they are "inferior." The thing that most gay women always objected to about GAA is all the leather and chains they hear clanking—which to them means supermasculinity.

186

MORTY: Something I've resented a lot which I've heard frequently in recent times from prominent women spokespeople in the lesbian-feminist movement has been to denigrate this swishy man, to make a point which could well be made without condemning feminine or effeminate men.

ALLEN: But Karla just said that she felt that the women responded negatively mostly to the supermasculine drag.

KARLA: Yes, but don't forget that women also object to so-called "effeminate" men. And the whole thing about very effeminate men is a double-edged sword. On the one hand, I admire effeminate men because they are breaking down roles, and transvestites because a lot of them are doing their thing very consciously to parody roles, especially men who call themselves effeminists and who do "gender-fuck." The latter often are not wearing female clothes but they have long hair and a "feminine" style. But the other side of the coin is the transvestite (the one who most often offends lesbians) who usually does caricatures of women for money, for entertainment, for exploitation. And there's a line between the ones who are doing it because they really believe that this is the way they feel naturally—this is how they feel comfortable—and they really see it as an anti-role thing, and those who are doing it for profit and entertainment. Of course, not all lesbians can see the difference because what you first see is the surface, which may look the same in both cases.

ROSE: Do you really think that all the men who are doing that are aware they're doing it as a breaking down of a role, or are they doing it to accept a role for themselves?

KARLA: I'm saying there's a difference of motivation. It's hard to see when you're looking at the surface.

ROSE: Some of the motivation is to accept the role, because I met a man who was—well, he wasn't quite a transsexual but he was in the transition stage of being one, I suppose. He got up at a panel at Queens College and said that he was more of a woman than I was, because he wanted to be "the little woman," and to do for his man and stuff like that . . . and I laid him out. I mean, he changed his mind after a few minutes, but the point is that their motivation is to be better at being women than even women are, while acting out conditioned women's things.

MORTY: I saw a very interesting drag act about three years ago when I was doing some organizing in the South. There was a bar there, and they billed drag shows. It was a very popular place. Lots of gays came. They even had a lot of straight people coming in to see what's happening there. Okay. One transvestite got up and was singing, doing the lip synch and the whole works, and then came a song, "This is My Life." And at the point he took off his wig, and he was singing, "This is my life, I am a transvestite," and he took off his eyelashes—"this is my life"—and took off his dress, and finally he came down to a pair of shorts, underneath it all. He was making a very personal statement. There are very few drag acts that I've ever enjoyed, or very few that even have any political messages.

KARLA: If you go into that: The thing that women object to about transvestites is just that, that a man can take off his oppression as he pulls off his false eyelashes and his wig and his dress. But we wear it all our lives.

MORTY: I think you're missing the point. He was making a comment about the clothes he was wearing—

ROSE: I think you're missing a woman's point right here, Morty, seriously.

MORTY: Okay, I'm willing to listen.

ROSE: Seriously! Because since he is, since he was (I don't know if he still is) in this particular instance acting like "a woman," Karla was trying to tell you her reaction to it, and what I heard you say was, "That's not valid because what he meant was something different." You have to hear the things that come across to women when men do this kind of thing. Otherwise, I don't think you're getting the point about when we say we can't work with men.

MORTY: If you're making a point about guys who are caricaturing women, that's one thing. If you're making a point about behaving in different role patterns, or dressing in different kinds of clothes, then I

188

would still reserve my position that that would be okay. Because you as a female can dress in many different ways, you can also behave in many different ways, and can put on or take off how society will perceive that oppression.

ROSE: That's not quite accurate. I can't really behave in many different ways. Not really. I mean if I put a man's suit on and a hat, and smoked a pipe and walked down the street, I might get beaten up by all the men in the neighborhood. I don't know. I wouldn't even try because I don't like to wear suits.

MORTY: Okay.

ROSE: The thing is that we have strata. My feeling in one very large area is that men who dress in what I call "unreal" women's clothing—the bouffant hair, the wigs, the eye make-up, the false eyelashes, whatever—they are *all* as far as I'm concerned, caricaturing a woman. They are caricaturing a women, 'cause that is not a woman, and they're saying, "It *is* a woman. We'll show you! We're better women than you are, see we have longer eyelashes, we have larger bazzooms . . . " (laughter)

ALLEN: How do you spell "bazzooms"? I'm going to have to transcribe this tape!

KARLA: B-a-z-z-o-o-o-m-s. Can we get off transvestites? It's almost like talking behind their backs because they really should have someone here to defend transvestites.

ROSE: Yes, let's get off transvestites.

KARLA: I don't know about Morty, but I think the three of us live kind of separatist lifestyles. I could talk from my own experience. I live with a woman. I have very little contact with men. I don't work on a job where I have to deal with men. There's a check-out woman in the supermarket. (Laughter) I interact only with women. In the feminist community in New York, you can kind of get women to do everything. If you need carpentry, a woman can do it. If you need your car repaired, you can find a woman car mechanic. And I live a separatist lifestyle.

189

And Allen lives on a farm with men. I mean, how often do you come into contact with women?

Being a separatist affects our lives. For me, part of being a lesbian separatist, which I kind of consider myself, three quarters, is that when I actually do come into contact with straight men, the shock is a lot ruder, because I'm leading a sheltered life, and in my life a lot of fantasies have developed about the way things can be—with gay men and with straight men—and so when I'm confronted with the reality of how people behave, I find it very shocking. And maybe some of the separatism then is bad because I almost forget the harsh realities.

ROSE: I don't think it's bad. I'm not terribly shocked when I come into contact with men. I expect men to be rude. When they're nice, that gives me a shock! I expect them to be the way they are, and they never fail to be that way, really. They're always obnoxious; they're always assholes.

MORTY: Come on, you're getting a little bit too heavy.

ROSE: No, I'm not going too far.

MORTY: Certainly you're entitled to, but I think you're doing so unfairly, because around a lot of gay people, both men and women, I find a lot of things offensive.

ROSE: Good, then you should say so. You see, I've been saying so.

MORTY: Okay, I do. But people are human, and I think you must also find a lot of women who are gay, lesbians, you must find a lot of their sensibilities—

ROSE: Why is it, Morty, that every time I answer Karla's statement about a particular thing that involves, as she said, being away from men, then going toward them, and I'm answering that particular thing, it seems incumbent upon you to jump in and say, "Well, women are bad, too!" Well, no one said they weren't, okay? (General pandemonium)

MORTY: You're attacking me very heavily and I think unfairly.

ROSE: I don't attack a lot of men enough.

190

MORTY: Maybe it's the categorical inference that I'm making from what you're saying.

ROSE: You see, Morty, we *are* at odds. There's a reason why we are at odds. You like men; they're your life. They're your sexual output, input, whatever. They're not mine; I don't particularly like them, okay? And when you say that people do human things, sometimes I find them to be doing inhuman things. And I'm not saying that women don't. There's a lot of lesbians I don't like also. We were talking about the shock that Karla receives, being a separatist, going out and seeing what men do, and I answered and I said that I was not surprised.

ALLEN: One thing. At first, my initial reaction to that little interchange was to be very sympathetic to Rose, but as a result of listening to you more, I could see why Morty responded that way.

ROSE: Of course.

KARLA: I don't understand anything. What am I doing here?

ALLEN: The sexual aspect . . .

ROSE: Where's my baby powder? . . . Allen, I'm sorry.

ALLEN: That's okay. The sexual aspect is somehow a part of it. It's sort of underneath all of this in a way. I've heard lesbians express this—very easily—because it doesn't cost them anything, expressing a disdain for the male body. Penises are somehow terribly distasteful and disgusting. But I just love to look at a man who turns me on and suck the cock of a man who turns me on.

ROSE: You just keep right on doing it! I'll find you all the men you want for you! I'm all for it. I think all men should be gay. I really do. I think they understand each other; I think they dig each other, really. This whole "brotherhood of man" is very true.

ALLEN: But you don't want that in a situation in which men have power over women.

ROSE: Oh, no. Personally, I think that if all men suddenly became

191

homosexual, I don't think you'd have all this hatred around. I don't think that the world would be the way it is because they would be finding each other, which is who they're looking for, you know. They're just fucking women over because of all the other oppression that's going on with them. I think they should be gay. I think women should be lesbians; and I think the world would be much better for it. But that's like, you know, a pipe dream, of course.

MORTY: It's never necessary, in fact I think it's inexpedient, for other people to be attacked in order for us, or one group to affirm.

ROSE: I don't agree with that, no I can't. . . . I know what you're saying. It's the whole conservative, or rather liberal viewpoint—

MORTY: No!

ROSE: I interrupted him. I didn't even give him a chance to say what he was saying. . . .

MORTY: Let's talk in terms of all of us as lesbians and gay men up against heterosexuals, especially heterosexual men. I think we're up against a repression of feelings. Now, we can go so far laying guilt trips on heterosexual men for being anti-feeling, and then they're going to find their backs up against the wall. I think in the long run what's going to get through to them more effectively is when we start to set a positive example in our own lifestyles of embracing and expressing our feelings. The things that have shocked heterosexual men most when we've been on demonstrations is not when we are out there on the picket line with our fists in the air, but when we kiss each other hello—two women kissing each other, two men kissing each other. That positive example, the expression of those feelings, that's my point, encouraging people, setting an example.

ROSE: All right, you're kind of saying, if we say, as the gay liberation movement seems to have been saying, "We are the same as you are. We're human beings. We love. We just happen to love a person of our own sex and that's just one of those things." Well, I can't.

MORTY: I'm saying more than that, though.

ROSE: I understand the political philosophy of that, and the strategy, but I can't really abide it because I am not the same as everybody else. My oppression doesn't make me like a heterosexual at all. The experiences I've had not only as a woman but as a lesbian makes me so different from a heterosexual—the way I think, the way I see the world, what I want from life. It's very different. I do not want to be like them. To be like them is death.

ALLEN: Morty is saying that we have something to teach them.

ROSE: I don't want to teach them anything. I just want to be left alone. I don't want them to harass me, or you either. But I don't want to teach them something. Even with gay men, in the gay liberation thing, it's like what women have to do for men, it's like servicing them again, teaching them how to be kind. And I don't believe that we're saying they don't have feelings. Heterosexual men have a lot of feelings—they're not very good ones, though.

KARLA: Morty's one step ahead of where the movement is at. We're still at the point of teaching ourselves, getting our own heads together.

MORTY: Just to put my thoughts into one sentence: I think we can fight our oppression through the affirmation of our feelings, our freedom.

ROSE: Well, I'm not sure. I agree that we should affirm our feelings. But I don't think that really in the long run it works. All right, the Stonewall Riot . . .

MORTY: We affirmed our anger then.

ROSE: We should still be angry.

MORTY: Absolutely.

ROSE: But to teach the heterosexual world that it's wrong to oppress people—I'm tired of that. Don't they know it already? What more do I have to teach these idiots? How many years do I have to be on the streets teaching these jerks they shouldn't oppress people?

KARLA: I don't think that we're ever going to teach them, because they know what's right and what's wrong, but it's not in the interest of the oppressor ever to give up his power. I mean, men know that women are oppressed, but they won't liberate women because they've got us where they want us, and they're benefiting by our oppression. We're never going to show them a positive example and "win their hearts." We're going to have to *take* it from them, and the only way we're going to do that is to get ourselves together and make them give it up.

MORTY: What we're saying is complementary. I don't mean to say one to the exclusion of the other. When someone shits on you, you get angry and show that anger. That's an affirmation of your feeling at that time.

ROSE: You're talking about the philosophy of working within the circumstantial thing. When circumstances dictate a particular kind of thing, you react to that thing. When they're nicer, you react to the nicety. Is that what you mean?

MORTY: I think when a heterosexual makes a real effort to communicate—

ROSE: Don't ever trust that, okay?

MORTY: I think they need positive reinforcement, if they're really showing an effort.

ROSE: Men are changing because they think it's expedient to do so. They think they're going to get something for it. They change abortion laws, for example, only because it's more expedient for them—because the ecology is asking for less babies. They know that women are oppressed with having abortions in back alleys, in small hotels, but they wanted the money. Now, they've decided there are supposed to be less children, so they'll give it to you. But then they'll change the law again if it suits them. So don't trust the heterosexuals, you can't trust them, because they're doing it for reasons unbeknown to us.

KARLA: After all, they're mentally ill, being straight to begin with! (Laughter) Maybe we should wrap this up. We do have enough.

194

SOME THOUGHTS ON
HOW GAY MEN RELATE
TO WOMEN

Allen Young

They say we hate women, fear them, are disgusted by their bodies, want to live in a world without them, want to be like them, worship them, wish we were women ourselves. They "blame" our mothers (and tend not to mention our fathers) for our awful fate. There are women who are disgusted by us, threatened by us, intrigued by us, contemptuous of us, and supportive of us.

I have seen many generalizations about the relationship of male homosexuals to women. Much of this is sweeping dogma that has little connection to my own reality. It is impossible, I think, to generalize about this topic for the simple reason that there are so many different male homosexuals and so many different women. But, on the other hand, the feminist movement and the gay liberation movement have attempted to forge a *group identity* for women and a *group identity* for homosexuals, so accordingly it is worth exploring the way that these two categories of people interact, the way that they are interrelated.

I do not feel that I have ever hated women or have ever been disgusted by women's bodies. But I have met male homosexuals who have such feelings. Where does this come from? I think it comes from a male supremacist society, one which adores masculinity. A homosexual man failing to achieve the treasured and sought-after traits of masculinity, then, could easily become a person who hates the *visible* source of "femininity"—namely, women. The rabidly male supremacist homosexual must be, on some level, a self-hating person. As this self-hatred subsides, as happens through gay liberation, gay men can be more loving toward women.

There are some well-established, uniquely close relationships between gay men and women. For example, there is a significant number of male homosexuals who gravitate toward certain gay professions which have a unique relationship to women—hairdressing, fashion design, cosmetics, interior decoration. Because some men in these fields fit the so-called stereotype homosexual, there is a tendency or a desire within the gay liberation movement to dismiss or ignore such

195

individuals—something which has always struck me as a bit anti-gay. Some feminists have suggested that men in such professions are complying in the exploitation of women, in that they help keep women in their most unliberated roles—sex object and housekeeper. These feminists may well be right; the fact that a woman seeks out a hairdresser voluntarily begs the question. Possibly some gay men choose these jobs because they have cultivated an appreciation for what they imagine to be feminine standards of beauty. Ours has been a society of "real men" and "real women." A faggot who accepts this dichotomy, and who doesn't make it as a "real man," has only one other choice—being a "real woman." This mentality, perhaps, motivates some transvestites (drag queens) and transsexuals (someone whose sex is altered surgically). Transsexuals like to think of themselves as women trapped in a man's body. Transvestism and transsexualism, however, are "extreme" choices, in the sense that few people have the inclination or the courage, so for some gay men, a better choice in this incredible role-playing game is to help "real women" fulfill the female role most perfectly and most beautifully. Perhaps both faggot and woman in such situations share a sense of joy, fulfillment, and beauty—while perhaps on another level they share a sense of pain, inadequacy, and ugliness. Possibly, of course, the gay men in such professions choose them for simpler reasons. For one thing, these are among the few professions where a homosexual has job security—he will not be fired if his sexual preference is known. In addition, gay men in such fields probably feel more comfortable being surrounded by women, simply because they perceive women as nicer, gentler, and less threatening than most straight men. There is a unique level of intimacy, confidence, and friendship, I am told, between male hairdresser and client.

I should take note of the fact that some women prefer the friendship of gay men because they discover that we can relate to them as people and not as sex objects. These same women are often disappointed, and sometimes angry, when we foresake their friendship in order to be with or search after a sex object (in this case, a man). *or to "choose sides" like Rusty & Toby*

Some women prefer the friendship of gay men above all other kinds of relationships, and in camp language such women are called fruit flies or fag hags. Some fag hags—the term seems ugly to me, both anti-woman and anti-gay—develop strong friendships with one or more gay men. I can't say what motivates such women, or why they enjoy an evening in a gay men's bar, but I know some lesbians believe that fag hags are closet lesbians, that is, women who know they do not wish to

196

be sexually dominated by a straight man but who are afraid to enter into the female side of the gay world. One comment I've heard about fag hags is that they are attracted to gay men for the challenge of it all—in the hopes of "curing" us or "making" us. Some gay men truly enjoy the company of such women, some are contemptuous of them, and some find such friendships convenient for straight-fronting (that is, putting on a heterosexual show) for family, employer, or social acquaintances.

Another special relationship between gay men and women is the incredible attraction of the gay male community for certain female entertainment stars. The late Judy Garland, of course, tops the list, and there is also Barbra Streisand, Liza Minelli, Bette Midler, Marlene Dietrich, Bette Davis, Katharine Hepburn, and perhaps others. I have often felt alienated from the gay male community because I do not generally worship these heroines. Why do gay men love these women so? Some say it is because of the imagery of strong independence that some of these women project. Judy Garland was popular, I was once told by a friend, because gay men could identify with her tragic struggle to survive. Some say it is merely the image of style and stardom that these women project. Whatever the reason, it certainly is a cultural phenomenon of considerable importance, and it gives the lie to the statement that gay men have no place in their world for women.

Is a male homosexual the ultimate male supremacist? Or are gay men likely to be among the males most supportive of the goals of women's liberation? Both ideas have been expressed by feminists. One thing is certain: male homosexuals are preoccupied with the fact that on some level we are womanly, or we are considered womanly by this society.

I have heard men call their asshole a pussy, and I have heard men express revulsion at the idea of smelling or tasting or even looking at a vagina. I have met *macho* bi-sexuals who would just as soon fuck a woman as a man (any hole will do). Some of these bi-sexuals really prefer anal sex with women—which I believe they experience as the ultimate in domination and humiliation. In camp lingo, gay men use such terms as "Miss Thing" and the pronoun "she" as a put-down. Some drag queens mock women or impersonate women on the stage in order to make a living. (Some lesbians have stated that they feel that drag shows are exploitive of women.) But it is the butch image that is the sexual preference for most gay men, and many male homosexuals cultivate a masculine identity with care and pride (as in, "I may suck cock, but I'm a man"). For most gay men it is still a compliment to be told, "Oh, you don't act like a homosexual—I never would have guessed!" Most gay men are turned off to drag queens and to effeminate men because the male homosexual's sex object, in the end, is a man. Some gay men are uncomfortable with lesbians—or dislike them—and are turned off to feminism because such women disrupt the well-established imagery of womankind. Even within the gay liberation movement, men have remained insensitive to the ways in which we embody a male supremacist society, and this has been a major factor in the establishment of an independent lesbian movement.

I say all of this to acknowledge the fact that male supremacist values, the internalization of stereotyped role-playing, infest the male homosexual community. A significant portion of gay men, at least superficially, have aligned themselves with men, have affirmed their manhood, and in so doing they ignore (at best) or combat (at worst) the goals of the feminist movement.

Gay liberation *without* feminism—and sadly this is the state of a significant part of the gay movement—cannot really deal with the source of homosexual oppression. For that source is the system of sex roles propagated by a male supremacist society. Gay men managing to obtain the privileges of straight men ("civil rights") may ultimately achieve the economic and political status given to heterosexuals. But, as long as the heterosexual nuclear family remains intact and respected, as long as the masculine image remains admirable, male homosexuals will continue to be marginal people. We will be misfits while others form their families; we will be cocksuckers and faggots (womanly nonmen), while only those men who fuck women will earn the cherished label "man."

Gay liberation *with* feminism is the only logical solution to the problems we face as male homosexuals in this society. My argument here, despite all that I have said about male supremacy among gay men, is that there are many indicators of an already well-developed unity in practice between gay pride and strong, independent womanhood. In other words, we are already well along the way, as gay men, toward a beautiful and strong alliance with women.

Well I remember the yellow brick schoolhouse in Woodridge, New York, where I learned to read and write. On one side of the building, the boys played a modified baseball game called "three feet." You had to throw a ball against the wall; there were teams, and if you didn't do well, your teammates would resent you. On the other side of the building, the girls jumped rope ("Down in Mississippi, where the boats

198

go *push*!"—see, I still remember). Was I a "male homosexual" at age six? Certainly not, but I was a fairy all right. I threw a ball "like a girl." And I found my place quickly enough with the girls and the jumprope.

It was simple enough, I think—the boys rejected me, or I rejected them and their competitive games, and I felt at home and welcome among the girls. Well, maybe I didn't quite feel "at home," because on some level I knew it was "wrong" for me to jump rope with the girls, I knew I belonged on the other side of the school, but the girls offered me affection and acceptance. I know from conversations with many dozens of gay men that this experience is almost universal among us: early childhood friendship and feeling of ease with girls.

My problems with relating to girls began with the emergence of my sexual identity at puberty. To a great extent, my easy friendship with girls continued all through junior high school, high school, and college. Many of these friendships were based on my attraction for the girls who, like me, got "good marks" in school. Later, some of it was political—my female friends were comrades in such groups as the Student Committee for a Sane Nuclear Policy. But I also was becoming an overtly sexual being for perhaps the first time (being unaware of such childhood sexual feeling). Much of my erotic energy went toward males, and I had sex occasionally from age thirteen on with boys (and once with an older man). But I tried very hard to be straight, and in so trying I found myself getting into relationships with some young women that can only be called contrived. In one case, when I was sixteen or seventeen, I purposely sought the company of a thirteen-year-old girl who, in the parlance of the times, had a "bad reputation," and we used to dry fuck together. I dated and necked rather compulsively, though I didn't enjoy this semi-sex very much, and I anxiously awaited the day when I would lose my hated and frightening virginity.

Throughout this period, I was not a self-aware homosexual. I knew I had a "problem," but I did not identify myself as homosexual entirely. Even after a long homosexual affair with a college roommate, I hoped to strengthen my straight identity. I expected to find my gay feelings fade into the past, just as the books said they would. As a straight-identified man, I of course did not encounter homosexuals in openly gay situations, though it turns out that still another roommate of mine was a closet homosexual. While I was living with him, I began a rather serious affair with a very nice young woman. I told her I loved her, and I suppose I did, and we even talked of marriage. But in all honesty I think what I really loved was the feeling of *belonging* that I had when I was with her in the company of my straight friends who had already formed into couples.

Shortly thereafter, I became fully integrated into a homosexual lifestyle, and I ceased making love with women altogether. Actually, I did try from time to time, but I couldn't keep a hard-on. However, I found that as I became a more sexual and sensual person, women began to find me attractive—much more so than before. Since I no longer desired the sexual company of women, but was afraid to tell them the reasons why, I found myself building barriers between myself and women. It became more difficult to have casual friendships with women. Especially as the cult of virginity waned in the mid-1960's, I found the casual company of women more and more difficult.

I did not like these barriers that I had built, and I did not really like the entire notion of a secret life. I was able, even before the gay liberation movement, to tell a few friends that I was gay—and most of these friends were women. And later, after gay liberation strengthened my sense of gay pride and identity, it was to women that I first opened up. It was easier telling women than telling straight men. This is another universal experience of male homosexuals. In our families, too, it is easier to tell our sisters than our brothers, easier to tell our mothers than our fathers. True, mothers wring their hands ("What did I do wrong?") and ex-girlfriends may feel a sense of loss and rejection, but there seems to be a level of understanding and acceptance of which men are not capable. And no wonder, did you ever hear of a woman beating someone up because he is a faggot?

I have noticed that my friendships with women I knew from our work together in the New Left in the late 1960's have in several cases been strengthened in this post-gay-liberation period. We are able to talk more openly, it seems, not about current events or Marxian analysis, but about our immediate human experiences. With straight men I know from similar days gone by, the contact is often more strained—if it has continued at all.

I am close to three women in my family—my mother, my sister, and an aunt (my mother's sister). Our relationships after my coming out have vastly improved. This is no doubt a result of three factors: first, my ability at last to be open and honest; second, my familiarity with feminism and my ability to use this knowledge to communicate better with the women close to me; and third, my new-found ability to be less intellectual and to be in touch with my feelings and other people's feelings, an ability I associate with nurturing feminine aspects of my personality.

As many people know, there is a theory very popular among professional and amateur psychologists that male homosexuals are created by dominant, overprotective mothers. Before my contact with feminism and gay liberation, I was to a great extent victimized by this theory, and as a result I did not feel good about my mother. I think, at the outset, we need to face up to the fact that most mothers can be described as "dominant and overprotective" if by that we mean that they are responsible for keeping up a home and assuming primary responsibility for giving a child affection (or any emotional response) and support. The entire line of thinking, I feel, becomes a sham.

I refuse to accept the notions of traditional psychology that certain behavior by parents will assure the sexual identity of a child. For example, I knew of many cases of families with so-called dominant mothers and weak fathers where the children are quite heterosexual. I know of homosexuals who come from homes where the fathers are tyrannical and the mothers silent and prayerful, while such households also produce heterosexuals. On the other hand, I will not say—as some gay liberationists do—that what parents do is unrelated to a child's sexual identity. It may be a factor. And if we feel good about ourselves, how can we "blame" our parents for anything?

For me, the crucial fact is that my parents did not force too many sex role stereotypes on me. For example, my father never pushed sports on me, for which I am keenly grateful, though sometimes I wish I had a stronger, more athletic body. I think people perceived my mother as dominant, but I know that she does not run things. While gentle and not a tyrant, my father is much more likely to get his way in a given situation. Given the conditions of most twentieth-century American marriages, however, my mother is quite an independent woman. I first heard the term "male chauvinism" from the lips of my mother. It was in the 1950's; I was but a boy, and if I am not mistaken she was talking about a certain cousin of hers who, indeed, is a male chauvinist. (My mother learned such vocabulary, by the way, from her association, since ended, with the Communist Party, and while she, true to the spirit of anti-sexist politics, has often used the ideology of anti-sexism in her personal life, the Party has seen fit to attack modern-day feminism in the name of its narrow brand of proletarian politics.)

My relationship with my mother, however, has not been all that great. My negative attitude toward my mother was quite simple; I knew

201

I was a sissy, I knew that being a sissy was a terrible thing, and somehow I associated my mother's care and affection and protective attitude toward me with the fact of my being a sissy. So I resented her and her ebullient affection, and most communication between us was spoiled by this dynamic. After coming out, and especially after understanding the undesirability of straight manhood, I was able to open up to my mother and to accept her affection. She can kiss me now as much as she likes, and I kiss her back not reluctantly but sincerely. My mother found out about my gayness accidentally—she spotted a gay liberation button I left carelessly on a sweater. I had been wanting to tell her anyway. She was not happy with the news, and she still has not recovered from the shock and disappointment. She is not one of those very rare mothers who will show up at a gay liberation march. But I think I have convinced her at the very least that there is much value in the improved communication between us, and she continues to respect and love me. She shares with me, too, in a way she did not before.

It is not uncommon for a male homosexual who is a fully grown man to live with his mother. While I once thought such an arrangement ridiculous, I could now seriously consider it—in general, I believe in communal living arrangements where there is a full age span from small children to old folks.

My sister and I (she's four years younger) were great friends and playmates throughout childhood, but when she became a sexual being she entered into awesome conflict with my basically puritanical parents. From that moment on, there was a great barrier between me and my sister. I couldn't be open with her about sex, I believed, because I couldn't reveal my own truths. I didn't want to know her side of things because then I'd have been obliged to tell about myself (out of the question). So I *seemed* to take my parents' side. Only many years later, after I came out, did we begin to get close again. Now we have a "no secrets" relationship which is by no means perfect, but which is unusually solid for sister and brother.

My aunt is someone I consider one of my best and most loyal friends. I have felt that way about her ever since I was a small child. She was the first relative I told about my gayness, and her response was consistent with this established love and loyalty and trust. Perhaps her involvement with people in the theater and the dance has been a factor. She is an open, incredibly self-aware person. Last year, while I was on a visit to Florida, she and her husband were quarreling, as they often do.

At her bidding, I went out with her several evenings to drink and dance at a nearby resort hotel. In the meantime, I discovered a lively gay dancing bar just a few blocks away from her apartment. Being somewhat bored by the straight scene she'd taken me to for several nights running, I suggested we go to the gay bar. She immediately accepted, and we both had a very nice time together, socializing and dancing, not only with each other but with people we met at the bar. Many gay men I know have close, loving relationships with an aunt or a grandmother.

Perhaps one of the most important relationships I have had with a woman is with Karla Jay, a lesbian with whom I have worked together on various gay liberation projects. To the extent that this working and social relationship has been successful, it is in part due to my conscious efforts toward respecting Karla's autonomy as a woman and as a lesbian, and in not permitting the straight male world to assume, as it is wont to do, that a man is always in charge. In any case, no matter what my intentions might be, Karla is not going to put up with any shit from me or any man.

It is one thing for gay men to have private relationships with women. We also are confronted with the reality of a strong, vital, growing feminist movement. We are men, not women, yet we cannot and should not remain aloof from the demands of angry proud women. As a starter, we can read feminist literature and support the demands of the organized women's movement. We should see such demands as being in our own interest.

One small group of gay men who call themselves "effeminists" have argued that gay men should place themselves virtually in the service of women. These men, I think, envision a world run by women with men in subordinate position. They want gay men to take the lead in this reversal of power. It is my understanding, however, that most feminists and most gay liberationists, most people of goodwill, seek a world of equality without power trips. That, presumably, is why we are busy combatting male supremacy. Having said this, I think it is worth pointing out that gay men are already more at home than straight men in such situations as cooking and housekeeping. It has been my observation that straight men tend to assume that women will serve them in certain areas, especially cooking and housekeeping. I do not think that gay men, when they live with women, make such assumptions, except, of course, married closet cases who can be typical husbands.

The area of child care and education, which our culture assigns to women, is of special interest to gay men. Many of us are exploring ways out of the trap set by society which separates us from the newer generations. It is no coincidence that among men who choose elementary education as a field, for example, the percentage of homosexuals is quite high. Many of the married homosexuals I have met say they are motivated to continue their marriages largely by their love for their children. Some gay men seek out work in child care centers, though unfortunately many of these centers, whether run by agencies or parents, do not welcome homosexuals or anti-sexists on their staffs. There are gay fathers with the custody of their own children, and there are gay men who'd like to adopt children, though this is usually impossible. Some gay men, of course, are not particularly interested in children, and though some may dogmatically label this as "privilege" or male chauvinism, it seems to me to be as much a matter of individual choice for gay men, as it is for straight married people or lesbians, to remain childless.

It is not always easy for a gay man to figure out how he relates to the half of humanity he is not involved with sexually—especially when society implies that sex is the main reason for men to relate to women. But relating to women is a part of gay life that is real and important, especially inasmuch as we define "gay" as more than just a sexual preference. The relationship of gay men to women is, in many ways, entering a new era with the advent of gay liberation and the Second Wave of feminism. Our tendency to relate more easily to women on many levels is a well-established fact, to the extent that we recognize and accept the parts of our personalities that are more "feminine." But, still, ours is a society which teaches men that women are for fucking. Our erotic impulses, for whatever reason, are in another direction. If we accept this most male supremacist notion of women—that women are for fucking and nothing more—then we have no use for women. As I said before, I believe there are a significant number of gay men who have such a view. (Straight men who have such a view—perhaps the majority of straight men—do indeed have a "use" for women, but often it is precisely within the confines of that word, "use.") I have indicated that gay men who are out of the closet, who have broken the barriers of shame and self-hatred and secrecy, are able to discover equal relationships with women. If we have love and respect for all human beings, in their fullest dimensions, we can find rich and fulfilling relationships with women.

OPPRESSION IS BIG BUSINESS:
Scrutinizing Gay Therapy

Karla Jay

The purpose of the following article is not to point a finger at a specific business, or to name names (either good or bad), or to imply that *all* lesbian/feminist therapists are corrupt, but rather to delineate the *patterns of corruption* of a few so that we can protect ourselves now and in the future from those who would exploit us. In fact it is even painful to me—having once sincerely believed as a Redstocking that *all* women are my sisters—to have discovered and then have to warn others of a flock of rip-off artists in our very midst. I would also like to point out that I have zeroed in on the therapy industry only as an example of *one* type of rip-off in the gay community. Therefore, the causes of corruption and the solution for it should be applicable to other rip-off businesses in the gay community, such as some gay bars, restaurants, and clubs, and to rip-off individuals such as some gay writers and entertainers who have gotten rich quick in the aftermath of Stonewall.

HISTORY OF THERAPY IN THE MOVEMENT

Some of us who first organized the radical gay women's movement tended to view all our problems as "class problems"; that is, all our problems stemmed from the oppressor—white, male, heterosexual society. All our hang-ups, therefore, were not individual problems with individual solutions but a class struggle with a societal solution. Consciousness-raising was used as a vehicle for women to realize our class oppression, to feel rage toward our true oppressors instead of turning that rage inward or onto other women.

Consciousness-raising was our answer to psychotherapy. Psychotherapy *usually* (I don't want to make pat statements about all types of therapy) encourages the individual to "adjust to" or "cope with" or "accept" society or oneself. Consciousness-raising, on the other hand, showed us that individual adjustment is not the answer and that society, not the individual woman, must change. Our pain, anger, frustration, and oppression belong to every woman and cannot be viewed as individual neurosis.

Needless to say, we were and are justifiably antagonistic to male-dominated schools of psychotherapy and their practitioners. Who hasn't heard horror stories of lesbians and male homosexuals being mistreated, traumatized, shock-treated, and even lobotomized by therapists? After all, didn't most of them consider us "sick," "perverse," or "abnormal" just because we were gay? Didn't they ignore our just grievances and attribute all our problems to our sexuality? Wasn't the thrust of therapy to "cure" us of lesbianism? And the "liberals" were and are perhaps even more disgusting with their patronizing attitudes. And even when they did accept us as homosexuals, they still laid other reactionary trips on us. In other words, while they considered it all right to be gay, a woman still had to look "feminine" to be considered a "normal" homosexual. The recent change in the labeling of homosexuals by the American Psychiatric Association is a good example of this liberal mentality: While they did change us from sick to merely "sexually disoriented," they didn't think of including some heterosexuals, who might want to convert to homosexuality, in the same category!

In any case, I suppose many felt that we had replaced therapy with consciousness-raising. Eventually, however, it became increasingly clear that problems existed beyond or perhaps outside of our oppression as lesbians (although pure "classists" would not agree with this position). Many consciousness-raising groups in which I participated or which I knew of became burdened by, obsessed with, or destroyed by the personal problems of one member of the group—problems which could not readily be tied with our general oppressions by straights. Another common problem was often conflict between members of the group. Another problem of the movement in general was that it was not easy to explain the suicides of "liberated, uncloseted" gays, who supposedly no longer gave a damn about the values of judgment of straight society, but who killed themselves anyway.

The entire movement, in fact, seemed to be burdened by those women who came into the movement to find a cure for their problems, or to find mediators for their relationships. Yes, a primary function of the movement is to support our sisters in every way possible, but it seemed increasingly difficult to make political progress, to formulate actions, and even simply to think when everyone was screaming, "Give me, save me, fill this need, fill that need!" In other words, women were draining strength from the movement instead of bringing strength *to* it. Instead of asking what they could do for the movement or to liberate other sisters, they were interested only in what would be done for them—and immediately.

The movement had not satisfied our needs, such as loneliness and despair, and the personal needs of our sisters are, of course, justified. Therefore, in response to this need, there grew a body of therapists, analysts, and peer counselors to deal with these problems. In New York, at least, being in therapy became somewhat of a vogue, and women followed and praised certain therapists in tones usually reserved for gurus. Shrinks were even called in to mediate at certain consciousness-raising groups—once the sacred grounds of political analysis. And now, although consciousness-raising groups seem to be losing popularity, the trend back toward psychoanalysis seems to be gaining, and it seems that psychologically many women have come a full circle.

PSYCHOTHE*RIP*Y: ADDLED FREUD AND FRAUD

With the rise of therapy, a variety of unscrupulous shrinks appeared and still exist in our midst. These shrinks have deceived us in many ways. First, we are being deceived because many of the so-called therapists are unqualified to be therapists. "Unqualified" is a tricky word, so I will try to give concrete examples of what I mean. To begin with, to call yourself a "therapist" in New York State, for example, you have to have certain degrees in psychology. Several of the therapists here have degrees all right, but in English, art history, etc. Personally, I have several degrees in literature and next year will be able legally to call myself "doctor," but I still would not dare tamper with another person's mind, let alone *charge* her for it!

Don't get me wrong: I'm not for qualifications in the legal or educational sense of the word. Twenty years of Freud and Jung will probably just rot your brain. However, I like to know what I'm getting, and I think all Americans are becoming wary consumers. When I go to the supermarket, for example, I read the ingredients of everything before I buy them because I'm a vegetarian and I want to make sure the producers aren't slipping a little meat in on the side. Applying this same principle of "truth in advertising," I want to know what went into my shrink. If she's a doctor, but a doctor of botany, I should know that because I'm not a plant. If she is on welfare for insanity, as is one counselor I know of, I should know that. Only with adequate information can you make a rational choice. You may still want to choose the woman judged insane by the State because that may mean she's the sanest person around, but you should still know what you're paying for. And in most parts of the country, you *are* paying for it—often to the tune of $35.00 per hour, although most shrinks do have sliding scales. I found, ironically, that the better therapists usually have lower prices.

In some cases, all the women are getting for their $35.00—even from certain "certified" shrinks—is fifty minutes of sex a week. If you dig that and that's what you go to a therapist for, fine. (I know that the issue of sexual relations between therapists and clients is a hot one, even in the straight world.) Personally, I believe that such sexual relations are wrong because there must be a certain distance in the therapist/client relationship in order for there to be some objectivity on the part of the therapist at least. Recently, one prominent lesbian therapist in New York admitted publicly that her sexual relations with her clients had been damaging to both parties.

Even some highly qualified therapists have dubious practices. It is unethical for a therapist to advertise, and yet I have seen at least one such ad. Some of the ads have even been misleading: One woman advertises a sexual fantasy workshop, which turns out to be her own personal recruiting grounds for victims of her sadistic "games." In addition, some "qualified" lesbian therapists are in worse mental shape than most of us. I witnessed horrendous scenes on several occasions when a lesbian therapist physically attacked her ex-lover and once even broke down someone's door because she thought her ex-lover was inside. The therapist had to be carried out by the police, but I thought the most unfortunate victims were probably her patients. Some of the best shrinks are said to have been terribly neurotic, but in this case I doubted how much this woman could help anyone else.

Finally, there is some doubt about what many shrinks are putting back into the movement, which has, after all, given them an extremely lucrative income—I haven't seen one starving yet! Let's face it—they wouldn't be in business, were it not for our movement; like the gay bars, they earn a living from our oppression, and I do think they owe us something in return. In my opinion, this concept should apply to all gay businesses—not just shrinks. In other words, if you live from our community, put something back into it. There are several ways to do this. Most of the better shrinks treat poor lesbians for free or for nominal fees, either privately or in groups. However, few shrinks, if any, have given any money to the Lesbian Switchboard in New York, for example, which refers people to these same lesbian or pro-lesbian shrinks, and which is usually desperately in need of funds.

THE CAUSES AND THE CURE

The above-mentioned rip-offs are caused by a certain naïveté and credulity as well as an overdose of optimism on our part. We are used to being conned by the straight world, but not by our sisters. We have said to others and to ourselves so many times that "Gay is Good" that perhaps we have begun to believe our own rhetoric, which might be modified to "Gay is *almost always* Good." Of course, we would like to believe that because a shrink is a lesbian or pro-lesbian that she is good and won't hurt us in any way, but it would not hurt gay people to exercise the same caution toward our own people that we would toward Establishment shrinks. After all, an honest shrink will be shown to be honest even after a bit of inquiry, while the bad ones might be exposed in the process.

In addition, those of us who are out of the closet face another problem. Although we can no longer be blackmailed, since we would be the first to proclaim our dykehood, we are powerless once we have been defrauded in any way by another lesbian. We are reluctant to go to the police or other authorities because certainly they are not our friends! Even if we do complain, the authorities are not likely to be sympathetic to our grievances. Even when a lesbian was murdered, the police were more interested in her movement activities than in finding her murderer. The fewer dykes the better is their attitude.

In any event, bringing in the police is always ugly. It is better to take preventive measures.

1. Demand to know who your shrink is. Don't give your head to just anyone. If you are interested in qualifications, ask to *see* the degrees. Don't let her tell you she flushed them down the toilet. Also demand to know whether she has a sliding scale. Is she charging you a fair price?

2. Ask around. Is this therapist stable? What is her sexual and mental reputation? Know what you're getting into. Check into "peer counseling" (counseling done by nonprofessional sisters) in your locality. Peer counseling has often proven to be better than that of licensed therapists. Find out if there is a gay or feminist therapy referral service in your vicinity. Such services include New York's Identity

House (140 West 15 Street, New York, N.Y. 10010, (212) 243-8181), which offers free walk-in peer therapy for gay singles and couples as well as for bi-sexuals, and Los Angeles' Gay Community Services Center (1614 Wilshire Boulevard, Los Angeles, California), which offers a wide variety of counseling programs.

3. Shop around. Talk to at least three therapists before picking the one with whom you think you will work best. You wouldn't buy the very first television you looked at, would you? Treat your head with the same loving care. Besides, most therapists from gay and feminist referral services offer free first sessions. In addition, the very process of choice gives you an opportunity to be active in your selection of a therapist, and you won't feel like a passive "patient." Also with the prospect of more than one therapist being available, there is less of a feeling of desperation, and you will feel freer to ask pertinent questions as to the therapist's methods and attitudes toward gays. (This interrogation is especially important when dealing with a straight therapist who might harbor anti-gay feelings or fears.)

4. Know when to get out. Even if thirty lesbians swear by her and light candles to her, if she's not helping *you*, split. Being X's patient may boost your ego in one sense but she can deflate your mind *and* your wallet.

5. Demand a fair return. Ask what she is doing for your movement and for your sisters as well as for you. Demand that therapists and all businesses thriving on our people put money back into our community.

Finally, remember that while unscrupulous shrinks are a *small minority*, we'd better stop them now before the problem grows. And we'd better clean out our own house first before we try to change the world.

THE SPIRIT IS LIBERATIONIST BUT THE FLESH IS . . . , OR, YOU CAN'T ALWAYS GET INTO BED WITH YOUR DOGMA

Karla Jay

It's been my experience that sex is the last area in which we reconcile the differences between our political ideals and our personal actions. And in no area have I seen such hypocritical dichotomies between what people preach and what they actually do. For example, I know several men who decry ageism, but they themselves sleep only with young men under the age of twenty-one. Then there was the case of the radical gay man who came over to my house for dinner one night. For several hours he raged and tiraded about how we have to sleep with "ugly" people so that no one will be excluded. To achieve this goal, he advocated promiscuity with a special emphasis on rejecting no one, especially not those usually considered "undesirable." I agreed with him heartily about the need to care for those who always wind up being rejected, and almost felt guilty about living with a woman of such physical beauty. Then, to my astonishment, he left for a "date" with one of the most attractive men I've seen in a long time, while I was left in my living room—standing and trying to close my jaw and thinking ironically of all the "uglies" who were to be *excluded by him* that night!

Don't get the impression that gay men are the main or only offenders. I can think of as many radicalesbians who are hypocrites in this area. I've heard countless sisters rant against any sort of sexual inequality in a lesbian relationship, only to hear later that their favorite sexual "sport" is sado-masochism, the very heart of which lies in power and submission—the ultimate in role-playing. Then there are other women who preach celibacy but who don't practice it, and some who denounce couples and wind up paired. There are also those sisters who decry looksism while choosing only fashion-model types for their lovers. Finally, let's not forget those lesbians preaching separatism and living with *men.*

Some of this hypocrisy must seem minor and harmless, but it can never be good for us, a movement whose base comes from our *experience*, not abstract theory, not to "practice what we preach," as the old adage goes.

Yet, I must admit that it is not surprising (to me, at least) that sexuality is the last area in which movement (and nonmovement) lesbians and other people reach a state of personal clarity and unity, for despite our so-called "liberation," we all probably still have some hang-ups about sex. For example, we are almost all affected by societal taboos (which are usually sexual in nature anyway), such as the taboo against incest. Although the lesbian community itself might not frown on incest, most people have their own built-in restraints in this area. In addition, I've found that many lesbians—even the most "liberated" ones—are hung up about talking about sex. In a consciousness-raising group I was in, the group suddenly got very abstract and theoretical, instead of personal, when the subject was masturbation.

In addition to our personal hang-ups, liberated lesbian society has created its own sets of taboos, based on what we perceive to be right or wrong. For example, while nothing would have been said critically about a lesbian using a dildo in 1950 (had anyone the nerve to discuss such things then!), anyone admitting to using a dildo today would probably be verbally castigated for enjoying "phallic" pleasure. Verbal criticism has thus *forced* some sisters into a second closet (that is, some sisters are "out" as lesbians, but cannot be proud of what their own brand of lesbianism entails—even to us, their sisters). Similar social pressure has also forced some sado-masochists and lesbians living as prostitutes to live in this second closet. And we have yet to admit that our own "puritanism" is no way to deal with what some of us may consider to be "problems."

These may seem to be extreme cases, although I believe them to be less rare than some may think. The main problem, however, is not that we all undergo a tug of war between private urges and public sanctions (although I don't want to underplay the role this type of dichotomy may play in some people's lives and the pain it has caused in too many lives). The main problem *is* that there is a large *irrational* (or perhaps it might be called *instinctual*) element to sexual attraction, activities, and response. Our fantasies are, by definition, beyond our control. Nor can we—most of us, anyway—program ourselves or raise our consciousnesses enough to *dream* the "correct line." For me, consciousness-raising has failed to blot Jane Fonda from my dreams. Furthermore, most of us (I can't vouch for *all* people) can't control who or what turns us on. When I see someone "exciting" to me, the immediate sexual response bypasses my brain and electrocutes my sensory endings *before* I can think long enough to say: "Sexist pig, stop that!" As much as I berate myself, my body won't listen to my intellectual appeals.

We may ultimately be able to program our sexual fantasies, dreams, and responses, just as many feminists have become lesbians out of a political choice, but my observations (and my own responses) tell me that true mental control is not yet a reality for the majority of lesbians. A real problem, however, arises when women feel guilty about their fantasies or instantaneous erotic responses, for I believe (and if I'm wrong, write in!) that attempts to repress such reactions can only lead to frustration, drive the impulses further into the subconscious, or create perhaps equally undesirable alternatives.

What we can know is the dividing line between our fantasies and our actions. I don't write passionate letters to Jane Fonda. Neither do I whistle at a woman who turns me on, nor do I approach anyone on what I would consider to be a sexist level. In short, I don't act on what turns on only my body. To begin with, for me a sexual experience would not be fulfilling if I were not also mentally attracted to an individual. In other words, although I acknowledge—and sometimes enjoy—my fantasies, I must act as my consciousness dictates.

Although I obviously believe in separating my fantasies and actions, many sisters feel that they should *act out* their fantasies, at which point they may crash headlong into movement ideology—or their own. For it is, alas, possible to hold two conflicting or completely contradictory sets of ideas. So what's the poor lesbian to do who sincerely believes she should act out or somehow explore her sexual fantasies, only to discover her fantasies center, for example, on sadism, masochism, or some sort of fetishism? As discussed before, sadism and masochism could contradict other beliefs regarding equality in a relationship. What such a woman with contradictory beliefs may ultimately do depends largely on which set of beliefs is the stronger, but her actual accessibility to an S&M experience also plays an important part. A final factor, which may be the most important one, is the social pressure—pro or con—from the lesbian community in her area.

Any such dualism in a person's beliefs must cause suffering, and in some cases depression, or perhaps even insanity. I wish I had the solution to such dilemmas, but I have only begun to analyze the problem, and the answers may not be easy or near—for me, at least. However, bringing the problem to the surface and raising the general

213

consciousness that such a political/sexual gap exists are the first steps toward finding an answer.

Equally important is a recognition of the struggle we and our sisters are going through in this area, and also a recognition that what is closest to our deepest selves is hardest to change. (It was not an accident that gay liberation was the last movement to surface, for isn't sexual oppression what lies closest to the soul?) And along with this recognition must come a certain tolerance toward others and toward ourselves into our struggle to change (not a tolerance for a complacency with the status quo). For the road toward the liberation of our deepest selves is hard and long, and I suspect that the ultimate definition of what is sexist, right, or wrong may be as fine as a razor's edge.

AGING

Riki

The stereotype of the lonely, old homosexual is one of the many anti-gay stereotypes we are constantly denying. We tend to say that this is a myth of straight society. We say that gay people can have long-lasting relationships, or perhaps we answer by saying, more to the point, that straight people get lonely and old, too. Yes, there is much too much truth to the idea that there are, in the gay community, many people who are lonely and old. The question of the aging homosexual is a complex one, involving such questions as sexuality, community, friendship, and money. I often wonder if the economic aspects of aging are overlooked when in fact they are the most important.

One thing is certain: the experience of aging changes from generation to generation. Awareness of the process of aging in the gay community is bound to become more acute as gay awareness itself intensifies. Some observations on aging, therefore, are very much in order.

I am now forty-four years old and have been working most of my adult life. As my salary increased, so did the cost of every other item, as well as taxes, in our inflationary world. Therefore, I am able to save little money, if any, for my old age. And I happen to work in a field that does not pay you what you are worth (no field ever does), offers no pensions, and is youth-oriented as is most of our society today. Since I know that I'll never be able to afford to live on Social Security, I'll probably have to go on relief when I retire. In addition, my physical condition is not the best, and I ask myself whether I will even be able to work another twenty years.

What of my lover? She will have a pension as well as Social Security if she can stick out the position she has already held for twenty years. But I am not eligible either for her rate of Social Security should she live, nor could I inherit her pension (as could a legal heterosexual spouse) should she die. (We might even have legal difficulties in inheriting anything from one another.) And so, while she may wish to retire comfortably, I would not be able to. Of course, even with her pension, she could not support both of us as she might wish to.

However, we are still better off than even older sisters who are now receiving small pensions or Social Security. Many are living alone on these small monies with few friends and sometimes with no families or lovers. We, this generation, do not see them at the bars, dances, and other events, because not only do they know they are living in a youth-oriented country where there is no place for them, but also they cannot really afford these social activities. Sometimes, they are also physically unable to attend, and no effort has been made to reach out to them to facilitate their presence at our community functions. Our youth (and I feel I am still young, until I see the 16-25-year-old group around) is what we thrive on. When that goes, we no longer have places to go where we will be welcome or comfortable with our younger sisters.

I want to try to make our sisters aware that we must start now to help those who might need friendship or a helping hand right away, partly because not too far in the future, that is where I—and all of us—will be. We will be needing younger sisters to help us if it is necessary. And I also feel that the awareness of ageism is a very important consciousness level for us to reach in our growth as lesbian women. To be aware, to grow, to bring our *total* community closer together, we must give a helping hand or lend an ear to those who have traveled the path before us.

Here are some of the practical things we can do. We might start an incorporated nonprofit organization in which money (such as dues) would be invested to buy and run a large house where those who have no one and very little money can stay. Lesbians would be encouraged to leave their money in their wills to the organization. Of course, this is a very complicated maneuver, but it is not impossible. Perhaps we could also set up a nationally coordinated pension plan to which interested gays could contribute.

But we need more than solutions to economic problems. We need social programs geared toward older gay people and their needs—that is, places where older gay people can meet one another and forums in which older gays can discuss their common problems. Some organizations, such as Gay Older Women's Liberation and the Gay Women's Alternative, do exist, but they are much too far and few between, and although they reach the lesbian over thirty, they often miss the lesbian over sixty. We also need not only to open the regular

216

gay liberation events to older lesbians but also to make an effort to *attract* them by having facilities to deal with physical infirmities and by having flexible admission fees to help those with fixed or limited incomes.

Naturally, we need more women and men to come forth to offer suggestions and their talents in order to come up with workable solutions to the practical problems of older gays. But right now, we also need all gay people of whatever age to raise our consciousnesses about the plight of older gays. Only then can we help older gays to help themselves and make all gay people, of whatever age, feel welcome, loved, and a valuable part of our community.

NIGGER IN THE WOODPILE

Thomas Dotton
—for Pepe

After five years of struggle, the gay liberation movement has failed to consider the freedom of black, Latino, Oriental, and other minority group gays. At times activist, abstract, mystified, reformist, and even aestheticized, the movement since Stonewall has plodded forward. But in general, it has nowhere addressed itself to what seems to be a fundamental contradiction between being black or Third World and being involved in gay liberation.

The particular situation of minority faggots has gotten lost in a labyrinth of conflicting movement methodologies and aspirations. Yet, because of faggot racism the unavoidable tension exists. And without substantial changes in movement focus, gay liberation will have to be denounced for the virulent racism it now seems to accept.

As a black I came to gay liberation a long time ago. My choice to identify myself as a faggot was motivated by both personal and political factors. In 1966 I allowed my name to be registered with the Dean of Columbia College as one of the seven founders of the Student Homophile League.

Like many others in those days before *Time* magazine sanctified our movement, I gave myself unconditionally to the cause of gay liberation. I knew I alienated myself from the wider black community, but only gay liberation appeared to offer me freedom as both a black and a faggot.

However, with the proliferation of gay liberationist groups across the country, it became clear the movement was unable to deal with Third World faggots. Attempts at our own organization in the larger cities received minimal assistance from white brothers and sisters; our nonwhite, non-middle-class organizations failed.

Personally, I withdrew, dissociating myself from a kind of gay liberation I couldn't honestly support. Following the advice of friends cautioning "All gays are equal," or, "Gay is good," I have been silent. I now feel I've been coopted by a long noninvolvement during which I've been content to wait, watch, listen, and try to understand why the

218

movement is not meeting its potential.

But the contradiction does not go away. If you are black, brown, or yellow, and you are out, you experience it daily. Each time you enter a bar, go to a party, attend a group meeting, read the gay press, or deal with white faggots on a social level, it is there. It is, outside of us, like a large beast looming omnipresent in front of us. Internally, like a crab with serrating pincers, it gnaws at us.

For years most of us have wished not to see it. We have been peripheral, shadowy forms, stepchildren, shuttled to the movement's edges. On faith, and only on faith, we've anticipated a turning inward by the movement, a process of self-criticism. Through it, we've thought, the movement might see its inherent racism.

This has not been done.

Now it is appropriate that we ask if gay liberation is doomed to be racist, and oppressive to everyone not white and middle-class. And it's time to ask ourselves, if gay liberation continues to refuse to deal with racism and sexism, how we can see it as anything other than a colossal waste of energy?

Our very problems in gay culture are ignored except for often confused Leftist rhetoric in publications such as *Gay Sunshine* or *Fag Rag*. Yet, the problems of our situation are neither transparent nor invisible; simply, they are not noticed.

And, as for the racism, which itself remains unseen, I am bored with the endless apologies and excuses. One need only look to the slick pages of the *Advocate;* to the dubious lily-white Fundamentalism of the Metropolitan Community Church (M.C.C.); to the unchallenged clichés of gay novels, poems, plays, films, and pornography; to the private as well as public opinions of individuals elevated to the ranks of gay spokespeople; to the blatant discrimination of bars, baths, nightclubs, and gathering places such as Fire Island and Provincetown; and to almost every other aspect of gay lifestyle from the individuals now promoted as heroes of gay history to the very locutions of what passes for gay idiom.

A thousand explanations could be offered. But, either through omission or distortion, gay institutions reveal debris inherited from straight society. With little apparent ill-ease, faggots have dutifully followed the lead of white, heterosexual America.

To us it can be of no importance whether the racism is deliberate or due to oversight; for us it *is*.

Repeatedly I have heard, "But it's because you people don't get involved," "You just don't seem to fit in," or, "You never join." Again we have here restatement of "normalization": that in situations of integration the burden of being accepted rests exclusively on the outsiders who must adapt to that which is not them.

Of most organizations along the East Coast with which I'm acquainted this has been the rationalization. Just as our low voting statistics are taken to mean we're not interested in government, our absence in gay liberationist organizations somehow says to white faggots we don't care.

It's time to face the fact that whites ask minority members to give up whatever ethnic identity they have to safeguard the cause. Or that groups across the country seem to be composed of white men and white women. Or that these white men and white women advocate from their middle-class perspectives a gay liberation that only makes sense if you're middle class. Or that for some reason, it's been virtually impossible for the blacks who have joined to assume active, visible roles in organizations. (I should note that Thomas Smith of the National Gay Task Force board is an exception: I can think of no one else.)

At this juncture, the example of a single city would be useful.

In Boston, "The Athens of the North," long active in civil rights and various progressive movements, we do not exist. There is no genuine, nonwhite input for the following groups: the Homophile Union of Boston, the Gay Media Action, the Homophile Community Health Service, *Gay Community News*, the Gay Academic Union, the Student Homophile League, the Gay Nurses Association, the Transsexual Counseling Service, Gay Youth. Third World participation is not sought for a variety of radio and television programs coordinated by the gay community. And last year's Gay Pride parade in Boston, for many reasons an absolute disaster, indicated the gay community's usual elitism, in being planned as a Mardi Gras to which marchers were asked to come dressed in costume for a midsummer carnival.

But by American standards Boston is a very cosmopolitan city. Elaine Noble, feminist and acknowledged lesbian, was just recently elected to a first term in the state legislature. Stuart Byron writes on film from a gay consciousness in a weekly selling tens of thousands of copies. With the exception of San Francisco, Boston might be the most faggot-tolerant of cities in the country.

Yet, within the Boston-Cambridge area, there exists a large black and Latin gay community ignored by and of little interest to white faggots clustered in fashionable Back Bay, South End, Beacon Hill, and

Cambridge gay ghettos. These minority faggots "don't fit." Those few black or Latin faces that can be seen in gay Boston belong to educated, mobile, middle-class, easily assimilated individuals.

Individuals from minority groups who are welcomed in the gay community are seen as separate, different from the unwashed masses of niggers and spics. At a fund-raising luncheon in a private home on Beacon Hill, I objected to racist comments from a prominent gay psychoanalyst; he told me I was mistaken when I protested, adding, "And, anyway, you're not one of them. I'm talking about the people in the ghetto. In Roxbury and Dorchester."

Obviously, in Boston, as in New York or Washington, gay liberation seems to be the province of the bourgeois. A general movement trend toward reformism (read: reintegration into straight society as happy, healthy, productive faggots) is just a projection of the same attitude into politics.

Activity of Boston Gay Media Action group is typical of reformism par excellence. The collective's politic could hardly appeal to members of the Third World.

While a staff writer for *The Boston Globe,* I was asked to join what was then a new group trying to form. I attended various meetings before I withdrew, disappointed with the group's politics.

Under the direction of Loretta Lottman, Gay Media Action in 1974 worked attacking straight media coverage in terms of the Houston horrors, or for not representing "positive" images of faggots in media, organizing a successful public protest to prevent airing of "The Outrage" in a regular *Marcus Welby* spot, and mounting a subway campaign around the group's lavender rhinoceros, "a misunderstood, but lovable animal."

Lottman's efforts are commendable, laudable, to a point. But is it surprising that Media Action as the most vocal group in Boston would fail to attract or involve Third World people?

With Media Action (as is the case with hundreds of groups around the country) we who are black or Spanish, if we are to participate, must admit the validity of the reformist overview. And reformism involves several articles of gay liberationist canon which shouldn't pass unquestioned:

1. Coming out is the cornerstone of reformism because it creates a hierarchy of liberated and unliberated faggots.

2. Reformism assumes that the goal of gay liberation, as

221

mentioned earlier, is to become as middle-class as the straights. It reduces the movement to normalization, betraying belief in the right and justice of straight society. It sings hosannas with each "more humane" reading of history, religion, psychiatry, sociology, ethology, and biochemical research. It does not see the totalitarian nature of these disciplines. No matter where it comes from, reformism rejoices in any suggestion that we are just like them, our heterosexual equivalents. It implies that if only straights learn to see that we're like them, we'll all be free.

3. Reformism also serves as midwife to the notion that the solution to political and social problems lies within the individual. All one has to do, the party line goes, is to pull oneself together. Finding oneself will transcend all the unpleasantness of the world.

But, without the sacred, traditional concept of the individual, reformism collapses. And we blacks, Puerto Ricans, and other Third World faggots have no individuality. Like our straight ethnic brothers and sisters, we are all of us created from an amorphous mass of the same invisibility. We have no look. We are looked at and not seen. Individuality, personhood, is a bourgeois luxury given and denied at will. We do not possess it.

So, if much of the movement has turned reformist, and reformism cannot include us, what then does the movement offer us? Does it mean to say to us that as dingy anti-faggots at the periphery we will somehow gain freedom in their personal liberation process? And can it convince us, we who have all our lives been no ones and who must understand that for its almost existential quality, that by basing a liberation movement on the individual, these white faggots even know what is the freedom they claim to seek?

In my particular case, the answers are all negative. Each black and Puerto Rican faggot must question for himself. I seriously doubt if replies to the questions can be "yes."

As similar questions must be posed in terms of every facet of gay subculture, of which politics is just reflection, an accumulation of "yesses" would be dangerous. These are questions which after five years should not have to be asked. To deny the "no" in these cases would be to destroy oneself. I can think of no reason why we should trust white faggots any more than we do white heterosexuals.

What we experience in gay institutions, we find again in bars, baths,

T-rooms, and other locales. Our social relations with whites are tainted with the same racial insensitivity and indifference. Their racism is a hundred-headed hydra reaching out in all directions.

First, we are screened for a stereotypic fear that we all are muggers, "gay knocks" (fag beaters) or general trouble. For many whites, this is implied in our "Latin looks" or pigmentation. Through the screening process, this quality is snatched away. Then we are permitted to enter baths, bars, or whatever. They neutralize us. Stripping us of their idea of black or Spanish, they then can safely see us from the perspective of fixed racist fantasies. In our vulnerability, we become Superfly or Miss Thing.

Obviously, no one is either Superfly or Miss Thing. Whites are oppressed by the same duality (butch or femme). But in our case, there is no compromise with these two mythical identities. Having no individuality for the racist, he makes us exist. And it is always at either pole. We blacks are, as Martha Shelley said of gay people, "the extrusions of your unconscious minds, your worst fears made flesh."

Over and over again, I have been told by whites, "But that's the way you people are." And nothing one might say is of consequence. As Richard Wright claimed a long time ago, in this country there is no Negro problem, there's a white problem.

Racism, like all positions rooted in passion, is an easy means for not dealing honestly with oneself. Deliberately, the racist chooses irrational unreason. Nothing on this earth will convince him that Puerto Ricans do not all have fourteen-inch cocks or that all blacks don't love to fuck. The words are heard, but a response exists before any information is provided. The racist has decided not to understand. He is white; others are not. He always must be white. He wants to be something, and white is something. The idea that man is only the shepherd of his being is unacceptable to him; for the racist the custodial nature of a being always in question will never do. Uncertainty terrifies him. Being something, anything, even just white is better than having to question. He has to know he is something and that something is white.

Otherwise, if he accepted being himself; that is, someone in this case, not white, there would be uncertainty. And uncertainty implies change. But he fears change because change cannot guarantee what he will become. He prefers not to change, however. He makes himself a white, a thing, merely a permanent something in the world. It's as an unchangeable white, like a thing, that he deals with the world.

But, since he lives in a world where nonwhites do exist, and since he refuses to admit change (which could lead him to see that despite this whiteness, he is like them), in front of them he is whiteness, whiteness pure and simple. They, these nonwhites, become Shelley's "extrusions of your unconscious."

And because this whiteness for him is special, God-given and all that, the racist values it. He values it, which makes it valuable. Accordingly, since others lack it and it is a thing like himself, those who don't have it must be plotting. They plot to take it from him or do him harm. He has to be on his guard. With each encounter with these imperfect, duskily tainted creatures, the thing that he is has to be reproven. With each nonwhite, the racist reaffirms his whiteness. Miss Thing and Superfly, things in himself which are among the many a racist fears, become useful tools. By them those of us who are nonwhite are mercilessly oppressed.

With these two insults, Miss Thing and Superfly, we are held in perpetual peonage. We are still on the plantation, in our nigger cabins; but now our masters prattle on and on about "the liberation of all oppressed peoples."

Our solutions can be diverse; yet, we must accept the fact.

We can become Exum, the baritone singing in operas, who prowls the streets at night in leather jacket, dirty denim, and boots, playing at a Superfly role he hates that's thrust upon him for no reason other than his appearance. He suffers with it. The role is not him. In Manhattan, that's what he's had to be.

Or one can be Delbert, a crippled person, the relic of a human being laid waste by white faggots' camp. In his case, his musculature, when he came out in his early teens, earned him the name "Crystal." He couldn't escape it. He became camp, which led to semi-drag, which led to drag, which led to johns, which led to a decade of the block. He didn't know any better. Being a faggot separated him from his own community. With whites he was like an affectionate puppy; they told him this was the way it is.

It would seem from whatever perspective gay culture is viewed, we lose. The institutions of white faggots are slambang closed in our faces; here we are superfluous. The movement proceeds onward without us; we are not even consulted. In social relations we are not desired; that is, unless we can become as culturally, intellectually as white as our "friends." And intimate involvements, whether they be one-night stands or mature and long-term, are contaminated with, at best, a subtle

224

racism that even in an ideal white-black relationship takes years to remove.

For us there is no excuse not to see. No justification not to realize. We are black, Chicano, Puerto Rican. We should stop allowing gay liberation to tell us this is not important. We have to cease playing their roles, playing at something we're not, something that probably doesn't even exist, except in their heads. We mustn't continue to live, as we do, in absentia, like the absent leg twitches of a recent amputee.

As always the movement asks for time. Shouldn't five years, three-hundred-odd years be enough?

The situation is similar to the great paradox of Plato's ideal state, the Republic, which could only come into existence if people were educated to accept it, overlooking the fact that he also tells us the only means of educating people correctly is the Republic. As members of the Third World, we cannot afford to wait for our white brothers and sisters "to get their shit together." We shouldn't forget that dealing honestly with us is one of the necessary steps in "getting their shit together."

No matter how loud or proud they might shout in the streets, white faggots are doomed to fail. As the movement is structured at this writing, the most they might achieve for us is more of the same with faggots rehabilitated into middle-class society's faithful. If their goals are attained, by becoming normal, they will join forces with the oppressive elements in our culture. One of gay liberation's implicit statements is, "Because I sleep with a man, that doesn't mean I'm not middle-class."

We should be wary. Many of us have gambled heavily in terms of gay liberation and lost. But there's no need for sackcloth, candle, and ashes. It is not so much the principle that failed us; rather, it was the middle-class faggots whom we believed when they told us they were different. They don't seem to be. And we have what we had when we started: our own black, Chicano and Puerto Rican selves.

Ourselves. This is where we should begin again.

Obviously, we have difficulties of our own: black faggots who would never touch another black because they are "too violent" or "too dirty"; the Latino who talks of "virgin assholes," claiming an anatomical reason why he can't be screwed; and middle-class black and Latino faggots (a subspecies beyond the scope of these notes) who further our oppression by their blind belief in integration.

But ourselves we should be able to understand. If anyone can help to solve some of our problems, it must be each one of us working together. Even at the risk of gay movement schism, we need to get close to one another. We need to free ourselves from white faggots to determine what, if anything, they have to offer us. We no longer should accept an entire gay subculture, like a bolus, stuffed rudely down our throats.

Practically, as a first step, we need a conference, a national Third World caucus. We've never had such a dialogue. Now we are black or Latino faggots apart from the movement in Detroit, Boston, Chicago, L.A., or Washington, etc. The movement of white faggots has kept us apart. Sitting down by ourselves with our Third World gay sisters (for whom I've in no way tried to speak), we need to know one another to be able to calmly discuss collective options.

Whites will accuse us of "separatism." Mention of Gay liberation's racism itself often leads to the charge. They will, for yet another time, claim there's greater political potential in a widely diversified gay liberationist movement. Anyway, we blacks, Puerto Ricans, and others haven't the strength to stand alone, they will say.

Yet they forget just how alone we already stand within their movement. And what we should want is not their support, but power, the power with which white middle-class America oppresses us. These "friends" share in that power. Like their advice, their objections would seem self-serving.

In no way should we spare them.

I think we have all been, perhaps, naïve to trust them. We were foolish to think we could be anything other than niggers. Now the time has come when we must reconsider. If we do not, if we remain as closely associated with their unrealizable white faggot liberation movement, we are rightly damned to remain right where we are, at the outside edges, the proverbial niggers in the woodpile.

WE'D BETTER ALL HANG
TOGETHER OR SURELY
WE'LL ALL HANG
SEPARATELY

Rita Mae Brown

The San Francisco Examiner, Hearst's newspaper, and *The Chronicle* blared the love affair between Patricia "Mizmoon" Soltysik and Camilla Hall of the Symbionese Liberation Army louder than Warner Bros. ever trumpeted for Errol Flynn and Olivia De Havilland. The papers hoped to ridicule the political group by focusing on the sexual preference of two of its members. The two women made no attempt to hide their love but deep feminism or gay awareness was never part of the S.L.A.'s communiques. The lesbian affair also gave the Federal Bureau of Investigation an excuse to psychologically loot the lesbian community of San Francisco and, to a lesser extent, the feminist and male homosexual communities in general.

Some of the F.B.I.'s tactics approached the absurd and are worth mentioning. A few days after the Hibernia Bank was robbed by the S.L.A. in April, 1974, Scott's, a popular women's gathering place, held a benefit for a child-care project. The place was jammed with women eager to support the project and to hear Rosemary Sorrells sing. In the midst of the crowd wandered an unidentified woman (relevant since people tend to know each other by sight if not by name in the lesbian community), tape recorder on shoulder, hugging everyone in sight and asking, "What do you think of the S.L.A.? Do you know any of the sisters?" For all her gushing affection the woman received no information. Did the F.B.I. think a hug and kiss on the cheek signified instant lesbianism? Of course, she may have been a lonely lady with only a tape recorder to fill those long hours of the night, but funny, nothing like that ever happened before in Scott's.

After the bank incident a few women were approached by women they didn't know asking essentially the same questions. The June 5, 1974 edition of *The Advocate,* a large West Coast newspaper serving the male homosexual community, reported that the F.B.I. thought members of the S.L.A. were being aided by friends. Apparently the authorities' concept of "friends" is anyone who is a lesbian or homosexual. The questioning continued, although there was no

227

connection between lesbian-feminist politics and the politics of the Symbionese Liberation Army. However, Marilyn Baker, a TV reporter from San Francisco, did find notes of the group's ideological statements in which the words "men and women" were crossed out and amended, "women and men." To the media and police this identifies a hotbed of feminist thought. To a male supremacist (be they female or male) any aggressive action on the part of a woman or women means they are in league with feminists. It's still terribly difficult for them to understand that a woman can take independent action of her own without coaching from anybody. Supremacists—and are the F.B.I. not male supremacists as well as a lot of other things?—revealed their bias when they first tried to tell us these nice, middle-class white women were hypnotized by that bad black man, Donald DeFreeze. From that they jumped to lesbian conspiracy, with no attempt to connect their hypnotic theory and DeFreeze with lesbians. Perhaps they thought Donald DeFreeze was a lesbian in drag after finding those inflammatory notes changing the order of the world from "men and women" to "women and men." This demonstrates one of the advantages of authority: you need never explain your theories, no matter how contradictory.

What lesbians need to realize from this is that as a despised group we can and will be blamed for any trouble involving women. If they can't pin it on us then they'll turn to that other reliable scapegoat, black people. Just as DeFreeze was dragged through the press mud, so were Camilla and Mizmoon. The white men of the S.L.A. never got the smear job that DeFreeze or the lesbians did. Camilla was the daughter of a Lutheran minister. Were Lutherans suspect? Can the point be more clear?

A strange rash of robberies hit the lesbian community right after the bank holdup. Strange, because the lesbian community has traditionally been far freer of rip-offs than, say, the male Left or the gay male movement. If those thefts were committed in order to break down the bonds between women in the community, they proved a dismal failure. On the other hand, perhaps the F.B.I. was searching for the Hibernia Bank money. Stranger things have happened in the history of that august, incorruptible bastion of American virtue, the Federal Bureau of Investigation. If they found any of the cash, $10,960, hidden beneath our mattresses, they kept it to themselves.

F.B.I. employees, who admitted to being on the payroll—a sort of coming out, first approached Mattachine thinking that long-lived organization included lesbians, or perhaps thinking that all homosexuals know each other.

The blundering of the F.B.I. in the lesbian community demonstrates one of the few benefits of exclusion from the American political process: we are so outcast that they don't know much about us. That gives us a thin line of protection, but not for long. Next time they will be more to the point.

The reaction of the lesbian, women's, and gay men's communities to the F.B.I. and the enraging insinuations of the press was heavy silence. Many people, learning from what was happening before their eyes, refused to discuss the S.L.A. with friends in public places while the F.B.I. rummaged through our lives. In some deep way women felt they had more in common with the S.L.A. women than they did with F.B.I. men or women. Most women disagreed with S.L.A. tactics, which makes the vow of silence even more impressive.

While the F.B.I. got to us first, other Americans had opportunity to observe their behavior later. The obscene spectacle of 500 policemen converged on those few S.L.A. women and men in Los Angeles, and covered by the press as though a shoot-'em-up Western, convinced many people that the "authorities" shoot first and ask questions later. The press, in living color, justifies them in this, even when they maul an innocent before the rolling cameras as they did when they threw an escaping woman to the ground and pinned her down like a calf at round-up. We might have confused this event for a John Wayne movie were it not for the Ford commercials. We also figured out that if the S.L.A. members had holed up in Beverly Hills, the chances of them being burned out would have diminished considerably. Class tends to dampen the police in their rowdy, red-blooded pursuit of criminals. Can you imagine an officer throwing a neighbor to the ground in her Oscar de la Renta?

Had many members of the S.L.A. lived and remained at large, I believe the pressure on the lesbians especially, then feminists and gay men, would have intensified. Their deaths got us off the hook much in the same way that the capture of the alleged Zebra killers relieved pressure in the black community of San Francisco. (Zebra was the police code name for the black men killing white men in the area.)

Since the shootout, many people seem to have forgotten the danger we are all in through no fault of our own. If one lesbian is a criminal, all lesbians are criminals. To the police mind, lesbian and criminal or pervert are one and the same thing. If Nixon is a criminal, it isn't assumed that all middle-class, upward-striving white men are criminals. But if one black man shoots a policeman, all blacks—women and men—in that community are suspect. If a black woman shoots a policeman, then all blacks and all feminists are suspect. If a lesbian shoots a policeman, then all "queers" get it, plus feminists. That's the nature of oppression: to hold an entire group accountable for the actions of one person who falls in that group. White men are allowed the luxury of individuality. We are not.

The fact that the San Francisco lesbian community is no longer closely watched doesn't remove the threat of such action in the future. All that is needed for police and federal backlash is another woman, lesbian, or gay man with a gun. As the Depression worsens, the chances of someone picking up the gun increases proportionally. We would be wise as a community now, before another "disturbance," to make plans among ourselves to protect ourselves. It's a sure bet no one else will protect us.

At the very least, the overground lesbian, feminist, and homosexual organizations can obtain the services of civil rights lawyers in their community, so we aren't left abandoned in a crisis, having to scramble for lawyers who aren't afraid to defend gay people. Another simple task is for groups to publish in their newsletters and as posters a citizen's legal rights. These should also be distributed in the bars, so that nonpolitical people who might not see a poster or read a newsletter are informed and prepared. Whether they are political or not, they will be suspect. There's a sad innocence in believing lack of political opinion will save you.

Another useful step, one that few of us want to take because of our experiences with these people, is to contact the police in the city and try establishing some exchange with them. If we have some slender contact with the police, it may make the difference between an all-out purge and a routine check. After all, we pay their salaries through our taxes. They need to be reminded that we are citizens and we are not afraid of them.

The most important step is for various groups in each locality to get the other groups in the area together to discuss how to protect each other. All of us who are scapegoats need each other. The more disparate we are, the more vulnerable we are. You won't get better treatment by the authorities if you aren't a member of a feminist or gay group. Remember, individuality is the luxury of the white man. In their eyes we are all the same. By-staying away from an organized group you

230

actually weaken yourself if and when a crisis does happen and the police make a sweep through your area. We are all we've got.

Considering the problem of increased harassment and potential brutality is no joy, but we can be thankful that the problem reveals hidden strengths to us. The years of duplicity in heterosexist culture taught us to protect each other with silence. Now we must protect each other openly with voice and body.

We must act as intelligent human beings and prepare for all eventualities, instead of waiting for something to happen to us. Humans can imagine a future. Let us imagine the bad and good things that could possibly come to us and do something about them.

Our experience with the Establishment media has taught us to expect nothing but distortion from the so-called free press when it comes to women, lesbians, male homosexuals, racial groups, and, of course, violence of any kind (except for state violence). We can't expect to learn the truth from television, newspapers, or radio. Therefore we must learn it from each other.

The possibility of renewed hostility, though frightening, should draw us closer, like iron filings to the magnet of a strong community. A new political maturity and pride are emerging among us. The bare bones of victory, so simple we neglect it, are being made clear to us by the harshness of our environment:

United we stand, Divided we fall.

PRESERVING THE PAST
FOR THE FUTURE

June Rook

The suppression of an oppressed group's history is probably one of the most effective methods of maintaining and ensuring that oppression. Without an historical or cultural background, people cannot authenticate their identities or provide role models which instill feelings of validation and self-worth. In his futuristic novel, *1984,* George Orwell portrayed clearly how this suppression of personal and cultural history helps destroy the human personality and creates instead a mindless, obedient, monolithic block of subhuman creatures.

Therefore, when an oppressed people begin to cast off their oppression, they must begin to find and control their own history. This process has been evident in the past two decades in the black liberation movement, and more recently in the women's liberation movement. For example, many blacks have reclaimed their African cultural heritage, worked to spread knowledge of black people of historical importance, and created numerous black studies programs in schools and colleges and in their communities.

Similarly, many feminists have begun digging in the past for information about ancient matriarchies, and many are researching biographies about women of more recent times. Some women have also become involved in setting up women's studies programs in colleges and universities.

And now that the first wave of gay liberation has passed, we lesbians and homosexuals must also reclaim our cultural heritage and our gay history. We must smash the false mirror-images of ourselves held up to us by our oppressors.

We should no longer have to hear that all-too-familiar story—my own story, and that of countless other gay adolescents, who in the anguish and confusion of emerging sexual feelings (and unable to tell anyone about those feelings), ran to the library and searched for some supportive, calming information on what it means to be gay. But at best we found condescending journalistic reports of the sordidness and sleaziness of the "gay underworld," by such writers as Jess Stearn and

232

Donald Webster Cory. At worst, we found the medical and psychological texts that dealt with homosexuality and lesbianism as a pathology—an ugly aberration that our "enlightened" society attempted to "correct," sometimes with the aid of such methods as electric shock therapy or lobotomy. In some cases the libraries refused to put even those books out on the shelves. And of course, how many of us dared ask for them?

The situation now is at least somewhat better. There are books such as this one, written by gay people, to give our sisters and brothers a more realistic, and supportive picture of gay life. But we still have a long way to go. For every book on gay liberation on the shelves there are four or five by people like Drs. Bieber, Hatterer, and Caprio who either try to change us or describe us as less than fully human.

In many places in the United States and Canada, gay women and men are organizing in order to recreate, gather, research and maintain our history which was mostly destroyed by a homophobic heterosexist society. In California, the Los Angeles History Collective, which was started in early 1974, is studying matriarchies, witchcraft and lesbian culture. In Toronto, *The Body Politic*, a gay newspaper, has founded the Canadian Gay Liberation Movement Archives. In Chicago, a lesbian library, called the New Alexandria Library for Lesbianwomen, has recently formed. At present it consists of a lending library numbering almost two-hundred books, a reference section including bibliographies, and an audio section containing tapes of music, poetry, and interviews. The library is currently being run by four women on a voluntary basis. And in New York City, the Lesbian Herstory Archives has recently formed and is now in the process of collecting and cataloguing material by lesbians and is working to establish a place where any gay women can have access to the work done by our sisters for research or just for "pleasure reading."

Although most of Sappho's poetry has been lost to us—burned by the early Church fathers—there exists a large body of work by lesbians that is virtually untapped, and that is in need of research and restoration, such as the works of Renée Vivien, Romaine Brooks, Radclyffe Hall, Wanda Landowska, Marie Laurencin, Liane de Pongy, Elizabeth de Gramont, and others.

In addition, we need to "discover" many lesbians whose very existence and whose contributions have been unknown to us. For example, many of us have heard of Rosa Bonheur, a major artist in the nineteenth century, but how many of us know about her companion of

233

forty years, Nathalie Micas, an herbalist, veterinarian, and inventor (the Micas brake for locomotives).

Gay archives should have several purposes. One goal of gay archives should be the establishment of records of all kinds, in all media—such as books, newspapers, pamphlets, posters, microfilm, tape recordings, videotape, and, hopefully, artwork by gay artists.

Another purpose is to make sure that the archives are used by gay women and men—that is, we must guard against the misuse of our material by straights who may seek in some way to distort it and discredit us. One way to do this is to try to remain as independent as possible. We must beware of accepting funding from any source that will put limits on our freedom or seek to tell us how to run our archives. They may, for example, dictate which gay people (such as academics only) have access to our material. Of course, it is difficult economically to get an archives going, but hopefully, even if we remain small, word of our successes will spread and other gay groups will form for the same purposes. Eventually, we might be able to put out publications such as gay history newsletters and magazines which would share our discoveries and reach more gay sisters and brothers.

Another way we can encourage the growth of gay history is to work for, even demand, the institution of gay studies programs in our colleges, schools, and community centers. Also, check out your school or local library—if they are lacking in gay materials, demand that they acquire books on gay subjects by gay people. We must organize wherever we can to reach as many gay people as possible, for almost as important as reviving our culture and passing it on to each other, is the establishment of a body of writing and works about the gay experience *that have been created by gay people.* We must no longer tolerate being defined as "the Other" by straights. Gay history is an ongoing and a snowballing process—the more works we have by gay people, the more gay history we will have. And it is up to us to make sure that there is a plethora of positive, knowledgeable, supportive and *firsthand* material for our sisters and brothers.

If you wish to donate material to a gay archives, or just wish to write for more information, here are addresses for some of the above-mentioned organizations:

Canadian G. L. M. Archives
c/o *The Body Politic*
139 Seaton St.
Toronto, Ontario, Canada M5A 2T2

Lesbian Herstory Archives
P.O. Box 1258
New York, N.Y. 10001

Lesbian History Collective
c/o Good Taste Productions
Post Office Box 1564
Santa Monica, California 90406

Mattachine Society
59 Christopher Street
New York, N.Y. 10014

New Alexandrian Library for Lesbianwomen
c/o The Lesbian Feminist Center
3523 N. Halsted
Chicago, Illinois

GETTING IT TOGETHER
JOURNALISM:
A View of *Fag Rag*

Charley Shively

When I first heard of gay liberation, it was exciting but like the evening news—something other people did. I read awesomely Carl Wittman's "Gay Manifesto" in *Liberation* (February, 1970) and through the "queen's network" knew people involved in Boston gay liberation, but I remained on the sidelines, cheering the action of others.

While I went to a few gay meetings, my loyalties and time went to the New University Conference (an adult spur of SDS)—where I helped mimeograph an underground paper and the Radical Historians' *Newsletter.* In a collective article I summarized my feelings in February 1971:

> Organization within all levels of NUC might listen to the experience of Gay Male Liberation Front in Boston. They have no organization at all, no officers, no committees and no chaired meetings. When they find a need, a task-oriented group gathers to do it.
>
> . . . Within the last nine months a community center has been established with a $700 a month budget, a letter-press newspaper (*Lavendar Vision*) published, a film is being produced, the gay guerrilla group is working on street theater, and any number of *ad hoc* groups have gone out to participate in various protest marches and demonstrations.

That hopeful vision shattered rapidly. A police agent made off with $700; the community center closed; and those males most involved in the *Lavendar Vision* left for San Francisco. I then felt strongly that something had to be done. Knowing from NUC how important publications were in keeping groups going—and feeling that I could do no less for myself and my people than I had done in the straight movement—I threw myself into the paper and hoped I could make a difference. A lot of other people felt the same way—particularly the

236

Gay May Day group in Boston. We met March 29, 1971, at Les Heuman, Kevin McGirr, and Craig Smith's place over a bar in North Cambridge and planned our next issue.

I contacted Sue Katz about *Lavendar Vision*. The gay women's collective had kept the paper going after the males had left for California. *Lavendar Vision* no. 1 (November 1970) had been printed in a sixty-nine fashion with the women's and males' sections printed opposite ways. *Lavendar Vision* no. 2 (April 1971) was an all-lesbian issue. I asked Katz if we could put out *Lavendar Vision* no. 3 as another joint issue or as an all-faggot issue. She said, no, that the women preferred that we take our own name, that they weren't into working with men, particularly when they didn't know them, and that a lot of women's energy had been drained by males in *Lavendar Vision*.

Meeting together, we came upon *Fag Rag*—a saucy, irreverent and bold name. (*Queer Times, Cumquat, Cocksucker, Boston Gay Glob*, and others I've forgotten were rejected.) Those very people who say we have no humor have attacked us for using such a name as *Fag Rag*. In a note about the name (issue no. 2) we wrote, "We're proud to take the straight Man's term of contempt and throw it back in his face; proud to admit, flagrantly, that we don't fit and don't want to fit Straight Amerika's definition of manhood."

Getting *Fag Rag* no. 1 out was the most exhilarating experience in my life. We were all high then, flushed by the "success" of May Day 1971—knowing somehow that faggots had made a difference, had made "history." And we wrote about it and worked together as faggots. What Bob Collins wrote about May Day was equally true of us in *Fag Rag*: "We didn't come together out of deep understanding and love but out of a need—willing to accept contradictions, willing to hope we could work together."

The number-one political problem is getting together. The "Establishment" is by definition already together and designed to stay that way. The closer any person or group is to that Establishment, the better they are able to organize. Freud talked about it in *Civilization and Its Discontents*. The "discontents" are by civilization's definition "haywire"—not about to join some loving circle of peace and harmony.

To be more specific: everyone working on *Fag Rag* has without exception been (and is) an egomaniac. We are mad, insane, among the worst of the "discontents"—perhaps the creepiest group of all. I say this neither romantically nor bitterly—but, I hope, realistically. Why

237

pretend otherwise? Indeed to assume that gay love and good wishes will carry any enterprise through is to neglect the most difficult political task of all, that of coming together.

To be even more specific, everyone here suffers from the princess syndrome—a star ready to criticize and denigrate others, unwilling ever to be criticized. The most easily recognized princess is the flamboyant, often gaudy one: with temper tantrums, dramatic entrances, well-timed walkouts, illnesses, suicide attempts, and other melodrama. Less well recognized is the cautious, circumspect, quiet, hard-working manipulator—no less bent on getting his way.

We've had many engagements between the two. The most poignant I remember was that between Garbo and Becal. Garbo's mother had just died; he had dropped out of school; maybe had a little speed and desperately needed encouragement and support beyond what any of us knew how to give. Garbo was yakking and camping and generally being outrageous. Becal yelled at Garbo to shut up, "We have business to take care of, if you don't want to listen, leave." Garbo stomped out in a near-Oscar-winning farewell. Becal was the personification of "straight" identity. He had been squeezed out of the Radical Therapists because he was going "bi-sexual" and passed through gay liberation on his way into the Communist Party. Becal wanted order, efficiency, and direction; had he stayed longer, doubtless he would have found some.

Since no one ever gets his way completely, resignations are forever pouring in. For anyone to work consistently on more than two issues has been a rarity (although since *Fag Rag* 6 we have had a tendency to stabilize somewhat). The difficulty centers around the necessity for compromise. Meeting others halfway requires respect and understanding of where the other person is coming from. But faggots tend not to respect each other; we can take an enormous amount of degradation and "compromise" ourselves with straight people (welfare, job, police, etc.), but never from another fag.

In addition there are dozens of people who come to work on the paper—perhaps call them "bewildered"—who want to do something but are appalled by the grinding of power politics of the forceful and articulate. At virtually every meeting someone is attacked, put down, humiliated. And those who just wanted to find some gay love or do something tend to drift off. Two artists contribute graphics but won't attend any meetings because they can't stand the "politics."

Working on *Fag Rag,* I have always felt I didn't belong: that something was wrong with me; that somehow I wasn't pure or good

238

enough to be there. I have felt the way I used to feel when my father was teaching me to drive: nothing I ever did would ever measure up to what he wanted; I would forever drive (as he said) "like an old woman." I'm not entirely sure why or how *Fag Rag* has come to project this feeling, aura; we've fought against it from the beginning, but the reputation tends to stick.

How should we deal with all our tensions and anxieties? I've always been an advocate of consciousness-raising groups—in which we become more human, vulnerable, personable to each other. But the people who are willing to work on the paper are not always those most willing to open themselves up in consciousness-raising. As Louis Landerson saw it, the C-R group would only become an extension of the power struggles in the paper. Opponents would master the weaknesses of each other and wait for a convenient time to pounce.

The struggle of getting together, working out who and what we are as a group, has been closely connected with the question of who our audience is or should be. We have belabored ourselves from the beginning about our relationship to the gay community. At first, I think we wanted to speak for and to reach every faggot. In *Fag Rag* 1, we worried that "it is very easy for any group of people to become elitist and cut off from the very people who they claim to speak for and about." We wanted to reach the "bar people," but they like many faggots have generally scorned us by making believe that *they* were not gay.

Rather to our surprise, *Fag Rag* has become a popular paper around the United States and abroad among those faggots looking for clues and support for a gay identity. We sell almost as well in San Francisco and New York as in Boston. And we get enthusiastic responses from groups in Ohio, Michigan, and Wisconsin that have kept us going in some weaker moments. Somehow all the hopes of the gay liberation fronts have come to be pinned on a few magazines like the *Amazon Quarterly, Lesbian Tide, Body Politic,* Detroit *Liberator, Gay Sunshine,* and *Fag Rag.* Almost through no choosing of our own, we have become a national publication.

This responsibility—somehow of keeping the fires and inspiration of the Gay Liberation Front, the battle against straightness, sexism, greed, and exploitation—has made it more and more difficult for us to be a consciousness-raising group. Our own needs by contrast with those of the "market" come to seem dilettantish or selfish. Being national also raises a question of the form of the paper. Should we become a "professional" journal of opinion—sort of a *New York Review of Books/Encounter/Commentary* for gay liberation? Doesn't the "dignity" of gay liberation require something more slick and impressive than *Fag Rag* has been?

I'm not sure what words to use to describe this question. I like to use "professional"/"amateur," but many will find the dichotomy unfair. In sports, they separate the "professionals" from "amateurs" by salary. In gay liberation, very few people can live from their salary as gay journalists. But professional/amateur causes less anger than gay/straight, counter-culture/establishment distinctions.

Let me try to paraphrase the arguments within *Fag Rag* on the issue. The "professional" side believes that we must be better organized, publish regularly, have an office, and do the other things any publication must do to continue. "Professionalism" also involves what kind of writing gets published. It means "high quality" writing; no half-digested, sloppy, lackadaisical work which would be rejected if we did not know the author. The professional also seeks "brand names" like Gore Vidal or W. H. Auden. These names inevitably sell papers because they are known and people want to know more about celebrities.

The amateur side argues that the people writing the paper are the most important. These people think that the distinction between writer and audience is less real than claimed. The amateur thinks only intermittently about continuity: today I'm working on the paper, but if Katmandu strikes my fancy tomorrow, I'll be off. That is, if freedom is important for the individual to get away from established society, it is equally important in the counterinstitutions. We almost have a *Fag Rag* shuttle between Boston and the West Coast. In writing, the amateur tends to believe not only "first thought best thought" but also that everything he writes must be printed—word for word—all is perfection.

Mostly on the amateur side myself, I don't think it means celebrating clumsiness and incompetence. What we need is a commitment of each person to control his/her own means of communication (a corollary to controlling the means of production and reproduction). No one should allow someone else to speak for him; specialization in this case is a form of robbery and exploitation. Too much mystification has gone into the "communications" industry: special skills exist but not one of them is out of reach of any faggot.

When the paper started, none of us had any previous experience with a newspaper. We all had a little training here and there (mimeograph, photography, typing) which we shared. *Fag Rag* has been a virtual school of journalism for us. We have emphatically tried to get everyone to share and do all tasks. Of course, in the rush of typing, layout and printing, someone with accumulated skills might have to do more. But a good typist should not be stuck with all the typing. Nor should those with layout training lock others out of decision-making in that area.

We have not solved the problem of unequal experience. The untrained often don't want to learn any of the accumulated wisdom about layout, writing, typing, etc. Everyone seems eager to be an "editor" (more often *the* editor)—that is, make decisions about what should be printed and how the paper should be run. But when it comes to shitwork, there are always some people off dancing. Yet the trained often hoard their skills and enjoy the power and leverage they have over the unskilled.

In writing, for instance. Verbal ability is a tremendous asset in our society. Every middle-class child learns it early and relatively easily; other children acquire literacy only as a great struggle. Being inarticulate is a social condition in the United States. I know this first-hand since my father did not read or write and my mother only finished grammar school. But I have also learned that writing is no magic gift of the gods, given usually to the rich and well born; it is a learned, communicable technique. (What a paradox: we are told that the art of communication is incommunicable.)

We have had many good writers who have passed our way; not one I know has done anything to pass their skills on to other faggots. And I have not myself been able to get anyone to listen to my ideas on writing style. Recently I argued against the phrase, "On the former, a most interesting and informative work is . . . " To me, that seemed hopelessly pedantic, and when I told the author that, he got very irritated.

Criticizing someone's writing is a very personal thing, like telling them they don't make love very well. We have by no means solved the problem of "editing": some articles need to be rewritten, need cutting, need criticism, need help. How can that be done without the sheer exercise of power? Most authors (sometimes the most established) won't listen to any criticism. And what about "slop"? Who is to take time to tell someone we can't print their high school book report on Hemingway's *Old Man and the Sea?* In a "professional" journal, a secretary just mails out a rejection slip and that's it. Literary rejection is just as painful and horrifying as sexual rejection. And some of the same

241

games are played on literature as in cruising places.

Fag Rag's editorial policy has been quite eclectic. Yet in choosing many different kinds of writing, we have generally agreed that conclusions should come from and out of personal experience. The idea of removing oneself from the battle and pretending that you are a disinterested bystander has seemed the height of intellectual treason and deception. As a result we have had a lot of first-person confessional pieces. And even those *Fag Rag*gers who are tired of true confessions still prefer first-person writing, anecdotal and specific. Interviews, for instance; whether of Sylvia Sydney or Gore Vidal, the interview is always first person.

What we have yet to create is a "gay" or "faggot" style of writing. We might be able to finger some writing as alienating, academic, straight, impersonal, and boring—but we still lack some common style, medium, vocabulary, or literature. There is the *Queen's Vernacular,* but much of that is more an affectation of a saloon society than a literature. Is it a first step toward a self-identity? Or only false consciousness?

An ideal I have often had myself has been group writing—either through taped conversation or passing drafts around for additions. In the beginning, we were much more socialist (even Maoist) in orientation than now. But whatever the politics, joint writing has been difficult. In *Fag Rag* 3 a group wrote "Hoover Goes Underground," and they had about the same disagreements as the three who worked recently on the Gore Vidal interview. We are not trained to work together.

Nor are our readers trained to accept an article by content rather than by the identity of the author. In the early issues, we did not include bylines; everyone's name was simply listed in alphabetical order at the beginning of the paper. But our audience responds best to big names and a paper must always be shaped by the social context—the society out of which it arises. We can criticize that society but at the same time we are caught in it.

Perhaps it is typical that I have talked so much about internal problems and said very little about our external difficulties. That is in some ways too typical; we turn in on ourselves, not adequately recognizing that we are not to blame for some of our troubles. They are laid on us by a hostile world.

Our first hassle has been in finding a printer. In ten issues we have gone to press with six different printers. The first printer who did mainly movement papers went out of business; the second dropped us

242

when we ran a picture of a nude black faggot; the third also went bankrupt; the fourth claims they're booked up for the next year; the fifth was in San Francisco for the joint issue; and our sixth is new and untried. Every one demanded cash in advance so they can't complain about our being slow paying their bill.

Beyond printing, the greatest single external difficulty is distribution. Publications get delivered in two general ways: subscription (either by mail or paperperson) or on newsstands. We did not take any subscriptions before *Fag Rag* 5 and since then we've been involved in an interminable hassle with the post office, keeping records, labeling, etc. Distributors are another story; they handle almost all publications on newsstands; most of them are syndicate-controlled (you have to bribe them to handle your publication); and all of them are greedy and inefficient. For better or worse (I'm not sure) no distributor has ever agreed to carry *Fag Rag;* and when we published a joint issue with *Gay Sunshine,* the latter's New England distributor dropped them. We are also banned in South Africa and have been under surveillance at various times by the Cambridge Red Squad, the New Hampshire attorney general's office, and doubtless others we haven't known about.

So how do we get distributed? Initially, we ourselves went into the streets and sold the paper; a thousand copies of *Fag Rag* 1 were sold at the 1971 Gay Pride March in New York City. Another two thousand on the streets of Boston. Through movement contacts across the United States we have located people or groups who help sell the paper or get it into stores. Now we have built up a network of people and stores who regularly sell the paper. Still, it's a lot of work, almost a full-time job; and lots of faggots have never heard of us or of any other gay liberation paper.

The resistance in distribution that has pained me most comes from fellow faggots. A distinguished New York poet once said to me, "Oh, my dear, imagine talking about such things in public; you should be ashamed." Their excuse for opposition usually (if verbalized) centers on the title: vulgar, insulting, disrespectful, etc. But the hypocrisy of that criticism was brought sharply home to me. I was selling copies of *Fag Rag* 6 in front of the East Village theater where Al Carmines' *The Faggot* was playing—seats $7 to $10; Faggot tee shirts, $5. All applause and cheers for the play. But cold stares for me at the door. And I got comments like these from some faggots: "What a filthy name for a paper!" "How can they let you sell *that?*" "Aren't you ashamed of yourself?" I sold two papers, one to someone trying to pick me up (his

243

lover/companion intervened).

If something appears straight, faggots find it twice as good as gay. Our dilemma is simple: the straighter, more "professional" we become the broader our "market." The marketplace is a tough one; even the straight *Rolling Stone, New York Review of Books, Partisan Review, Ramparts, Liberation,* etc., are in a squeeze between rising paper, printing, mailing costs and the competition of more visual media like TV, concerts, and dances. Breaking into this market is not easy, you have to be hard and lucky.

Fag Rag will probably never get into that league because we have set as our goal to express, project, articulate, experience our gayness into print. The existing media and distribution networks are designed to keep out any such values. As Jill Johnston says, the existing media are "more an obstruction than a channel . . . Somehow the incoming information is blocked or distorted instead of passed through intact at all. the media is its own agency, or else it's a strict customs agency and very little cargo is permitted to pass."

Fag Rag like other outsider publications should build another network where we can develop and discover some of our destroyed sensibility. Faggots need to speak to other faggots in order to build a way of speaking and a self-awareness of our being beyond that imposed on us by straight society. If *Fag Rag* can continue as a medium for poetry, short stories, history, essays, plays, reviews, and personal testimonies—then we might develop a consciousness which will strengthen and activate us to be gay. A consciousness that will give a glimmering of how we can change, overthrow the straightness around (within) us; how we can become whole people.

In our "unmanifesto" (*Fag Rag* 6) we said, "In publishing, we do not wish to block someone else but to share ourselves and to provide a place where other faggots might wish to sing about themselves. Hopefully, our readers will find echoes and reverberations of themselves in our writing and will respond to us, not by accepting everything we write, but by loving us for taking the time and energy to write for other faggots." Perhaps our greatest achievement might be to show other faggots that they can start their own paper.

LIST OF GAY PERIODICALS

The following is a list of periodicals reflecting various aspects of the gay liberation movement. The list includes periodicals oriented toward both gay men and lesbians, those oriented primarily toward men, and those published by and for lesbians. For information about subscriptions, send a self-addressed, stamped envelope to the periodical. Or send $1 for one or more sample copies of any publication.

PERIODICALS OF GENERAL INTEREST

Gay Community News
22 Bromfield St.
Boston, Mass. 02108

It's Time
Newsletter of the National Gay
    Task Force
80 Fifth Ave.
New York, N. Y. 10011

PERIODICALS ORIENTED PRIMARILY TOWARD GAY MEN

The Advocate
2121 South El Camino Real
San Mateo, Calif. 94403

Arcadie
61 rue du Chateau d'Eau
Paris, France

The Body Politic
Box 7289 Station A
Toronto, Ontario, Canada M5W 1X9

Fag Rag
Box 331 Kenmore Station
Boston, Mass. 02215

Faggots on Faggotry
Box 227
Old Chelsea Station
New York, N. Y. 10011

The Gay Alternative
232 South St.
Philadelphia, Pa. 19147

Gay Crusader
c/o U.F.G.O.
Box 872
Chicago, Ill. 60690

Gay Liberation Press
P.O. Box A76
Sydney Sth 2000
New South Wales
Australia

Gay Liberator
Box 631-A
Detroit, Mich. 48232

245

Gay News
1A Normand Gardens
Greyhound Road
London W 14 9SB

Gay People's Union News
Box 90530
Milwaukee, Wisc. 53202

Gay Sunshine
Box 40397
San Francisco, Calif. 94140

Gay Tide
2142 Yew St.
Vancouver, B.C., Canada

Manroot Poetry Journal
Box 982
South San Francisco, Calif. 94080

Pa'fuera
Apartado 5523
Estación de Puerta de Tierra
San Juan, Puerto Rico 00906

Pittsburgh Gay News
Box 10236
Pittsburgh, Pa. 15232

Pro-Me-Thee-Us
The Eulenspiegel Society
Box 2783
New York, N. Y. 10017

R.F.D.
Rural Gay Journal
Box 161
Grinnell, Iowa 50112

Weekly Gayzette
Box 15786
Philadelphia, Pa. 19103

PUBLICATIONS BY AND FOR LESBIANS

Ain't I a Woman
Box 1169
Iowa City, Iowa 52240

ALFA Newsletter
Atlanta Lesbian Feminist Alliance
P.O. Box 7684
Atlanta, Ga. 30309

Amazon
2211 East Kenwood
Milwaukee, Wis. 53211

Amazon Quarterly
Box 434
West Somerville, Mass. 02144

Cowrie
359 East 68 Street
New York, N. Y. 10021

Desperate Living
Box 7124
Baltimore, Md. 21218

Dykes Unite
S.U.C. Geneseo
Fraser Box 354
Geneseo, N. Y. 11454

Focus: A Journal for Gay Women
c/o Boston D.O.B.
Rm. 323
419 Boylston St.
Boston, Mass. 02116

Lavender Woman
Box 60206
Chicago, Ill. 60660

Lesbian Connection
Ambitious Amazons
P.O. Box 811
East Lansing, Mich. 48823

The Lesbian Feminist
Box 243 Village Station
New York, N. Y. 10014

The Lesbian Tide
1005 Ocean Ave. #B
Santa Monica, Calif. 90403

Lesbian Visions
c/o The Lesbian Collective
Box 8265
Stanford, Calif. 94305

Long Time Coming
Box 161 Station E
Montreal, Quebec, Canada
H2T 3A7

The Purple Cow
Box 10
1739 High St.
Columbus, Ohio 43210

Sappho
BCM/Petrel
London WC 1V
England

Sisters
1005 Market
Suite 401
San Francisco, Calif. 94103

Tres Femmes
Gay Center for Social Services
2250 B St.
San Diego, Calif. 92102

Wicce
Box 15833
Philadelphia, Pa. 19103

BIBLIOGRAPHY

The bibliography published by the Task Force on Gay Liberation of the Social Responsibilities Round Table of the American Library Association includes listings of books, articles, periodicals, audio-visual materials, and directories. For a free copy, send a self-addressed stamped envelope to Barbara Gittings, Coordinator, Box 2383, Philadelphia, Pa. 19103.

POWER TO GAY PEOPLE:
A Los Angeles Experiment in Community Action

Richard Nash

Although social service agencies are not generally thought to be revolutionary tools by which a society is changed, I believe the Gay Community Services Center in Los Angeles has been developing into just such a tool.

This is the case because it has geared its programs and services to meet real needs of an oppressed minority, and because it has devised a unique style to enable gay people to work together on our own behalf. If power is defined as the ability to get things accomplished, then GCSC is making it possible for heretofore largely powerless people to mobilize the power necessary to change our own lives, and, growing out of this, the larger society in which we live.

Let's look, in turn, both at how the center's activities are matched to the actual needs of people in the gay community, and at the special way it brings gays together in the pursuit of our goals.

MATCHING ACTIVITIES TO NEEDS OF THE OPPRESSED

Before GCSC leased the central building in the fall of 1971 at 1614 Wilshire Boulevard, ten blocks west of downtown Los Angeles, it had rented first one house and then another, which were called *Liberation Houses*. The direct experience of the early workers, who emerged almost entirely from the Gay Liberation Front, showed the immediate need for housing. Street people wanting a place to stay with other gays were being put up in numbers up to forty a night at the GLF building, which was never designed to house anybody. We began, and have continued ever since, by creating programs in direct response to the needs that our firsthand experience told us were priorities. We began with little administrative structure and still less money. But that did not keep us from responding to the human needs of our gay sisters and brothers.

One by one, additional services were developed to deal with the human needs of oppressed gays.

There is discrimination in hiring and on the part of employment agencies, especially against the more feminine-identified men and the more masculine-identified women. Our *job placement service* has been highly successful in searching out employers with fewer prejudices and in many cases finding jobs where gays can be up-front at work.

Gay men and women still often face moralistic lectures, insulting comments, or incomplete examinations (not checked for anal VD) from doctors, but not at our *medical clinic,* which is staffed completely by gay doctors, nurses, technicians, and others who welcome this opportunity to serve their brothers and sisters.

Our *draft and military program* worked first (with one-hundred percent success) to keep men out of military service from which gays are officially excluded, when they wished to claim their gayness as the reason for avoiding this oppressive situation. Since the end of the draft, the attention of this program has shifted to getting dishonorable discharges upgraded and to helping gays get out of the service on the basis of their gayness. Both men and women approach us for this help.

Gays arrested are oppressed by many uncaring lawyers and public defenders who overcharge and/or give poor counsel. Our *legal services program* provides legal counseling and referral to competent, friendly lawyers. Next, as we face court proceedings, all too often our rights are overlooked and/or our sentences are cruel and extreme. Our *arraignment intervention program* arranges for gay law students to be in court to advise gay arrestees of their rights and to intervene on their behalf to get minimal, sensible judgments, often involving the person in center programs as an alternative to jail.

Gays serving time in jails, prisons, and state hospitals, or who are on probation or parole from these institutions, face some of the most inhuman treatment, ranging from being held indefinitely to being brutalized, to not being allowed to associate with other gays. Our *prisoner, parole & probation program* assists people in each of these categories, providing services relevant to their needs and dealing directly with corrections officials at all levels to improve their treatment of our brothers and sisters.

Gays with personal problems who turn to private therapists or mental health centers regularly encounter professionals who want to "cure" their gayness or refuse to explore the problems as manifestations of a messed-up society. The *peer counseling program* at the center gives troubled persons the chance to work with a person who not only shares his/her gayness, but also is prepared to use methods more relevant than the traditional medical model for resolving personal problems.

Young gays are harassed by parents, school officials, and peers. Teen-agers who are kicked out of home or school often appear at our doors, having no other place to turn. The *under-21 group,* which is operated entirely by the young gays, gives young people the chance to rap and socialize together, to develop activities for mutual support, and to act as an avenue to any of the center's programs.

Gays whose experience of their oppression is overwhelming often abuse alcohol and other drugs as one way out. As with VD, alcohol and drug abuse is rampant in the gay community because relevant help has not been provided. Our *alcohol and drug abuse program* has taken this situation seriously and is designing services, in cooperation with interested members of Alcoholics Together (the gay counterpart to Alcoholics Anonymous), to give realistic help to chemical abusers who want to rehabilitate their lives.

This list illustrates that what we do has developed in response to real, existing needs in the gay community, but does not exhaust our range of services. We also have a twenty-four-hour hotline for crises; social alternatives, including dances; a transvestite/transsexual program; a parents of gay people group; and a speakers' bureau.

The programs already listed assist people in cases where oppression is direct and obvious. The oppressor, whether a person or an institution, is easily identified. There are more subtle forms of oppression experienced by gay people, often denied or not understood because their sources are not so readily apparent.

For example, there is the isolation of the young gay who believes he/she is the "only one," which is a function of social censorship of honest and complete information about us.

In our society there is a double standard in which nongays are permitted to give free expression to their sexuality in public, but gays are warned not to. We are expected to be sexual neuters, not holding hands, kissing, discussing our love affairs, etc. By limiting the expression of our natural human emotion to private settings, we do tremendous psychological damage to ourselves.

In a predominantly nongay society, our sexuality is typically the source of negative experience: shame, guilt, hostility, compromise. When people experience their gayness in consistently bad ways, it is inevitable that they will develop a low self-esteem.

Because we have been up-front only at great risk of ostracism, we have lived closeted existences which keep us isolated and alienated from each other. This loneliness is expressed by a large majority of people coming to GCSC.

Growing out of this oppression is the fact that we are not whole people on the job, at school, in church—in the many social institutions where most people make most of their friends. Consequently, we have another circle of gay friends, with whom we are not whole either, since they are not typically our coworkers, classmates, etc. Having different sets of friends and sharing only limited parts of our lives with them means that our lives are disintegrated, with our sexuality fragmented from the rest of our existence.

How people view themselves is a product of the conceptual tools available in their culture. It is no coincidence that a great many of us should have limited and/or negative self-images when the conceptualization offered by our society has been the term "homosexual." Not only is the term a direct put-down because of its connotations, it also limits our vision to a specific behavioral pattern: what we do in bed. It focuses attention away from *who we are* to *what we do*. The possibility that our lifestyle can be a consistent whole, informed throughout by our sexuality, is ruled out. The exploration of the ramifications of our gayness for politics, religion, lifestyles, etc., is discouraged. That many think of our identity in terms of what we do rather than who we are is a tragic consequence of the conceptual tool offered by our society. And, since the distinction is subtle, many miss its enormous importance.

It is to meet the needs of gay women and men oppressed in the more subtle ways just described that the Gay Community Services Center began its *self-development program,* including gay awareness rap groups, growth groups, consciousness-raising groups, and the counseling program already mentioned. By helping people become a part of a mutually supportive community, by giving solid encouragement for more openly gay lifestyles, in providing different settings in which gays experience their gayness positively, in offering a wide variety of groups in which we experience ourselves and each other more fully, and in developing new conceptual tools encouraging us to explore all the implications of our sexuality for our total lives, the center helps people realize their full potential as gay human beings.

We have believed from the outset that a careful analysis of our oppression is the starting point for program planning. This is the gay consciousness we believe necessary to meet the needs of an emerging people.

251

The Gay Community Services Center has been a service agency (and certified as such by the state) combined with a community center. As a service agency the center helps people who come with particular needs. As a community center we provide a setting for people who want simply to enjoy themselves and to have a good time with others who share their gayness. Actually, a majority of people come to the center with this second motivation, rather than for help with problems.

So far I've written about how our programs grew in response to the real needs of emerging gay people. Now I turn to the other reason mentioned at the beginning for why the center has a revolutionary impact on its community: the special way it brings gays together in the pursuit of our goals.

CREATING COMMUNITY

Every worker at the center is gay. There have been only rare exceptions to this generalization. Every person on the staff is also a volunteer. Only a few people—some of those who are full-time volunteers—have received small "survival stipends," $50 to $150 a month, when money was available. The staff has been ingenious in finding other means of support.

The center has become a vehicle for gay people with special skills and talents to give of themselves to their brothers and sisters. A great variety of people who experience the mystique of the center are motivated to see it as the place where they, too, will offer their particular contribution. Doctors, nurses, technicians, psychiatrists, psychologists, social workers, clergy, teachers, law students, businessmen, accountants, corrections officers, and others have volunteered their services to the center. Many of these people are up-front gays; others have to do their work anonymously. Not only are there gay people who have all the skills needed to staff our kind of center, our experience also shows that they are willing and ready to work at a gay center where they serve their sisters and brothers.

All our workers are peers with the people who come to the center. We are gay people helping each other. Some staff have academic credentials, some have advanced training, some have professional experience. But all this is incidental, in most cases, to their becoming workers. First we look for people who are really together gay human beings. Then we welcome whatever other resources they bring.

The peer relationship existing between people at GCSC means to the

252

person coming to the center that he/she will have the opportunity to deal with somebody who in large measure shares where he/she is coming from. Women with women, men with men, transvestites with transvestites, alcoholics with alcoholics, young people with young people, and in all cases gays with gays. Our experience tells us that, because of the peer nature of our service, people come with more confidence, open themselves up more comfortably, have fewer resistances due to fear and suspicion, and save much time in explaining detail.

The peer relationship also has implications about how a service is rendered. Staff, with certain exceptions, are not seen as experts, but rather as other human beings. Whether or not a special expertise is part of the service rendered, the quality of the interaction can be described as human. We—all people at the center—share our experience and insight, develop emotional involvements, and relate with each other at many levels in the several programs there. We discourage the clinical detachment of some agencies and encourage the personal involvement natural to people who share a common oppression and a common struggle for liberation.

We charge no fees for any activity. Many of the people are poor, but there is a more fundamental reason for not charging. It is inconsistent with our larger goals. Payment implies an inequality between a giver of services and a receiver of services. It defines the relationship as being built on the need of the client and the expertise of the professional. That very relationship is what we avoid at GCSC because it is inconsistent with our longer-range goal of creating a sense of community among those who use the center.

By our understanding, community means having that kind of relationship to others in a group of people in which a person receives according to his/her need and gives according to his/her ability and in which people define for themselves the ways they will be givers and receivers. In that setting the exchange of money makes little sense. Should I pay you today for something I receive from you, when tomorrow you might return the money for something you receive from me? We invite all people to join us in our larger community-building effort.

The center needs money to operate. Many people are in a position to give money, and we always welcome contributions, from people using our services as well as others. Our basic support has always been of this kind. We make appeals regularly. But, we do not charge fees, thus not defining ahead of time who will be givers and who will be receivers and how that exchange will operate.

Notice that I've written at this length without mentioning the names of anybody at the center. This is purposeful. From the beginning there was a sizable group of workers involved. To mention the names of a few would falsely imply that their special contribution was more important than that of others. But, more importantly, it would divert attention away from the more fundamental reason for whatever success the center has achieved. Without denying the courage, clear vision, and extensive talent of many people identified with GCSC, I think it is more important to focus attention on the nature of what happens at the center. We are organized to make possible the coming together of people from many lifestyles and with many talents to interact in ways that are mutually satisfying. It is the positive, supportive experience of this interaction which is contagious. It continuously draws more people, who, having felt this special mystique, want to make it available to still more people.

POLITICAL IMPLICATIONS

The political implications of the center's existence may now be evident. We are not political in the usual definition of that word. But we are highly political by our definition of the term, which would have to do with bringing power into people's hands to take charge of their own lives and destinies.

Certainly, the objective oppression outlined above keeps us from controlling our own lives. But, so also do the repressive attitudes in our own heads which we've internalized from the larger society. Freeing people internally is the first step in preparing them for dealing with external oppression. The center works at both levels, but our assumption is that gays are going to have to win our own freedom rather than have it handed to us by somebody else.

We focus our attention less on our oppressors or on the people in control of the standard means of social change than we do on our sisters and brothers. We are not trying to change the world or even our city; we are trying to make more real the notion of community among gay people. Where external oppression still has power over us it is where we have not freed ourselves internally, individually and collectively.

Kahlil Gibran said it well:

And what is it but fragments of your own self you would discard that you may become free?

If it is an unjust law you would abolish, that law was written with your own hand upon your own forehead.

You cannot erase it by burning your law books nor by washing the foreheads of your judges, though you pour the sea upon them. . . .

For how can a tyrant rule the free and the proud, but for a tyranny in their own freedom and a shame in their own pride?

That speaks especially to me because I was arrested, without justification, on an unjust law: solicitation for prostitution. I finally won when the city dismissed charges, after a two-year struggle, in and out of the courts. I did not do it alone; I didn't have to. The community of which I am a part at the center mobilized the resources—and a great many were needed—to defeat our opposition. We stood together in our conviction of our rightness and our pride. Our very oppression turned out to be the theater for victory. When we turn our oppression around and use it to our advantage as stepping stones to our freedom, we become victorious.

That is what the Gay Community Services Center is all about. We are trying to facilitate a self-defining, self-affirming, mutually supportive community of gay men and women, not only as the road to freedom for individual gays, but through us, for the larger community in which we live.

For an up-to-date list of gay organizations, consult *The Gayellow Pages,* Renaissance House, Box 292, Village Station, New York, N. Y. 10014.

INFORMATION ON VD FOR
GAY WOMEN AND MEN

Julian Bamford

Venereal diseases aren't terrible, shameful, or mysterious things. They are diseases like any others, but they are a taboo subject because they are connected with sex.

VD affects all communities, but until now almost every written handout on the subject has ignored or been confusing to gay people. We gay people have a right to the facts and need them for our own health care.

For example:

FACT: Men can get gonorrhea in the rectum (ass), something that most doctors overlook because they assume they are dealing with non-gay men.

FACT: Syphilis and gonorrhea seem to be almost nonexistent in communities of gay women.

WHAT IS VD AND HOW DO GAY PEOPLE GET IT?

VD stands for venereal disease. A venereal disease means any disease that is spread by intimate body contact with an infected person. This usually means sex, because sex is one of the few times we enjoy close physical contact with another human being.

The two most common venereal diseases are syphilis and gonorrhea, and they are caused by different germs, have different symptoms, are detected by different tests and are cured by different treatments. Contrary to popular myth, you don't get VD by contact with door knobs, toilet seats, spoons and forks, or by shaking hands. It's impossible because the germs cannot live away from the infected part of the body. There is no immunity to VD. If you get either syphilis or gonorrhea once, you can get it again. You can even have these two separate diseases together at the same time.

256

WHAT IS SYPHILIS?

Syphilis is a disease caused by a germ called a spirochete. Although starting in one spot, it enters the bloodstream and infects the whole body. You can get it by contact with the innocent-looking infectious sore or rash which an infected person may not even be aware of. The syphilis sore is usually in the genital area but can be anywhere on the body. This means you could get it from any kind of sexual contact with an infected person—possibly even by kissing if the sore is in their mouth. The disease runs as follows:

Men: The first (primary) stage of syphilis involves a usually painless sore which may develop anytime between ten and ninety days after you were exposed to the infected person. This sore is called a chancre (pronounced "shanker"). It appears at the place where the germs entered your body. This usually means in, on, or around your penis, rectum, or mouth. Because the sore is often small and usually painless you may never discover it. The chancre may be an open sore or closed like a pimple, and is full of syphilis germs.

In this early stage, syphilis germs taken from the chancre can be detected under a special microscope. However, a syphilis blood test may not turn positive for up to four weeks after the sore appears. So, if there is any doubt in your mind or your doctor's that you might have syphilis, make sure you have a blood test taken one month after your chancre appeared. Only if this test shows negative can you be sure you haven't got syphilis.

Even without treatment the chancre will disappear but this does *not* mean that the disease has ended. The germs are still increasing in number and spreading throughout the whole body. Once diagnosed, syphilis is cured quickly and easily.

The second stage (secondary syphilis) appears from two weeks to six months after exposure. A rash that can take many forms may develop at this time. It may cover the whole body and even include the palms of the hands and the soles of the feet. It probably won't itch. Infectious sores sometimes develop in the mouth and around the rectum, and you may lose patches of hair. Because secondary syphilis can resemble many other diseases, some people are unaware of the true nature of their illness. Only a medical examination and blood test will tell with certainty if you have syphilis. Secondary syphilis can also be easily cured.

257

Untreated, these secondary symptoms, like the primary chancre before them, will disappear in time. *But the disease is still active in the body.* You may continue to feel fine and may go along for years thinking you are healthy and not infected. Untreated, syphilis may then eventually lead to blindness, crippling, heart trouble, and brain damage. These are some of the consequences of late syphilis. In this late stage further progress of the disease can be halted by appropriate treatment, but damage already done cannot be reversed.

Women: As mentioned before, syphilis is very rare among gay women. However, it is possible, particularly through the increase of bi-sexual behavior, that more gay women might be contracting syphilis. The symptoms of syphilis are the same as in men—the appearance of a chancre where the germs have entered your body. The chancre is likely to appear somewhere in the genital area: on the labia (the outer lips of the vagina) or somewhere inside the vaginal canal or on the cervix where it would be noticed only if we examine ourselves regularly using a vaginal speculum. The chancre may also appear in the mouth or possibly in or around the rectum. As with men, the chancre disappears in a month or so but you will still be infected if you have not been treated. The progression of the disease runs the same in both sexes; the same microscope and blood tests are used to detect the disease and the same antibiotics are used to cure each stage.

WHAT SHOULD I DO IF I THINK I HAVE SYPHILIS?

Go to a doctor or clinic.

BUT SINCE I MAY NOT NOTICE SYMPTOMS AND STILL MAY BE INFECTED AND CAPABLE OF PASSING SYPHILIS TO OTHERS, HOW CAN I BE SURE I DON'T HAVE IT?

Routine blood tests are the way to make sure you don't have syphilis, or of detecting it early if you do. (Remember, blood tests detect only syphilis, not gonorrhea.)

HOW OFTEN SHOULD I HAVE ROUTINE BLOOD TESTS?

Since the chances of getting syphilis are directly proportional to the number of sexual contacts you have—

Men: If you go to the baths, tea rooms, or trick frequently, you

258

should have a blood test *every three months*. If you have only a few sex partners you should have a blood test *every six months*. Write the dates you are due for tests on your calendar. Make it a habit to have routine blood tests.

Women: It may not be necessary for exclusively gay women to be tested as often as gay men. However, it is a good idea to have a blood test for syphilis if you've never had one. If there's *any* chance that you may have contracted syphilis, be sure to be tested.

WHAT IS GONORRHEA?

Gonorrhea (the "clap," "dose," "drip") is the most common of the venereal diseases. It is caused by a germ called a gonococcus. Unlike syphilis germs, which enter the bloodstream, gonorrhea germs usually stay in the original area of infection. This can be the penis, vagina, cervix, rectum, or throat.

Gonorrhea can be passed only when the germs are transferred directly from an infected part to someone else's uninfected parts. It is almost always passed during anal or vaginal intercourse; from an infected penis to a rectum or vagina, or from an infected rectum or vagina to a penis. It is sometimes passed during oral sex (sucking or licking) when it may pass from an infected penis or vagina to a throat. Only on very rare occasions do gonorrhea germs seem to pass from an infected throat to a penis or vagina. It seems even less likely that they pass from an infected throat to another throat during kissing. Unfortunately very little is known by anyone about gonorrhea of the throat (pharyngeal gonorrhea).

Men: Gonorrhea in the penis, rectum, or throat may or may not produce symptoms. Symptoms for gonorrhea in the penis will usually be noticeable several days (two to ten) after having intercourse (screwing) someone with an infected rectum or vagina. You'll probably first notice a burning sensation or uncomfortable feeling in the penis, usually when you urinate. This is often accompanied by a whitish discharge (pus) from the penis. As these symptoms may be caused by other diseases (described later), you should ask for a smear test (microscopic examination of your discharge) to see if you have gonorrhea. New research has shown that many people may have gonorrhea in the penis and not have the symptoms (asymptomatic)—perhaps two-thirds of all gonorrhea cases! You should try asking for a culture test to be taken from your penis (using a sterile loop). You can do this when you have your routine syphilis tests.

If you were screwed and the gonorrhea infection is in the rectum, you will probably have no symptoms at all. You may have rectal itching or pain; or you may have a discharge of blood, pus, or mucus from you rectum or on your feces (shit). Any of these symptoms are good reason for you to go for an examination and have a culture taken from your rectum (obtained with a cotton swab) to see if you have gonorrhea or not.

If you get gonorrhea in the throat from sucking an infected person, you will probably have no symptoms, though you may develop an ordinary sore throat. As said before, lack of research means little is known about pharyngeal gonorrhea.

Gonorrhea of the penis, rectum, or throat can be cured with appropriate antibiotics. Treated early, no complications are likely to result. Untreated gonorrhea can lead to scarring of the urinary passage, infection of the prostate gland, testicles, blood, or joints. Untreated gonorrhea can block the flow of urine through the urethra, or the flow of sperm from the testicles.

If you develop symptoms that might be caused by gonorrhea, or if you suspect that you may have been exposed to gonorrhea, but haven't developed symptoms, it is important that you be tested and possibly treated. The test for penile, rectal, or pharyngeal gonorrhea requires that a culture specimen be grown and you must *ask the doctor* to take a specimen from those areas. Penises, throats, and rectums are not routinely tested.

Also, if you are treated for gonorrhea of the penis, stay away from alcoholic beverages until the symptoms have completely disappeared. Alcohol will irritate the infected urethra and may prevent the sores from healing.

Remember: Blood tests do *not* detect gonorrhea. They detect only syphilis. You *must* have a smear or culture to detect gonorrhea, and you must *ask* to be tested in the penis, throat, or rectum if you suspect exposure in those parts.

Women: The question is often asked whether a women can pass gonorrhea to another woman when they have sex. In theory, the germs of gonorrhea might be passed from a finger to a vagina or from a tongue to a vagina if the infected person has an exceptionally heavy discharge, to provide the germs with an environment capable of keeping the germs alive outside the body for a longer time than is normal. Some cases of mother-daughter transfer have occurred where poor hygiene conditions existed (in the bathroom, for example). In actual fact, woman-to-woman transmission is extremely rare. If you have *exclusively* gay sexual conduct you can be fairly certain of never contracting gonorrhea.

If you relate sexually to men and contract gonorrhea, you have a serious problem, since the disease seldom produces symptoms until the disease is well advanced. Most women are unaware that they have gonorrhea until a male sexual partner develops symptoms and tells her.

If you have symptoms of gonorrhea, you *may* notice a yellowish discharge from your cervix, and you *may* experience abdominal cramping around or shortly after your menstrual flow. If you go untreated, the infection will progress from the cervix, through the uterus (womb) and go into the fallopian tubes and ovaries, causing serious and painful inflammation of the various glands, tubes, and pelvic organs. A condition known as pelvic inflammatory disease may result in permanent damage to the Fallopian tubes, causing sterility, and may require surgical removal of the infected organs.

If you are having sex with men, and if you or they have several partners, you should make a habit of having routine cultures taken for gonorrhea, perhaps every three to six months.

Women, like men, may also contract gonorrhea in the rectum or the throat. If you have rectal or oral sex, you should request that cultures also be taken from those areas.

WHAT SHOULD I DO IF I THINK I HAVE GONORRHEA SYMPTOMS OR SOMEONE I HAD SEX WITH HAS SYMPTOMS?

Go to a doctor or clinic. Request gonorrhea cultures from the parts of your body where you may have been infected.

Remember: You must *ask* to have cultures taken of your rectum or throat. Also, since rectal, pharyngeal, and cervical gonorrhea seldom produce symptoms, *routine* examinations are recommended for sexually active persons.

WHAT IS NONSPECIFIC URETHRITIS (NSU)?

NSU is an infection of the urethra, the precise cause is not determined: there can be burning, or a discharge.

NSU may be caused by a variety of microorganisms, by chemical or

261

physical irritation of the urethral lining, or after a true case of gonorrhea in the penis. Usually the precise cause is not determined, therefore the name "nonspecific," or as it is sometimes called, "non-gonococcal" urethritis.

NSU will often disappear in several weeks without treatment. Treatment with tetracyclines will usually be effective in providing a more prompt cure.

Drinking alcohol and sexual activity should be avoided until the discharge has been cleared, as any irritation of the urethral lining will prolong the healing process.

Men note: Not everything that drips is gonorrhea. In males, a discharge from the penis or painful urination can be caused by organisms or problems other than gonorrhea germs. Only a microscopic examination of the drip can determine whether its cause is gonorrhea or something else, although the discharge from NSU is usually thinner than that of gonorrhea.

WHAT IS VAGINITIS?

Vaginitis is a problem of women, and is a catch-all term for any inflammation of the vagina. Most women get it at some time in their lives. Gay women, however, avoid much yeast and other infections because they don't usually take birth control pills. There are different kinds of vaginitis with different causes and cures, the most common being yeast (*Monilia*) and *Trichomonas*. The others are usually referred to as nonspecific vaginitis.

A yeast condition is caused by the overgrowth of an organism which is normally present in the vagina. There is a cottage-cheesy discharge from the vagina, together with itching. Yeast commonly follows antibiotic treatment for something else, though you can get it spontaneously if you are run down. Yeast can be passed between women living in the same house and sharing towels and washcloths, or during lovemaking. Wearing non-breathing nylon underwear may aggravate it; cotton or no underwear will not. If you notice your yeast early enough, you can often restore the healthy balance of your vagina by giving yourself one acidic douche (two tablespoons of white vinegar in a quart of warm water), or by putting plain natural yoghurt in your vagina. If douching doesn't work the first time, see a doctor who will prescribe medication—frequent douching does more harm than good. Meanwhile, you can relieve the itching somewhat by sitting in a bath of cool water or applying cold compresses over the vagina. You can also give yourself instant relief for an hour or two by dissolving a generous amount of baking soda in a pitcher of warm water and pouring this over the inner vaginal lips.

A *Trichomonas* infection usually involves a thin, yellowish, unpleasant-smelling discharge together with itching and burning of the vagina and vaginal lips. *Trichomonas* is passed during sex or sometimes on shared waschcloths, towels, or clothing. The trichomonal organism can also lie dormant for long periods in the body, causing no symptoms or problems. The infection can therefore seem to occur spontaneously. If you notice the symptoms early enough, you can try one vinegar and water douche (as above). Otherwise, a doctor should take care of it.

If you are not sure what you've got, a doctor can diagnose your condition by making a microscopic examination of your discharge, and treating it accordingly. If your vaginitis keeps recurring and your doctor doesn't seem to be helping any, it's worth finding out more about vaginitis from somewhere like a local feminist health group. More and more medication without finding out what you have and why you have it probably won't help.

WHAT ARE VENEREAL WARTS?

Both men and women sometimes get warts in the anal or genital region. These seem to be caused by a virus similar to that which causes warts on other areas of the body, and it seems to be transmitted by sexual activity. In moist areas such as the clitoris, in the vagina, on the cervix or inner vaginal lips, and in or near the anal canal, the warts are small, cauliflower-shaped pink or reddish growths. One or more may appear together. On the outer vaginal lips and the shaft of the penis, they are harder and look more like ordinary warts. *IT IS VERY IMPORTANT TO TREAT VENEREAL WARTS EARLY* as they can spread and be even more difficult to treat, especially in the anal canal or vagina.

WHAT IS HERPES?

Herpes is another skin condition, caused by a virus which is closely related to the one which causes cold sores. More women seem to get it than men. Herpes is probably, though not always, spread by sexual contact. The virus lies dormant in the body until it is somehow

263

activated; this sometimes happens to women following another vaginal infection.

Small, very painful blisters appear, usually in crops or bunches. They may be somewhere on the vaginal lips, clitoris or cervix, on the penis, or in or around the anus. In a few days the blisters burst and become sores, which gradually become less painful and heal over. The whole cycle takes seven to fourteen days, after which the virus may remain dormant and cause no more trouble. Sometimes, however, it recurs, blistering and fading in cycles.

Herpes can be treated by a doctor, who should also check to see if you have syphilis. Putting cold compresses, or a mild anesthetic cream or spray on the blisters (check with your doctor) will help relieve some of the pain. New techniques have been discovered for treating herpes, though many physicians may not yet be aware of them. A dermatologist might be able to help you.

WHAT ARE CRABS?

Crabs (pubic lice) are pinhead-sized insect parasites that live in the hairy parts of the body, usually around the genitals. Some people have no symptoms at all while others experience intolerable itching. Crabs are passed by physical contact when having sex or even while sleeping in the same bed. They can sometimes spread throughout a household by sharing clothes and towels. You can sometimes get rid of them with A-200 bought at a drug store, but Kwell (prescribed by a doctor) is usually more effective. Be sure to follow the instructions for using the medication so as to eliminate both the crabs and their eggs. Your sex partners and roommates should also be treated at the same time to avoid reinfesting each other.

WHAT ARE SCABIES?

Scabies are tiny (you won't see them with the naked eye) insects which burrow under the skin and cause sporadic itching, which usually gets worse at night. They can be passed by skin contact with an infested person anywhere from the neck down. If untreated, they slowly spread over the whole body. The only thing you may see are some raised areas or red bumps. You may think they are mosquito bites and only realize they are scabies when they won't go away. A doctor's prescription of Kwell will banish them (A-200 doesn't work). All roommates and sex

264

partners should be checked and treated to avoid reinfesting each other.

WHAT CAN I DO ABOUT PREVENTING THE SPREAD OF VENEREAL DISEASES?

1. *TAKE RESPONSIBILITY FOR YOUR OWN BODY.* Learn about the enemy. Study this article. Ask questions. Genital diseases, especially VD, can be eliminated. There's no need to be ashamed or frightened of them. The bad feelings you have come from society's repressive attitudes toward sex.

2. If you are a woman who examines herself regularly using a vaginal speculum, you are much more likely to notice venereal diseases and vaginal conditions in their early stages. And sharing other women's experiences in a self-help clinic can help you to understand and take care of your body.

3. Visit a doctor or clinic if you are ever at all suspicious about your health. Better safe . . .

4. Have routine VD check-ups: a syphilis blood test and the appropriate gonorrhea cultures. Have them as often as necessary according to the number of sexual contacts you have. Men: every three to every six months.

5. Spread the word to everyone about routine check-ups. Talk to your sex partners about them.

6. Inform the people you have had sex with if you are diagnosed as having syphilis or gonorrhea. This may involve going back as far as a year in the case of syphilis (depending on the stage), but usually no more than a month from the onset of gonorrhea symptoms. Your sex partners may be infected and *not know it.* They need to be examined, tested, and possibly treated.
Remember: You can have syphilis and gonorrhea *without any symptoms.*

7. Never try to treat what you think may be syphilis or gonorrhea yourself with left-over antibiotics. It is important that the disease be accurately diagnosed and fully treated. Never share your antibiotics with a friend—you need them all for your own infection, and your sex partners need a full treatment too.

265

A NOTE ABOUT CONFIDENTIALITY OF MEDICAL RECORDS IN CALIFORNIA

The California State Code, Title 17, Section 2636(b) protects your medical records. They are available to no one without your written consent. Subpoenas from courts, police or government agencies are not honored. No one will know that you have been seen or treated for VD unless you personally tell her/him. Doctors and laboratories are required by California laws to report cases of syphilis and gonorrhea to the County Health Department. Your medical record at the County Health Department is also protected by the same law quoted above.

Minors: If you are twelve years of age or older, and find that it is difficult or impossible to discuss your health problems with your parents, you may be examined and treated for syphilis and gonorrhea without the consent of your parents under the law (AB-656), which was effective November 13, 1968 in the State of California. *Note:* The above is not necessarily true in other states. You can call your local Health Department (listed in the phone book) and find out the law in your own state.

Even knowing the above facts about confidentiality, if you are still uptight, it is better to give false identifying information than to withhold treatment from yourself. But make sure that you check back with the clinic for the results of the tests they have taken, as they won't be able to get in touch with you.

WHERE CAN I GO FOR VD CHECK-UPS OR TREATMENT?

Free VD treatment is provided by the public health departments in every state. There is one in every city, listed in the phone book under City or County Health Department. In some areas there are also free clinics and feminist clinics, organized by concerned local people. These can be found through the phone book or through local community information sources: e.g., gay groups and centers, college student unions, and hotlines.

BOTTOMS UP:
An In-Depth Look at VD and Your Asshole

Edward Guthmann

> "I'm convinced that God loves and approves of gay men, and that's why he put the prostate gland right above the asshole so we could enjoy the pleasure of being fucked."
> —a gay man from Berkeley

> "Don't give him anything but love."
> —slogan for anti-VD poster put out by Los Angeles Gay Community Services Center

The joy of anal sex is a mystery and sounds unpleasant unless your body has known it and adjusted to it. To the squeamish man who calls it "unnatural" or fears being hurt, I would compare the ignored potential of the asshole to the many muscles and organs which seem useless only when we don't explore and exercise them. I would say, remember that your rectum has a mucous membrane lining, just like your mouth or a woman's vagina, which allows for a highly erogenous union of bodies once the fear of fucking and rimming is overcome.

It's really an incredible discovery. But unfortunately there are at the same time serious risks, in the form of a whole spectrum of anal VD: warts, anal syphilis, anal gonorrhea, herpes, hepatitis, and more that can be transmitted in gay lovemaking when two men don't know what precautions to take.

I decided I had to write this article when two friends of mine discovered warts in their rectums, neither of them having heard of anal warts before. Now, after a year of treatment, including hospitalization, they're still infected and still wearing invisible chastity belts on their backsides.

Getting into all forms of lovemaking, fucking and rimming (oral-anal) included, wouldn't be a hazard if we had more information on anal venereal disease. But medicine has largely shied away from it (and most other gay health needs), even more so than with "straight" or genital VD. Facts are scarce and research is slim. It wasn't until 1967

267

that statistics on male-to-male transmission of VD were compiled by the American Social Health Association.

If a doctor neglects to take an anal culture, the patient will usually have no way of knowing he's infected, because there are rarely any symptoms. He's then more likely to reach an advanced, serious condition. And this is only one of the complications of anal VD.

What's more, the rectum seems to retain viruses and bacteria much more than the genitals, because they thrive well in warm and moist regions, and also because it's so much harder to clean your asshole really thoroughly than all the other parts of the body.

So again, it's very wise to know the ramifications of anal sex, to be able to fully enjoy it as a physical and/or spiritual self-expression, as much as any other type of lovemaking.

Reading this article needn't make anyone panic, or cease their preferred sexual activity, but rather be aware of possible risks, and to avoid them with the right precautions.

ANAL WARTS

Anal warts, especially, are a big problem. Even though they're an epidemic with gays, very little information is available, and their treatment is somewhat crude. Since they're highly contagious, though, you should seek treatment immediately.

Warts most often result from anal intercourse. Doctors know they're caused by a virus, but the virus hasn't been identified or isolated to the point where an efficient cure or vaccine has been developed.

Usually you'll see small tumors just outside the rim of the anus when you get warts. Unlike hand warts, they're pink or red, soft and moist with an indented, cauliflower-like appearance. They can sometimes form a large tissue mass. Some clear up quickly, others take years despite treatments. They can recur even if you've had no sexual contact since before your first treatment. Sometimes there will be itching or bleeding, but most often you'll have no symptoms. You won't feel anything.

My friend recalled his experience: "When I first felt them, I assumed they were hemorrhoids. So I went out and bought some Preparation H. I'd never even heard of anal warts!" First, he went to a general practitioner who spent six unsuccessful months trying to kill the warts with acid. Then he found a good proctologist who had to operate and even then spent a full year more (at this writing) of weekly check-ups

268

to burn or freeze recurring warts.

During that time, my friend couldn't be fucked by anyone for fear his infection would spread to others, as well as the possibility of the contact ruining the effectiveness of the treatment. He didn't stop enjoying an active and healthy sex life, but still couldn't help feeling inhibited by the warts. He liked being flexible, and it bothered him to fuck his partner and then not be fucked.

The hassle of warts is made worse, as with all anal VD, by the nature of the rectal canal. The mucous membrane lining of the rectum has no sensory nerve endings, so you can have them up inside your ass and never know it while they multiply and grow larger.

The rectum can be compared to an elastic tube that stretches and contracts, so in its normal folded state you wouldn't be able to feel all the way up your asshole to know if any warts have formed deep inside. Only a doctor with an anoscope could do it.

When you spot warts or suspect them, go immediately to a proctologist or a doctor who's equipped to treat them. Most VD clinics can only diagnose them, and they aren't in a position to refer you to good doctors. You have to call the local medical society for referrals, or call any gay switchboard or community center for the names of good proctologists or gay doctors.

Bear in mind, treatment is fairly unsophisticated and unpredictable. The freezing technique, called cryotherapy, is the newest and best. A San Francisco proctologist I know now uses this almost exclusively. He says, "I'm very encouraged by it from two standpoints: (1) it can be done in the office; and (2) the amount of pain is minimal. And it's more accurate. I feel I can limit the treatment and know what I am treating."

He said he hopes a vaccine or immunization for warts will be developed, "but it's not forthcoming." He said, "I feel cryotherapy works not because we've destroyed warts but through the process we're stimulating an immune reaction in the body."

Podophyllin, an "acid," is the most common treatment. It's not always reliable as it affects people differently. It can severely burn and spread to other parts of the body. It should never be used on the tender inner rectal lining, only on the outside anal skin.

When warts are up inside the rectum, cryotherapy or electro-coagulation (burning with the help of an anesthetic) should be used. The latter requires hospitalization, but can be very effective depending on the individual and the extent of the infection. Surgery of course will run into hundreds of dollars, on top of your check-ups, and without some medical insurance or a fat bankroll, the cost could be prohibitive.

The point is to go out of your way to get the best treatment. Many general practitioners are ignorant of the problem, and they can waste your time with limited treatment, such as using podophyllin indiscriminately, or by treating only those warts observable on the skin and not looking for intra-anal warts.

Doctors should always take a gonorrhea culture and blood test for syphilis when treating warts. The rash which comes as a secondary symptom of syphilis looks just like warts. If the doctor mistakes them for hemorrhoids, which are inflamed blood vessels appearing as tabs of skin, you probably need a new doctor.

Proctology clinics are located in San Francisco at University of California, Mt. Zion, Children's Hospital, SF General, St. Mary's and Presbyterian Hospital. In Los Angeles, the Gay Community Services Center's free clinic can treat warts.

Penile warts are much less common, and generally less of a problem, though under a tight foreskin they can be awfully painful. They can be transmitted to, or contracted from, a sexual partner very easily. Treatment is the same, but usually easier for the patient as access is direct.

ANAL CLAP

Anal gonorrhea strikes more often (same as with genital clap) than anal syphilis. In eighty percent of the cases, you won't have symptoms—very different from the burning discharge of penile clap. So, check-ups every three to six months are necessary if you're active. A doctor can't see the gonococci in the rectum but a culture will determine it.

(The symptoms of anal clap that rarely do occur are a moistness, discharge, or discomfort when shitting.)

Having no symptoms is dangerous because as an unknowing carrier you could infect many partners and possibly reach an advanced stage. Unchecked gonorrhea can cause sterility, an infected prostate, or, in rare cases, blindness.

The clap is infectious and will live in your body until you're cured. If you've just fucked someone with anal clap, you can reduce chances of infection by pissing because the gonococci enter only through the meatus (penis opening) in that condition. If you're being fucked by a man who's got a dose, you'll almost for sure contract it because the rectum is such a contained receptacle.

Rimming or sucking cock can result in pharyngeal (throat) gonorrhea. When it does, a throat culture will define it and antibiotics will cure it as with all forms of the clap.

(To digress from anal VD, a word about penile clap: fifty percent of men with discharge complaints really have NGU, or nongonococcal urethritis, which is the same as NSU. It's defined as any infection of the urethra not caused by the clap, and is usually a milder discharge, and not continuous like the clap. So always demand a culture.)

ANAL SIFF

Anal syphilis, too, rarely infects the body with any signs. In the primary stage, a chancre sore may appear, but unlike oral or genital chancres they're "atypical" and have no common characteristics, except that they're painless. When they form inside the rectum rather than the rectal opening (anus), they won't be visible. When chancres are visible (as well as "secondary" siff symptoms) they often resemble the symptoms of other diseases. Syphilis is called "the great imitator" because it mimics other infections: a blood test or darkfield exam of serum from the sore are sometimes the only way to identify it.

Chancres will form precisely at the spot where the spirochete germ enters your body, anywhere from ten to ninety (usually twenty-one) days after contact. So you could have negative blood tests for weeks until the germs are numerous enough to be recorded. The chancre disappears if untreated, followed sometimes by a secondary stage of a skin rash. The rash usually appears as raised bumps all over the body, including inside the mouth, palms and soles of the feet. Usually the rash won't itch and will be so mild as to go unnoticed; but it's highly contagious.

This same rash will resemble anal warts when it appears near the asshole. Other possible secondary symptoms: hair falling out, and a low-grade fever and swelling of lymph glands. Even without treatment, the secondary symptoms vanish, like a chancre, within two to six weeks. Siff then becomes latent (no signs or symptoms) for years. Once it goes this far, you've a thirty-three percent chance of getting an advanced condition, which can lead to a fatal heart attack or paralysis, or insanity (remember Al Capone).

271

Remember, there's a very small (about twenty-five percent) chance that any of these primary or secondary symptoms will develop. And without any siff symptoms, you're still infectious, and the spirochetes remain in your blood until cured.

FISSURES, ABSCESSES, AND FISTULAS

The rectum is particularly vulnerable to some infections when no precautions are exercised. Aside from the nature of the mucous membrane lining, further disease can flourish in what's called anal crypts. These are pockets leading to anal glands located where the lining of the bowel meets the skin, one-half inch inside the anus. When these become infected you'll get problems with fissures, abscesses, and fistulas. These are very often caused not by sex but by diarrhea or other bowel problems.

A fissure is a split or tear in the anal canal, from an infected crypt. It appears like a small raw spot, and could be mistaken for a chancre. In severe cases, minor surgery is needed.

There's a theory, by an Englishman named Dr. Peter Lord, that says the relaxed muscles one gets from anal intercourse will make the body less, rather than more likely to get a fissure.

Abscesses will develop when the infection of the crypt goes deeper, causing a highly painful swelling. Once a doctor drains an abscess and the pus is released, the patient's pain will subside. But in eighty-five percent of abscesses, once they're drained a fistula develops, which is a tunnel boring outward from the abscess infection. It must be surgically opened and troughed.

Fissures, abscesses and fistulas are not a large or significant problem and shouldn't be considered a major risk in anal intercourse.

HEPATITIS

When two men are rimming and the tongue and lips enter the partner's asshole, there's a definite possibility of hepatitis infection, caused by the bacteria and viruses in human feces. Rimming, in addition to any oral-genital activity, can also cause oral syphilis and oral gonorrhea, pinworm, typhoid, and salmonellosis, though none are as frequent as hepatitis.

Dr. Erwin Braff of San Francisco's City Clinic says, "These infections of the gastrointestinal tract are a very significant hazard that one doesn't really think of as being a venereal disease." He added that the incidence of pinworm, typhoid, and salmonellosis isn't common enough to be considered a significant risk. Again, the rectum is very difficult to clean thoroughly, so you might say the cleaner the man the less chance of disease for the man who rims or fucks him. A gamma globulin shot within a week after contact will prevent or at least minimize the onset of hepatitis in seventy percent of cases.

Yellow skin, or jaundice, is the traditional hepatitis symptom, when really only one out of three persons get it. It usually resembles the flu: no appetite, aches and pains, a fever, abdominal pains. The urine is very dark and feces become a light clay color. Hepatitis is serious, in that it can permanently weaken the liver, and can put you on your back for weeks with a long, slow recovery. Often when hepatitis symptoms have left or are slight, the disease is still communicable.

HERPES

Herpes genitalis, though it's more common to women, can infect men who enjoy anal sex. If infected, men will get the same fever blisters women get, pinkish with a red border. Herpes are exquisitely painful if located on skin outside the anus (or on the genitals) but usually not felt at all if inside the rectum.

The blisters fester and merge together as they grow so that you can't sit down, let alone have sex, without agonizing pain. After four or five days they start to heal, and then another ten days pass before they disappear without scarring. The sores won't be communicable unless they're open.

Herpes can return as they will lie in remission, and the virus can be reactivated by the chafing of buttocks (especially with overweight people), or from sex, or from irritating material in the feces which don't get washed off completely. So, unlike most VD, when herpes erupt it's not always because of the last sex you had, but rather the original infection could easily have been reawakened. This is also true with anal warts sometimes.

Herpes cure is a matter of simply alleviating the symptoms until the virus leaves the body and the disease cures itself. To stop their spreading, it's good to rub sulfa cream on the sores, Vaseline on the skin near the sores. A tub of hot water helps too, as will a surface antiseptic or pain pills. Washing well instead of wiping with toilet tissue is good.

273

It's possible to get herpes in the mouth—either from rimming or sucking, or by transferring the virus from hand to mouth after urinating.

PROSTATE AND SPHINCTER

The prostate gland, from which much of the erotic pleasure of anal intercourse stems, can become infected if the sexual partner uses undue force when penetrating the rectum, especially if fists or dildos are used. Any kind of rough sex could also injure the rectal lining, and here's where tears and splits resulting in abscesses or fissures might occur.

Otherwise, if the partner is gentle and takes his time, allowing the sphincter muscle to relax and the rectum to stretch and expand slowly, there's little chance of infection or damage. Lubrication is also a good way to facilitate fucking without really taking out any of the enjoyment.

A finger or tongue are the perfect preliminary. Boston's *Fag Rag* (issues 7 and 8, Winter/Spring 1974) ran a story "Rimming As An Act Of Revolution," by Charley Shively, which says it so well:

Rimming is a wonderful way to prepare an anus for a penis. Who is so tight he cannot accept a tongue, soft and slippery and easy as it is in its message of love into the rectum? Once softened, resistance melts like butter in the summer sun. Stiffness becomes softness becomes yielding ecstasy.

The approach is what matters.

Approach, really, is the main consideration in all forms of sex and their relation to venereal disease. There's a saying that "the stiff prick has no conscience," but a man does, and if he wants to enjoy all forms of lovemaking, he'll want his sexual partner to share the joy of sex without fear of infection.

PREVENTION

Thus, prevention of VD is a two-way street. You take steps to protect your lover/partner from infection, as well as precautions to guard yourself. Preventing VD is a mixture of hygiene, caution and positive thinking.

First of all, washing clean before and after sex is necessary, and fine for esthetic reasons too. A bath or shower enhances the natural body scents and makes the skin smooth and soft. Washing your asshole *before* sex will decrease the chances of the man rimming you getting hepatitis or other gastrointestinal diseases. To wash after sex with warm and soapy water will kill most siff and clap germs. And pissing after sex will help eliminate any possible clap germs from the urethra. (This is debatable, because who really wants to jump up and dash to the john after an orgasm? Most people would rather lie with their lover and linger in the beautiful afterglow of sex, and I'm not about to suggest you neglect that.)

Of course, don't ball anyone who's infected with any of the above infections. You're not only courting the germs, but you'll possibly pass them on.

A quick examination of your partner might reveal symptoms that he hasn't noticed.

A periodic self-examination is wise, not only to protect yourself and partner, but to understand and be in touch with your body. Try kneeling on your bed, and looking backwards while holding a mirror to your ass and genitals. Lift your balls to get a better look.

Check-ups can't be stressed enough, especially if you trick a lot or frequent the baths. Remember, you usually won't know when your ass is infected with VD unless a partner tells you he has it genitally, or if there are symptoms such as itching or discharge (very rare). *So even if you've no reason to suspect, even if you haven't balled in months, you should go for a blood test and gonorrhea culture. Always request that cultures from your mouth and rectum be taken.* Many public health clinics, such as San Francisco's City Clinic, see many gay patients, and take throat and rectal cultures of all patients as part of the routine.

Always tell everyone you've balled once you've found an infection, and encourage them to go for tests. Although direct communication is the best method, if you don't tell them, then make it a point to give their name to your doctor or clinic worker, for the simple reason that you're protecting them and aiding in the abatement of the disease. The names of persons with any communicable disease are required by state law to be confidentially reported to the Department of Health.

As further prevention, most doctors will encourage using a rubber. This is really controversial, mainly because for most people a rubber ruins the pleasure of sex. It should be said here, though, that it will be very effective in preventing most VD, including warts. (Dr. Braff of SF's City Clinic suggested to me that there needs to be research for a suppository as an alternative to rubbers. An antiseptic for the rectum or vagina, tasteless and odorless, inserted before balling, wouldn't be nearly as repulsive as a rubber.)

A vaccine against warts, let alone one against the clap and syphilis, has yet to be developed, but would ultimately be the easiest and most efficient deterrent to infection. What's needed is public support and demand for continued research into a vaccine.

If you think you can cure siff or clap or any VD by treating yourself with tetracycline or penicillin at home, you're wrong. Don't try it: the amount or kind of antibiotic you take may be wrong, allowing the infection to linger. Seek out the best treatment.

A positive state of mind, your mental attitude, shouldn't be discounted as a means of prevention or partial cure. Try to mellow out and don't become too identified with the disease. The infection is possibly being sustained by the overwhelming depression that can accompany it, as by the virus or bacteria. Perhaps your attitudes and emotions will help where medicine cannot.

Above all, don't be unnecessarily alarmed by all this information. Just take heed, and continue to enjoy! -

ALCOHOL USE AND ABUSE
IN THE GAY COMMUNITY:
A View Toward Alternatives

Kevin J. McGirr

THE IMPORTANCE OF BARS FOR GAY PEOPLE

It seems that bars have held a more prominent place in the life of many gay people than is true for their straight counterparts. The range of responses to gay bars varies from exhilaration to repulsion or to just plain relief.

Most discussion on the bars omits any discussion on the use and role of alcohol—this is what I would like to consider in this report.

Until recently, there were few other social outlets besides the bars for gay people. There are now alternatives, though few, and many gays, for many reasons, continue to gravitate to the bars as their primary social outlet. For some the bars are quite satisfactory, for others oppressive.

Straights have the world at large in which to develop their social-sexual network. This is a privilege and a right not available to gays, whose individual rights are still unprotected by laws. Even with the advent of gay liberation and more public sorts of gatherings and places to meet, the bar still retains a prominent place in the culture, which is fine for those who enjoy going to bars, not so fine for those who would rather not yet don't feel there are alternatives suitable to their needs and lifestyles. Very simply, there still remains a need for meeting places out of the public view.

It is imperative to growth, and indeed to survival, that gay people find places to meet each other. The bar has traditionally offered a semi-dark, secluded setting in which one is reasonably secure from exposure and hassles. The risk of exposure is minimized, and the impact of identification softened should one unexpectedly happen upon a co-worker in a gay bar. An anonymity is offered by the bar; it also is a common ground ("we're all in the same boat").

These are important places, for it is here that gays become acculturated to a social interaction not learned through childhood and adolescence. Bars are our social space, to have good times, to dance and meet new friends. For many the only purpose in going to a bar is to meet someone to talk with. Another side of the picture is that these are not relaxed, comfortable environs in which to meet people. One perhaps has questioned, "Are you having a good time?" and a not unusual response, "Are you kidding!"

Many people enter bars prepared with an assortment of hopes, and the fears of possible rejection, which, for many, materializes as often as not. These are hopes that include the wish for a pleasant evening, meeting friends, making new friends—maybe for someone to spend time with, perhaps someone to spend a long time with. The fear of rejection, of not being desired, can supersede all other emotions toward bars. For those for whom the bar scene would not be a first choice in another kind of society with different attitudes, the bar becomes a place of competitive tension.

It may be worthwhile to take a look at the role of alcohol in the bar setting; after all, the purpose of the establishment is to sell alcoholic beverages to patrons. As the pattern of patronizing bars develops, so too develops a pattern of alcohol use.

A few of one's favorite drinks lends a relaxed and willing-to-wait atmosphere to the environment. Drinking becomes a part of the bar pattern—drinking to relax the search and numb the wait. Alcohol use becomes an integral part of going to bars, of visiting with friends, of making new acquaintances, of dealing with loneliness and the fear of being rejected, of going home alone or even of going home with someone.

For most people, drinking remains as a useful, acceptable social tool, often used and only occasionally, if ever, abused. For others, the pattern quietly changes to tolerance and unconscious acceptance of a routine. And what once was accepted, and perhaps desirable, becomes a problem. One of the primary questions put to people as a barometer of their alcohol use is, "Do you ever drink alone?" How many gay people spend their entire evenings drinking alone in a crowded bar?

ALCOHOLISM AND THE GAY COMMUNITY

The pattern of bar drinking is, of course, not the only way problem drinking develops. For many gays, participation in the bar scene is but a brief experience. For others, the bars are too much of a commitment to the label "gay," and they never enter a bar. The ways in which alcohol is used and the reasons for which it is used go a long way in determining

278

whether alcohol will become a problem. Generally, people who feel okay about themselves, okay about their world, don't get into trouble with drinking. Although more and more gay people are feeling okay about themselves, it remains difficult to feel okay about a world which continues to work at making us feel not okay.

Gays as a Minority

Gays, as any other group, in society face tensions and conflicts which in some way need to be resolved or relaxed. But gays as a group hold the status of being an unaccepted and concealed minority. With this comes specific and additional problems for the individual. Her/his sexuality and lifestyle not being in the mainstream causes conflict with society at large on a daily basis. With each individual there is variance of approach and personal resource in solving this overall conflict; for some, that may include alcohol.

Problems for Gays

There are numerous situations unique to the gay experience which most certainly cause tension and conflict.

For example, there is the situation that we as self-defined gays must live with, that being the context of our less-than-accepted status. It is something we learn from early childhood. New situations confront us daily as a result of our being different, of our resisting the pressures to fit into molds, to get married and have a "family." Integrated into the pressures is our gender role and the need to maintain a veneer of feminine or masculine identity so as not to raise suspicions in the world about our sexuality. Situations constantly arise, and in response we must cover, lie, or perhaps just withdraw rather than be exposed. There are repeated instances that we face—creating varying degrees of uneasiness, an uneasiness we want to eliminate.

Consider too, the time in our lives during the process of coming out—a time of transitions and transformations in our self-concept. Developing a valid identity as a gay person is usually not problem free. Carl Rogers states that a valid identity is a congruence between the image we have of ourselves, the image we project, and the image the world has of us. All too many gays have not achieved that congruence, that harmony of personal/social identity which flows freely through our days. The tensions around the double life, the fears of exposure

279

with the possibility of rejection, beg for relief. Coming out can be a time of heightened emotions and struggle within ourselves—pitted against the values of society. One must deal with the fears and apprehensions over being different, with telling friends and family and with the looming possibility of being rejected by them. It is a time (and potentially a long time) when in making the transition the problems seem too large and perhaps one feels no support. We may prefer to retreat, deny our sexuality and/or seek out ways to tranquilize.

Another dilemma which many face: being closeted and perhaps being closeted all of one's life. Some people are not in a position to express anxiety over their sexual feelings, perhaps only having cursory or partial contact with the gay world (i.e., visiting tea rooms, paying for sex) while leading a very separate existence. Then too, there are those for whom their sexuality is wholly unrealized, suppressed to a confused recognition; perhaps, no recognition at all.

Eliminating Conflicts

There is a need for people to eliminate or at least minimize conflict in their lives. As mentioned, there are various psychological recourses, such as sublimation, denial and compensation to deal with problems. Alcohol, as well, in its very immediate way serves to relieve tensions—helping to forget—relaxing the cerebral functions.

In some cases, use becomes habit; habit denies the problem. Problem drinking often progresses from social drinking. Drinking that was a social escape becomes a psychological escape; the drinking pattern changes, becomes different from that of her/his friends. People around the problem drinker begin to comment on the change in the drinking pattern. The drinker may begin to feel guilty about drinking, may begin to think about controlling the amount or frequency. The fact that one is feeling a need to control the drinking may signify a drinking problem.

Problem drinking doesn't always result in drunken behavior. Many people drink themselves into a relaxed state and maintain themselves there. As the problem progresses, blackouts occur (episodic amnesia—forgetting what one said, or did, the night before, for example). Hangovers become more frequent and painful. Alcohol begins to interfere with relationships, jobs, interests and concern for others.

At some point, habit becomes addiction, and when the drug is alcohol, a progressive illness occurs which can be stopped only by a

280

total cessation of drinking. A drinking problem is alcoholism, characterized by a loss of control over drinking alcohol. The person who is alcoholic may not drink every day, may refuse drinks at times, but when she/he starts to drink they cannot guarantee when they will stop or what their behavior will be like at the end of a drinking session.

The stereotype of the alcoholic is being destroyed as treatment becomes more accessible and available earlier in the illness. Alcoholics come into treatment at all ages and from all social conditions. To describe a typical alcoholic is as difficult as describing a typical American. Since the Skid Row alcoholic population represents five percent or less of the alcoholic population, the other ninety-five percent are not readily identified as alcoholic except by the closest persons in their lives.

Where to Turn to for Assistance

The usual estimate is that one person in fourteen is alcoholic. That figure alone indicates that alcoholism is a significant problem in the gay community. Treatment, specifically for alcoholic gays is just beginning to come alive; and the need for such facilities mandates more exposure and discussion. But alcoholism information and treatment resources are available. In addition to active Alcoholics Anonymous and Al Anon (for friends and family members) groups, there are detoxification centers which offer in-patient treatment with counseling and education programs, out-patient clinics, rehabilitation programs, and in most major cities there is a twenty-four-hour counseling and referral service sponsored by the National Council on Alcoholism, listed under "Alcohol Information" in the telephone directory.

Specific Needs of the Gay Alcoholic

Hopefully, we can look to the future when gay health agencies will have facilities to assist a gay person with alcoholic problems. Presently such programs are being developed—a description of them will follow later in this article. There is also a need to induce a sensitivity to the gay alcoholic in existing facilities.

Consider the situation of a person who has come in contact with existing facilities and counselors, time and time again, unresolved in their sexuality. There are limitations in these facilities coming out of pre-existing biases well ingrained in social value.

281

It is true that one must focus on one's alcoholism and receive the necessary assistance, but just as one must admit to their alcoholism, isn't it also important to create supportive environments in all facilities, to allow individuals to open up to their conflicts related and/or concealed by their alcoholism?

Presently, there are gays working in the field of alcoholism; we can appeal to their ability to come out, identify themselves and begin to educate co-workers. Gays should be able to serve as role models and resource persons for their patients and co-workers.

ALTERNATIVES FOR GAY ALCOHOLICS

San Francisco

One such development has been the institution of a pre-treatment counseling and referral service for gay people in San Francisco. This service is funded by the Whitman Radclyffe Foundation (a California-based organization which assists in funding special projects for the gay community), as well as by some monies from the City and County of San Francisco.

The service, which is under the direction of Rusty Smith, offers counseling, education and referral for gay people with alcohol problems. The need for such a service has been evidenced by the overwhelming response from the gay community as well as the numerous requests for advice and information from other alcoholic treatment facilities. Since the service has begun, Smith has counseled an average of seventy people a month and has made many appearances before alcoholism facilities, establishing a rapport in the field of alcoholism and sensitizing alcoholism staff workers to the needs of gay people.

"We've had instances of staff being openly hostile to gays. Often times gays would enter treatment facilities for their alcoholism; however, when they were identified as gay, staff response would be that they had to cure their homosexuality to eliminate their alcoholism," Smith said. A more serious problem has been the rejection of gays by other alcoholic clients in treatment facilities. The most critical discrimination has been the lack of acceptance of gays in heterosexually dominated Half-Way Houses. The impetus for the counseling service came out of a specific need to establish half-way houses for gay people. Thus with a one-year, $50,000 grant from the State of California and the City and County of San Francisco, a half-way house was established as of October 1, 1974, serving both men and women with a capacity for twelve people over a three-month period. The half-way house will be a transition space, a supportive environment for gays with a view toward helping people make choices in life as gay people without the use of alcohol. The house will offer a time to develop new patterns and positive approaches to a lifestyle in the gay community and not the usual re-integration into the nuclear family setting so often the orientation of traditional half-way houses. Special half-way houses will be a necessity until such time when there has been marked increases in the awareness and sensitivity to the needs of gay people.

Another impetus for the creation of this service is that many gays would not seek treatment, largely because of the fear of being rejected or mistreated in alcoholism facilities. Not that this fear is unfounded but there still exists the need to assist gays in finding a facility that is sensitive and responsive. It needs to be reiterated that alcoholism is the disease and not his/her sexuality and that alcohol is the problem to be dealt with—thus the need for continuing education and rapport in the existing facilities. Smith points out that there is an increasing sympathy in all facilities and also notes that gay people working in these facilities can be relied upon more and more to support gay clients.

ALCOHOLISM AMONGST GAY WOMEN

Karen Hall, also a counselor at the San Francisco service, has been instrumental in bringing about needed awareness and response from women to the service. Hall had a drinking problem herself, as she explains:

> Once I got into the bars I never got off the stool. This was when I was just coming out. I needed to identify; therefore, I thought that I had to go to bars, drink and dress a certain way—and this was what being gay was. By the time that I had caught myself I found that I just liked to drink, and it has nothing to do with being gay. I had juxtaposed various associations with homosexuality—being depressed and being alcoholic. In other words I was carrying out a script that I had written in my head—I didn't like gayness, I didn't feel that I had made any choices about my life until I stopped drinking. For all that I was feeling, I drank and I was gay, a sick association that I had projected. Having to

283

socialize in a bar helped me along in a drinking habit. I became addicted to the bar itself and it got so that I didn't want to go anywhere if I didn't know that there was going to be booze there. I didn't make a social life outside of the bar—I stayed in my lonely corner, liked it there and liked being miserable. Before I realized that I was not in control others had to make choices for me. I now realize that I had emotional problems that I had to straighten out regardless of whether I was straight or gay.

With regard to women relating to the service, Hall finds that the response has been very strong and was surprised to see so many willing to seek help. "Women in general are hard to get out of the woodwork and women with a drinking problem can almost be impossible. Alcoholism is just as much of a problem for women in spite of the stigma that drinking is 'unfeminine'." When Hall first joined the service she found that the service needed more exposure, a face to identify with. Besides advertisements in the bars there have been a number of television programs devoted to the subject. There's a need to bring information into the community, to make people aware about how patterns develop and how they can be stopped. In addition to the counseling service, women's rap groups have been organized.

Commenting on the dynamics of the bar, Hall feels that a lot of younger women (under twenty-five) are actively seeking alternatives to the bars. For a lot of older women the bars are the place, and the social atmosphere of the bars puts a drinking problem right up front. Hall feels that a lot of women will be heavy drinkers because of stigmas and roles that they have internalized through socialization. She feels that this is part of the oppression but also feels that this is over-emphasized and that a lot of women will force a role, a role that is not at all themselves, and drink through that role. Drinking covers up a lot of discomfort, and helps one to feel normal—that is, just like the next person.

The address of the service is:

Whitman Radclyffe Foundation
2340 Clay St.
Room 405
San Francisco, Calif. 94115
Rusty Smith: Coordinator (415) 567-0526

NATIONAL TASK FORCE

In April and May of 1974 in Denver, Colorado, at the National Conference on Alcoholism's annual meeting a paper was delivered on the "Alcoholic Gay: Stigma and Sobriety." The paper was well received and a desire was expressed for more information and means to eliminate discrimination against gays in the field of alcoholism.

Brenda Weathers, while attending that conference, called for a National Task Force on alcoholism in the gay community. With the number of people who have responded there is hope that the Task Force might obtain funding for education and outreach into the gay community as well as the Alcoholism field; with a view to offering technical assistance in setting up programs for gay alcoholics in various parts of the nation.

Los Angeles

Alcoholics Together is a group founded in October, 1970 as an alternative to Alcoholics Anonymous for gay men and women. The group is modeled on the philosophy and method of A.A., but with an awareness that gays do not share in the lifestyle orientation of most A.A. members. Since that time the group has expanded from Los Angeles to many other cities throughout the United States.

The *Gay Community Services Center* in Los Angeles is a multi-serviced facility that provides counseling—both individual and in groups—for gays with alcohol problems.

Van Ness Recovery House. In conjunction with Alcoholics Together and staff at the Gay Community Services Center a live-in recovery house was established in 1973. The house has a capacity for twelve to sixteen people in a post-medical detoxification for a thirty- to sixty-day period. The house also serves as a meeting place for Alcoholics Together and other related rap groups. Currently, the house depends on stipends from its clients and private donations for its financial operation although a $25,000 grant from the state of California for program evaluation and strengthening came through in the Fall of 1974.

Addresses:

Gay Community Services Center
1614 Wilshire Blvd.

Los Angeles, Calif. 90017

Telephone: (213) 482-3062

Van Ness Recovery House
1322 North Van Ness Ave.
Los Angeles, Calif. 90028

Telephone: (213) 463-4266

WOMEN'S PROGRAM

Through the efforts of people associated with the Gay Community Services Center a special program for women in Los Angeles was launched on October 1, 1974. This is a million-dollar, three-year grant from the National Institute on Alcoholism and Alcohol Abuse (a division of the Department of Health, Education and Welfare)—the largest funding ever granted an openly gay organization and the largest funding ever granted for a comprehensive rehabilitation program for women alcoholics.

Brenda Weathers, project director of the women's alcoholism program and one of the writers of the proposal to the Institute, explains that the impetus for the proposal came about as a result of gay women alcoholics and alcoholism staff workers who were very aware of discrimination in existing agencies—discrimination toward gay women as well as the overall inadequacy in most facilities to deal with women's problems. The program will be designed to serve all women, although the primary outreach will be toward gay women.

The proposal put to the NIAAA included documented evidence of existing agencies blatantly denying services to gay women. Defense for such discrimination on the part of existing agencies stated that gay women were incompatible in programs where the rehabilitation process included reintegration into nuclear family settings. Weathers feels that a lot of the discrimination is basic homophobia; particularly when the defense for discrimination state such fears as: "Gay women might rape other women in treatment facilities." And as in other cities, when gay women are accepted in treatment facilities a not unusual response is to attempt to eliminate their homosexuality rather than deal explicitly with their alcoholism.

The feeling of the staff working in the alcoholism project at the Gay Community Services Center is that alcoholism is a critical problem in

286

the gay community and that the incidence of alcoholism may very well be higher than in the straight community. Data collected through the Gay Community Services Center and Alcoholics Together estimate that twenty-five percent of the gay community have problems with alcohol use—and this is felt to be a conservative estimate. It is acknowledged that many who have contact and awareness of alcoholism in the gay community feel this figure is an exaggeration. Perhaps there is a fear of associating problems and sicknesses with homosexuality in the public mind. But as already elucidated in this article—the oppression of gay people and the fact that the bars have traditionally been important meeting places for gays can be critical factors contributing to a higher incidence of alcoholism.

The Los Angeles program includes a recovery house and numerous supportive services. The recovery house is a post-medical detoxification for a period of thirty to sixty days and includes peer counseling, exposure to alternatives and group support. There is also a re-entry house, less structured and defined than the recovery house, but which serves as an intermediary atmosphere hoping to build group support with a view toward alternatives to the bar and drinking lifestyle. This is available for a one- to six-month period after the thirty-day recovery period.

Supportive services include: job development, vocational rehabilitation, child care (for mothers previously not able to receive any treatment because of children), criminal justice diversion, prison probation and parole outreach (assisting women who have been arrested for alcohol-related offenses).

The recovery house serves twelve to sixteen women at a time and it is estimated that the entire program will eventually serve 750 women a year—most of whom will only be seeking the supportive services in a one-time contact. But the importance of participating in many of the services is emphasized. Much contact and consciousness-raising is a necessity in dealing with the years of oppression as well as the group support for success in dealing with one's alcoholism.

Another very important aspect of the service is prevention outreach—inculcating an awareness of the bar syndrome, making known those existing alternatives to bars as well as the need to create more alternatives both personally and socially. There is also hope that this outreach can be national which ties in with the Task Force. If the funds can be acquired this project can sponsor staff members to travel—to bring the word elsewhere inducing people to come out, to discuss the problem and offer the technical assistance to formulate more programs.

Inquiries regarding the Los Angeles program should be addressed to:

Women's Alcoholism Program
Gay Community Services Center
1614 Wilshire Blvd.
Los Angeles, Calif. 90017
Telephone (213) 482-3062

Anyone in the New England area interested in the problem of Alcoholism in the gay community should address correspondence to:

Gay Community News
Alcoholism Project
22 Bromfield St.
Boston, Mass. 02108

CONTRIBUTORS

Gary Alinder, San Francisco, Calif.—"Sometime writer, sometime vagabond, sometime cabdriver."

Julian Bamford, Los Angeles, Calif.—"I'm twenty-five, grew up middle-class in England. Presently live in a gay men's collective in Los Angeles and do house-cleaning for a living. Lately I've been writing songs, enjoying time outdoors, and pursuing personal growth. Am tall, dark and handsome, and beginning to be aware of social oppression. Sometimes I'm lonely."

Konstantin Berlandt, San Francisco, Calif.—Cabdriver, writer, feeling trapped in an unsatisfying 40-hour week job, is trying to free-lance his way out of it. A shy San Francisco queen, who at this writing is living with a lover/companion/friend, "wants more out of life than capitalism has to offer."

Rita Mae Brown, Cranbury, N.J.—Author of *Rubyfruit Jungle*, has worked in the women's and gay movements since 1967. She plans to continue that work until November 28, 2044, when she reaches the age of 100. She's recently finished a second novel, *In Her Day*, and has started another. She wishes you all "kisses and revolution."

Jeanne Córdova, Los Angeles, Calif.—Received her lesbian education from the Camp Fire Girls and the Roman Catholic convent, and her less imaginative learning experiences from the University of California, Los Angeles. The former curriculum has led to a long and fulfilling career as a dyke activist and also has brought "many personal rewards." The latter experience (as a community organizer, Master in Social Work) was fortunately thwarted in its liberal bud and has, for the last five years, been used for more righteous purposes in the lesbian, feminist and gay liberation movements. Yet these two paths of wisdom have led to a third. Having founded *The Lesbian Tide* four years ago, she accidentally learned to write, and lo! (sayeth the goddess), is now a nationally syndicated feminist columnist, with a book (*Sexism: It's a Nasty Affair!*) to match.

Louie Crew, Fort Valley, Ga.—Has written widely as a scholar, poet and fiction writer. In February 1974, he and Ernest Clay were married in Fort Valley. They live as an integrated couple in what is otherwise the white part of town. Ernest is a model, fashion coordinator, and a licensed practical nurse, now training as a hairdresser.

Laura Della Rosa, New York, N.Y.—"I'm a neurotic goddess—ready to soar with gazelle-like sleekness, but rooted/locked/attached to therapeutic ruminations. I'm a city person, a dancing person, an eating person—intrigued with the many roles and act-hungers I want to play out. I've been involved with psychodrama and still believe that the most confusing and complicating technique is the core of it all—*role-reversal*. I tend to sleep with friends, or those I've known for a while. I'm finding there are limits—I'm not an innocent primitive—and that people, and myself, are not to be trifled with. (Did I mention how much I hold in as I go through my school/work days in a Masters in Social Work program?)"

Karla Dobinski, Madison, Wisc.—Born and raised in a small Wisconsin town, Karla is presently in law school. She works part-time for a local newspaper and spends her spare minutes doing far too many things: assisting women with their divorces, giving energy to the lesbian community, and writing for the newspaper *Whole Woman*.

Thomas Dotton, Worcester, Mass.—"I have been a reluctant scribbler for the Boston *Globe* and for *Newsweek* in New York and in Paris. I should like to be identified as a novelist and translator at work on a lengthy analysis of homophobia and the movement."

Edward Guthmann, San Francisco, Calif.—"I work in a small graphics shop as a typesetter and layout artist. Currently working on a children's book. Also do some acting. I live in a flat overlooking Dolores Park with three other men, and ride my 10-speed bicycle to work. I have a voracious appetite for all types of films, and I love to travel. I spent some time in Central America this past fall and will return later this year. I study Spanish at San Francisco City College."

Tom Hurley, Watertown, Mass.—"Right now, I live with a bunch of faggots in the Boston area and earn my living by teaching at a local university. I plan to quit teaching, leave the city, and join an intentional community in Maine—very soon. I write for *Gay Community News* and hope to continue writing about gay and other forms of life."

Karla Jay, New York, N.Y.—"I am in exile from California, an urban person, and a meeting dropout. I am looking for people who want to grow, to share love, to be mutually supportive, and to build a world together. I have not survived gay coupledom but still feel that the lifestyle is beautiful and valid."

Robert LaRiviere, Salem, N.H.—"Perhaps the only thing you should print is that I am presently living in New Hampshire and seeking employment in an alternative education situation."

Julie Lee, Fanwood, N.J.—"I am a middle-aged lesbian-feminist radical, and a lesbian peer counselor for Daughters of Bilitis in New Jersey. Since accidentally finding D.O.B. in the mid-1960's, I have worked with and for that organization. Trained as an industrial scientist, I left the field in 1961 because my feminist consciousness would no longer allow me to tolerate the mistreatment accorded women in the laboratory. Since then I've devoted full-time to movement activities: writing, lecturing, and counseling."

Edward E. Loftin and Join Hands—Eddie Loftin needs no more introduction than the beauty of his letters. Join Hands (P.O. Box 42242, San Francisco, Calif.) is a group of gay men doing prison support work toward the following ends: "to help connect gay prisoners with sisters and brothers on the streets for our mutual help and education; to work toward the day when all oppressed people run our own lives and when prisons, if they exist at all, will be to protect us from corporate executives, U.S. presidents, war criminals, and other such enemies of society."

Don Mager, Detroit, Mich.—"I came out in 1972, directly into gay liberation activities in Detroit. I am a poet and playwright, supporting myself with a medley of jobs including teaching at a day-care center. I've worked on *Gayly Speaking*, the weekly gay liberation radio show in Detroit, the Committee for Gay Rights, and as a writer for the *Gay Liberator*. I've published poems in about thirty magazines and journals in England and America, both gay and straight; and my play, *Kepler*, was performed in Puebla, Mexico, in 1971. I share a household with my two children and a lover, with hopes eventually to escape from urban life for northern Michigan."

Kevin J. McGirr, Somerville, Mass.—"For two years I've worked at the Pine Street Inn, which is a multi-service shelter for the homeless men of Boston, most of whom are alcoholic. In addition, I am writing about various topics pertinent to the gay community—becoming conscious and living a lifestyle which was described in a Boston weekly as that of the 'artificial poor.' "

Richard Nash, Los Angeles, Calif.—Has been on the staff of the Los Angeles Gay Community Services Center from its inception in 1971 in several capacities, including counselor and group facilitator. Before that he was active in the Gay Liberation Front of Los Angeles. He sees "separation as the historically and politically necessary stage for the gay movement to come into its own and to support the efforts of gay people to develop our own lifestyles."

Catherine Nossa, St. Louis, Mo.—"I am twenty-six and presently putting most of my energies into developing skills in writing and painting, for which prostitution has provided much interesting subject material. I am gathering material for a handbook on prostitution, and for an overview of prostitutes in literature and art."

Jeanne Perreault, Edmonton, Alberta, Canada—Jeanne, Jennifer and cat (Susanna Moody) live in quiet ways. "Read, drink tea, water the plants, hassle about housework. Laugh, cry, fight. Ordinary. We both go to school, scrounge for money, visit our friends. The style of our lives grows out of who we are—leaves space for who each of us is becoming."

Riki, Brooklyn, N.Y.—"I was a late bloomer, having made my decision to 'come out' at a late age. Since I've never married, I was always aware that I would have to take care of myself in my old age, which is why my 'Aging' article is so important to me, as well as to everyone living a 'single life.' "

June Rook, New York, N.Y.—"Currently involved in radical politics, lesbian history, the art of batik painting, and, most of all, 'deep communication' with women."

Jane Rule, Vancouver, British Columbia, Canada—"I am a novelist, short story writer, sometime teacher and essayist. My most recent book is *Lesbian Images*, a kind of common reader, and I am now working on a novel called *The Young in One Another's Arms*. I was born in the United States in 1931 and grew up there in the suburbs of various cities, except for summers in the redwoods. I lived in England for a while, and then in 1958 I came to Canada. I have been a Canadian citizen for some years. I live in a rain forest on a small island off the west coast between the mainland and Vancouver Island."

Nina Sabaroff, Portland, Ore.—"I teach sexuality at a community college, and work with other women writing and speaking on the 'biology of women.' I have been photographing women for four years and in other ways exploring and feeling my woman-vision, which swings back and forth between *any day now* and *not in my lifetime*. I would like some day to live with my sisters/friends/lovers and comrade lesbians in NozamA, a planet of our own making."

Charley Shively, Boston, Mass.—"Saggitarius, born 8 Dec. 1937, Stonelick Township, Ohio. Sucked first cock at five; was fucked at twelve. Father couldn't read/write and mother finished 8th grade; got Ph.D. from Harvard in history. Until sophomore year expected to be President, then realized faggots couldn't run; chose cocksucking and have ever since been a 'happy homosexual' anarchist. First book of poems: *Nuestra Señora de los Dolores* (Boston Good Gay Poets, 1975)."

George Whitmore, New York, N.Y.—"Poet and playwright." He is also a free-lance writer and often writes for gay publications. His forthcoming book of poems is called *Getting Gay in New York*. He organized the gay caucus at the 1974 (MORE) magazine journalism convention and was one of the coordinators of the Gay Academic Union conference in November 1974.

Allen Young, Royalston, Mass.—"After growing up on a chicken farm in the Catskill Mountains, my burning ambition was to be a Latin American foreign correspondent for a major American daily. Shortly after the 1967 march on the Pentagon, I dropped out of all that into S.D.S. and the underground press, and I secretly hoped I might become editor of *The New York Times* 'after the revolution.' Now, my main ambition is to have a prolific vegetable garden and to finish the octagonal house I'm building in the woods. I live in a decentralized rural community with several friends; we are attempting to build a community where we can live in harmony with each other and with the rest of the planet. I feel that my involvement in gay liberation and the back-to-the-land movements is an expression of my attachment to socialist, anarchist and pacifist traditions."

292

continued from page iv .